'A quirky fact here, an interesting tale there, an anecdote to relate ... I have always loved the world of stories and few tell them better than Joy and Abhishek. The Great Indian Cricket Circus will be so much fun.'

HARSHA BHOGLE

THE GREAT INDIAN CRICKET CIRCUS

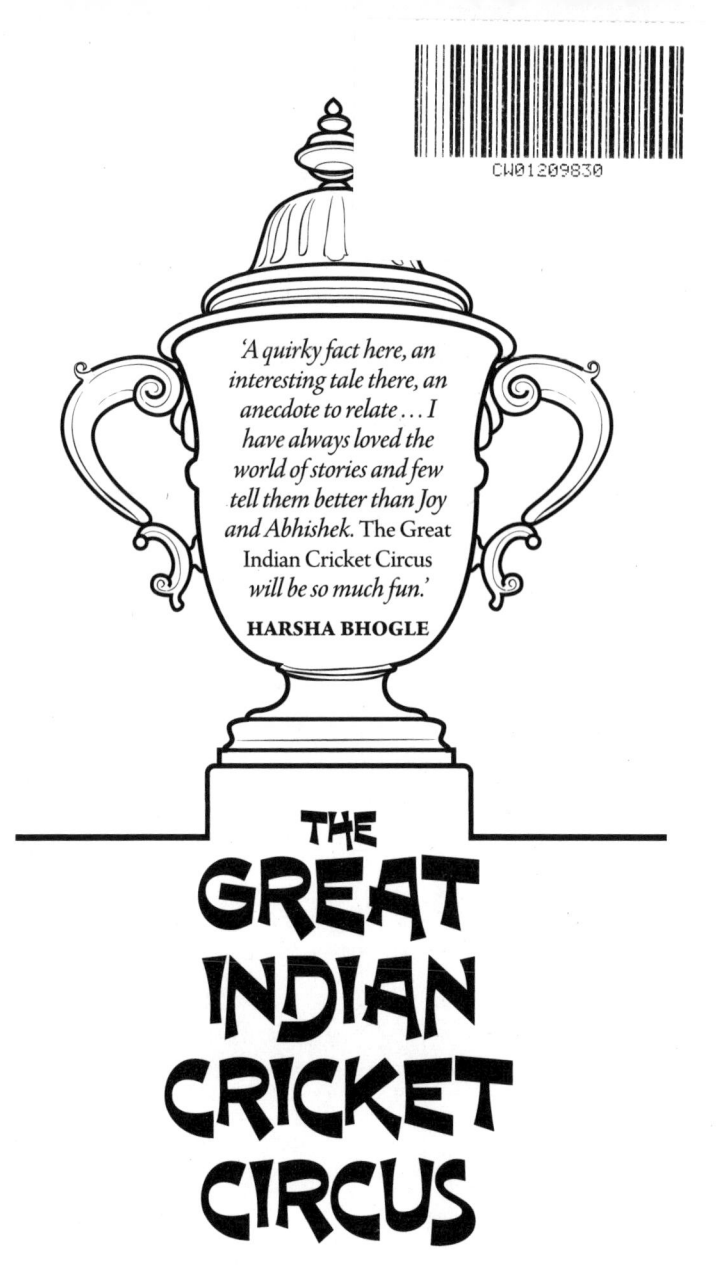

Celebrating
30 Years of Publishing
in India

THE GREAT INDIAN CRICKET CIRCUS

Amazing Stats, Facts and Everything in Between

ABHISHEK MUKHERJEE
JOY BHATTACHARJYA

FOREWORD BY R. ASHWIN

HarperCollins *Publishers* India

First published in India by HarperCollins *Publishers* 2023
4th Floor, Tower A, Building No. 10, DLF Cyber City,
DLF Phase II, Gurugram, Haryana – 122002
www.harpercollins.co.in

2 4 6 8 10 9 7 5 3 1

Text copyright © Abhishek Mukherjee and Joy Bhattacharjya 2023

Illustrations on pages 32, 69, 102, 136, 165, 192, 218, 243, 268, 298,
318, 348 and 386 by Surojit Bhattacharjee

P-ISBN: 978-93-5699-115-6
E-ISBN: 978-93-5699-149-1

The views and opinions expressed in this book are the authors' own.
The facts are as reported by them and the publishers
are not in any way liable for the same.

Abhishek Mukherjee and Joy Bhattacharjya assert the moral right
to be identified as the authors of this work.

All rights reserved. No part of this publication may be reproduced,
stored in a retrieval system, or transmitted, in any form or by any means,
electronic, mechanical, photocopying, recording or otherwise,
without the prior permission of the publishers.

Typeset in 11.5/15.2 Dante MT Std at
Manipal Technologies Limited, Manipal

Printed and bound at
Nutech Print Services - India

This book is printed on FSC® certified paper
which ensures responsible forest management.

To
The memory of my grandparents, who defined my childhood.
All four would have exaggerated while describing this book.

Abhishek

To
Vivek, who bowls a nifty out-swinger
and Neel, his steadfast fan.

Joy

Contents

Foreword	xi
1. Indian Cricket in Fiction: English Literature	1
2. Indian Cricket in Fiction: Films	9
3. Cricketers in Unusual Professions	17
4. Butterfly Effects: Off-the-Field Incidents that Changed Indian Cricket	23
5. The Real Stakeholders: Iconic Indian Cricket Fans	35
6. Against All Odds: Indian Cricketers Who Vanquished Pain	45
7. Parallel Universe: You Didn't Know They Were Cricketers	59
8. Unusual Scorecards	65
9. Numbers Game: Indian Cricketers and Music Albums	73
10. The Diaspora: Indians Playing Domestic Cricket outside India and England	77
11. The Reverse Diaspora: Non-Indians Playing in Domestic Cricket	83

Contents

12. All-Rounders: Indian Cricketers Representing
    Their Country at Another Sport   89

13. Tournaments: Iconic, Unusual and Forgotten   95

14. Indian Derbies: Famous Rivalries   107

15. It's a Match!: Unusual Cricket Contests   115

16. Ranji Trophy Remix: Defunct, Modified, Renamed,
    and Returning Teams   123

17. PETA on the Pitch: Indian Cricket and Fauna   129

18. Family Matters: Related Indian International Cricketers   137

19. Family beyond Cricket: Indian Cricketers Related
    to Famous Personalities   149

20. Nominal List: Nicknames of Indian Cricketers   159

21. What's in a Name?: Cricketers Named after
    Other Cricketers   169

22. Why Me?: Cricket Venues Named after Unusual People   175

23. Remember My Last: Lesser-Known Last Names of
    Indian Cricketers   181

24. Time Out: Abrupt Halts and Unexpected Endings
    in Indian Cricket   185

25. Silver Screen: Cricketers Who Acted in Movies   197

26. Sharma Ji Ke Bachche: Highly Qualified International
    Cricketers   205

27. Early Prowlers: Outstanding Indian Fielders
    before the Modern Era   211

28. Cricket in the Crown: Royalty in Indian Cricket   217

Contents

29. Curious Selections	225
30. Indian International Cricketers Born outside India	233
31. The Radcliffe Curse: Partition 'Transfers'	237
32. Curious Legacies: Things Named after Cricketers	241
33. Did You Know?: Unusual Feats by Indians outside International Cricket	247
34. The Rovers: Cricketers Who Played for Several Teams	257
35. Did that Really Happen?: Popular Myths in Indian Cricket	261
36. Unholy Smoke: Cricketing Effigies and Posters Burnt in India	273
37. Microphone Men: Iconic, Controversial, Unusual	279
38. Standing Out in the Stands	287
39. Divine Acts: Religion and Indian Cricket	293
40. Not Quite Cricket: Indian Cricketers Who Faced Racism	301
41. Comebacks Like None Other: Cricketers Who Overcame Grief to Return to the Field	309
42. Pieces of Wood: Famous Bats of Indian Cricket	315
43. The Plate Group: Food and Indian Cricket	323
44. They Did *That?*: How Indian Fans Have Followed Cricket	333
45. Big Hits: Iconic Sixes in Indian Cricket	339
46. End of Innings: Indian Cricketers Who Died Unnatural Deaths	347

47. Player–Coach Feuds	355
48. Coats, Caps and Bails: Indian Umpires	361
49. SOS: Famous Call-ups in Indian Cricket	369
50. Commercial Gain: Iconic Advertisements in Indian Cricket	379
51. And, Sold!: Facts about the IPL Auctions	389
52. What Do They Know of IPL Who Only IPL Know?	399
Why This Book?	409
A Note from the Authors	411
Acknowledgements	413
Bibliography	417

Foreword

Where does cricket end and the rest of life begin? In India, you never know. Most of us grew up on a steady diet of book cricket in classrooms, tennis-ball matches at lunchtime, and noisy action at the local parks near our homes. And then, of course, there were days when all this was forgotten, when India played, and we would anxiously check, on TV, or even on the radio at the local tea stall, whether Sachin was still batting.

I have been lucky enough to live my dream and make the transition from book cricket and tennis balls to walking out there in the middle for my country. Still, like all of you, I will also always remain a fan of this beautiful game.

The Great Indian Cricket Circus is an unabashed celebration of this incredible sport. In these pages you will meet international footballers who captained in Ranji finals, monks who were brilliant bowlers, cricketers who were musicians, actors, nightclub owners, and even fingerprint specialists. There are amazing facts about iconic tournaments, seemingly insignificant incidents that totally changed Indian cricket, famous rivalries from the clubs of Mumbai to IPL teams, unusual scorecards and cricketing families, and some that debunk popular myths in Indian cricket. It also contains fascinating trivia from the world of women's cricket.

I am indebted to the game forever for coming to me and revealing my purpose in life. This book tells us how many others like me found theirs.

Intrigued? Dig in and enjoy! Start with the first chapter like a Test opener, or just jump to any topic that strikes your fancy—either way, you're in for a treat!

R. Ashwin

Indian Cricket in Fiction
English Literature

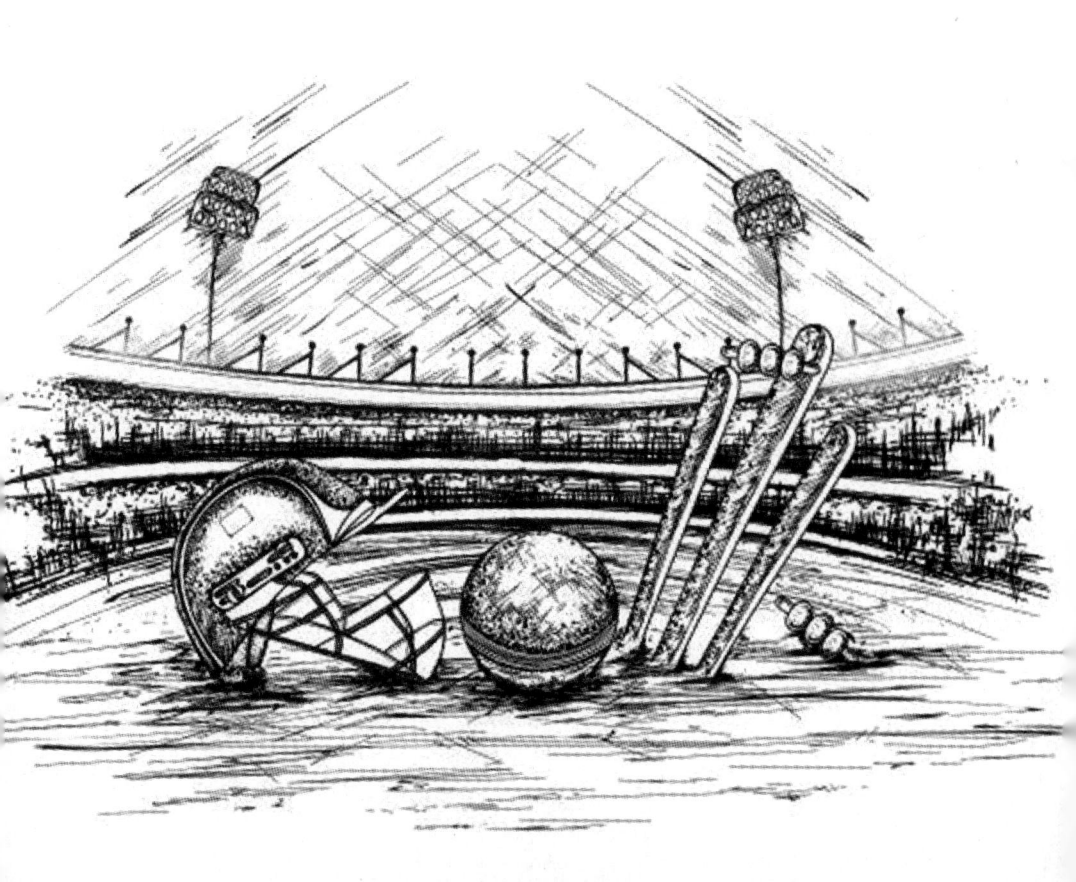

The Pickwick Papers *has a cricket match, as does* Tom Brown's School Days. *Sir Arthur Conan Doyle wrote* 'The Story of Spedegue's Dropper.' *Wodehouse created Psmith and Mike Jackson. Douglas Adams had Arthur Dent and Ford Prefect show up to Lord's on a Chesterfield sofa two days before a Vogon invasion. Garry Sobers and Ted Dexter, no less, have lent their names to works of fiction as well.*

But what about Indian cricket in fiction? Journalist-turned-novelist Moti Nandy had set a trend in Bangla sports fiction, as have some others, albeit to a lesser extent. There have been writers—Indian and otherwise—writing in English who have chosen cricket in India as their subject, or at least a part of the plot.

R.K. NARAYAN, *SWAMI AND FRIENDS* (1935)

At the Board School, young Swaminathan becomes part of the MCC (Malgudi, not Marylebone, Cricket Club), and quickly earns a reputation for his bowling. He is given the nickname 'Tate', after Maurice Tate, the famous Sussex and England seamer, and in Swami's own words, 'the greatest player, the greatest bowler on earth'.

Tate had toured India and Ceylon in 1926/27 with the M.C.C. (Marylebone, not Malgudi). On that tour, he took 128 wickets, of which 116 came in first-class matches. This still remains a world record for most first-class wickets in a season outside the British Isles. One cannot blame Narayan—or Swami.

Swami and Friends mentions Don Bradman, Jack Hobbs and K.S. Duleepsinhji as well, but it is Tate who takes centre stage.

JEFFREY ARCHER, 'THE CENTURY' IN *A QUIVER FULL OF ARROWS* (1980)

Archer was impressed by Mansur Ali Khan Pataudi in their Oxford days together. They remained friends even after, and his adulation for the Nawab ('the last among old-fashioned amateurs') is well-documented. There is little doubt that the leading character of 'The Century' is based on Pataudi.

Archer has taken the odd liberty with facts—it is a work of fiction, after all—but nearly everything about the character matches Pataudi's profile, even something as specific as Iftikhar Ali Khan Pataudi's hundred for Oxford against Cambridge at Lord's.

MIKE MARQUSEE, *SLOW TURN* (1986)

Marqusee is known for his political writings, but he was also the greatest American cricket writer—though, to be fair, he never had to encounter much competition. Before his two cricket classics, *War Minus the Shooting* and *Anyone but England*, he wrote *Slow Turn*, a thriller (well, of sorts).

The protagonist is a foreign cricketer, and the location is Tamil Nadu. The story begins with the gruesome murder of an umpire. However, as the plot unfolds, crime and cricket become a supporting act to contemporary politics. Not his greatest work.

ROHINTON MISTRY, 'SQUATTER' IN *TALES FROM FIROZSHA BAAG* (1987)

One of eleven stories in Mistry's brilliant anthology, 'Squatter' has cricket as a central theme. Nariman Hansotia, who drives a 1932 Mercedes-Benz, sports a Clark Gable moustache, and tells tales to the children at Firozsha Baag, narrates the story of Savukshaw.

Savukshaw walks out to bat at 38–5, with India still requiring 350 to avoid an innings defeat. He starts hitting the ball so hard that the fielders are too afraid to stop or catch it after a grave injury to one of them. Almost every shot ends up demolishing a ball, and the MCC exceeds their budget. The bat survives because Savukshaw used a special oil based on a formula he had acquired from a sadhu.

SALMAN RUSHDIE, *THE MOOR'S LAST SIGH* (1995)

Abbas Ali Baig helped India save the Bombay Test match of 1959/60 against Australia. As he walked back, caught Ken Mackay off Ray Lindwall for 58, a woman of about twenty in a dress jumped the fence of the North Stand, ran onto the ground and kissed Baig.

Around the same age as the girl, Baig was petrified, for his parents were at the venue that day.

Aurora, mother of Moraes Zogoiby aka Moor, the protagonist of Salman Rushdie's *The Moor's Last Sigh*, painted a work called *The Kissing of Abbas Ali Baig* that dates to 1960.

But that was probably the lesser of the two cricket references in the book. There was also the boy who used to ask for 'just one fielding' opportunity from the cricketers. Raman 'Mainduck' Fielding preferred to be called J.O. Fielding. After all, did C.K. Nayudu, no less, not address him as 'so, my little just-one fielding?'

Of course, he does not quite remain 'little'. Cricket becomes 'fundamentally communalist' in the eyes of the cartoonist Fielding.

IAN BURUMA, *PLAYING THE GAME* (1991)

It is not usual for celebrated Dutch authors to write novels on cricket, let alone with K.S. Ranjitsinhji as a character important enough for his photograph to feature on the cover. However, while Ranji is relevant to the book, his cricket is not. The same cannot be said of Gandhi, who bowls underarm and even 'Mankads' Ranji in an inter-college match (before Vinoo Mankad was born, of course). Gandhi and Ranji even watch cricket together in London.

None of this is, of course, remotely true—though Gandhi and Ranji did meet in real life.

ARUNABHA SENGUPTA, *BOWLED OVER* (2004)

Along with several cricket-themed short stories, Sengupta's anthology consists of a novel, *Gilbert Jessop Mystery*, which is a thriller involving Gilbert Jessop, the legendary pre-War cricketer of Gloucestershire and England, and India, immediately after Independence and the 1990s.

There is also *Cricket in the Mirth*, a play where William Shakespeare, G.B. Shaw, Charles Dickens, P.G. Wodehouse, Rabindranath Tagore, Richard Bach, Vikram Seth, Sydney Sheldon and others watch a Test match.

CHETAN BHAGAT, *THE 3 MISTAKES OF MY LIFE* (2008)

Bhagat's third book is set amidst the 2002 Gujarat riots, but also features cricket. The three protagonists sell cricket goods, watch cricket, and one of them spots a rare talent. The narration often mentions some iconic moments of twenty-first-century Indian cricket.

ANUJA CHAUHAN, *THE ZOYA FACTOR* (2008)

Zoya Solanki was born on 25 June 1983, at the very moment when the Indian cricket team won their first ever World Cup. A client-services representative, she now has to work with the 2011 edition of the team. The time of Zoya's birth, combined with the team's continued success in her presence, quickly establishes her status as the team's lucky mascot.

The genre is romance.

PRAMESH RATNAKAR, *CENTURION* (2012)

A cricket book like none other, *Centurion* is a fictional work about Sachin Tendulkar—and yet it is not. It is difficult to classify the book, for how often do you come across a first-person narrative of Tendulkar himself, a man of flesh and blood and cricket and, er, *philosophy*?

JOY AND VIVEK BHATTACHARJYA, *JUNIOR PREMIER LEAGUE: THE FIRST XI* (2014)

The novel recreates the excitement of the IPL with its natural extension, a Junior Premier League. The principal characters are Sachin, a Ranchi boy with an indecipherable bowling action, and Neel, his closest friend and a decent batter. There are lots of references to the actual IPL and meetings with actual IPL players, including Chris Gayle. The action takes the boys to some of the most hallowed Indian cricketing grounds: Eden Gardens, Feroz Shah Kotla and the Cricket Club of India.

RUSKIN BOND, *CRICKET FOR THE CROCODILE* (1986)

The parents of little Ranji (yes, Ranji) use the sport to trick him into focusing on mathematics ('you might need maths to work out your batting average') or history ('famous cricketers make history'), but cricket remains his priority. One faithful spectator of the enthusiastic village matches is Nakoo the crocodile, whose interest has mostly to do with the personnel (the 'juicy bank manager', for example).

The match begins with an unexpected pitch invasion—and gets funnier. Bond does not let his readers down.

HOWZZAT!

In 1997, Jagmohan Dalmiya became the first Indian President of the ICC.

Indian Cricket in Fiction
Films

The only astonishing thing about Indian movies on cricket is how few they are. Casual references are, of course, aplenty. In Kawal Sharma's Maalamaal, for example, Rajkumar Saxena (Naseeruddin Shah) has to splurge money so he hires Sunil Gavaskar to play against his Dharavi XI.

In Dayal Nihalani's Karm Yodha, Sameer (Raj Babbar) faces a different predicament. Chased by goons, he finds his way inside a cricket ground, where a match is on. He grabs a cricket bat, presumably the batter Kapil Dev's, to bash up the antagonist.

However, not many movies actually revolve around a cricketer, culminate in a match, or are generally about the sport itself. Here is a list of some that attained iconic status—some for sheer quality, others, not quite.

The list includes only works of fiction, and thus does not include the biopics of Mohammad Azharuddin (Azhar), M.S. Dhoni (M.S. Dhoni: The Untold Story), Pravin Tambe (Kaun Pravin Tambe?), Mithali Raj (Shabhaash Mithu), and Jhulan Goswami (Chakdaha 'XPress) or 83, based on one of the most significant moments of Indian cricket.

LOVE MARRIAGE (1959)

The genre, as hinted by the title, is romance. Sunil Kumar (Dev Anand), the protagonist, is an aspiring cricketer who arrives in Bombay and rents a room. A highlight of the film is the action of a fast bowler that is modelled on Ray Lindwall's, rated as one of the finest bowling actions in the sport by many.

And then, there is also the little matter of Mohammad Rafi singing 'She *ne khela* he *se aaj* cricket match, *ek nazar mein dil bechara ho gaya* LBW'.

ALL ROUNDER (1984)

It was only fair that at least one cricket movie would be made immediately after the 1983 World Cup win. Ajay (Kumar Gaurav), the protagonist, is the eponymous all-rounder in this otherwise forgettable movie, one that even Kishore Kumar fails to salvage with his *'Pawan purvaiya chale'*. However, the sheer spectacle of Shakti Kapoor playing a superstar cricketer makes up for everything.

KABHIE AJNABI THE (1985)

Unlike the other names on the list, *Kabhie Ajnabi The* featured international cricketers in key roles along with actors Poonam Dhillon and Debashree Roy. Much of the hype around the movie was largely around the two cricketers, Sandeep Patil and Syed Kirmani.

While Patil was approached for his role as the protagonist (a cricketer called Sandeep), Kirmani's role was not part of the script initially. However, once the role was created, an action sequence between the two attained great publicity.

Decades later, Patil reminisced about a day's shooting at the RCF Ground in Chembur, Bombay. The unit required a group of twenty-one young cricketers. One of them was Sachin Tendulkar, then barely ten.

CRICKETER (1985)

Not much is known about Bish Mehay's movie that starred Deepti Naval, Saeed Jaffrey, Marc Zuber and, er, Kapil Dev. The movie was heavily promoted as 'entirely shot in England', and one of several posters sums up the storyline as 'he became a Test cricketer but his emotional life was a mess'. Another poster features Bob Willis.

The IMDb page of *Cricketer* provides some interesting bits of trivia. For example, it was released on 1 January 1985, in *Iceland* of all places; the role came to Kapil Dev only because Sunil Gavaskar turned it down; and the movie had problems with an Indian release because Mr Wouhra, the producer, was an NRI.

AWWAL NUMBER (1990)

Dev Anand plays Vicky, a former cricketer, president of the BCCI, deputy inspector general of police, the antagonist's elder brother, a crack shot, and Cindy Crawford's son. And that is only his on-screen role; he also wrote, directed and produced the movie. Such was his impact that Aamir Khan—who plays Sunny, a young cricketer—signed up for the movie without knowing the script.

The climax shows an ODI between India and Australia at Wankhede Stadium. Like many movies on cricket, the protagonist needs to score 6 runs off the last ball. Unlike any other movie, however, *during the last over*, Dev Anand's brother, a cricketer-turned-terrorist, hovers in a helicopter near the ground, ready to assassinate fifty thousand spectators and all twenty-two cricketers.

LAGAAN (2001)

It was only a matter of time before Bollywood figured out a way to amalgamate cricket with patriotism. They then roped in Bhanu Athaiya and A.R. Rahman, and brick by brick, built the magnum opus of Indian cricket movies. From practice under floodlights to handmade pads to match-fixing, *Lagaan* has everything, including tributes to Palwankar Baloo and Bhagwat Chandrasekhar, and a mention of W.G. Grace.

Despite its deviations from cricket, or at least from its 1893 laws, *Lagaan* manages to stand the test of time. The film also made its way to the Academy Awards nominations.

STUMPED (2003)

Stumped is a throwback to the summer of 1999, when India fought Pakistan at Kargil and in the World Cup. The film deals with the residents of Happy Home Society, all but one of whom are focused on the cricket. Reena Seth (Raveena Tandon) awaits news of her husband, Major Raghav (Alyy Khan), missing and presumed dead, at Kargil. The poignant ending features Kapil Dev, Sachin Tendulkar and Yuvraj Singh in a moving message.

IQBAL (2005)

Iqbal (Shreyas Talpade) has multiple hurdles to conquer. He comes from a humble, rural background, and is speech and hearing impaired. To make things worse, his father (Yatin Karyekar) considers cricket a waste of time. However, he gets unwavering support from younger sister Khadija (Shweta Basu Prasad), and convinces former cricketer Mohit (Naseeruddin Shah) to coach him.

One of Nagesh Kukunoor's finest works, *Iqbal* is a tale of struggles told beautifully, with subtle humour, and outstanding performances from everyone.

CHAIN KULII KI MAIN KULII (2007)

There is no 'yer a wizard, Harry' moment for Karan (Zain Khan), a bullied orphan. Nor is he given a wand. However, he gets a bat—the same one with which Kapil Dev made 175 not out in the 1983 World Cup. The bat transforms Karan into an extraordinary cricketer who is catapulted into the national side in no time.

VICTORY (2009)

The IMDb page of *Victory* can pass as a Who's Who of international cricket. From Tony Greig to Allan Border to Waqar Younis to Sanath Jayasuriya to Brett Lee to Muttiah Muralitharan to Graeme Smith, *Victory* featured enough cricketers to field its own IPL team. The predictable match-winning last-over onslaught from Vijay Shekhawat (Harman S. Baweja) comes against Stuart Clark.

DIL BOLE HADIPPA! (2009)

'Veera Kaur gets selected for the men's cricket team disguised as Veer Pratap Singh in this romantic comedy' may sound bizarre, but it is an accurate summary of a rather peculiar storyline. Whatever the intent had been, it does not work. The humour is dated and the cricket far from authentic. Rani Mukerji's comeback effort fell flat on its face.

PATIALA HOUSE (2011)

Patiala House tells the story of Gattu (Akshay Kumar), an Indian based in England who wants to play cricket. He has the talent for it but his father, Gurtej (Rishi Kapoor), threatens to commit suicide if Gattu plays *for England*. All ends well, especially after Gattu bowls like Lala Amarnath to dismiss Andrew Symonds. The movie features Sanjay Manjrekar and Nikhil Chopra commentating in Hindi during an Anglo-Australian match.

CHALO PALTAI (2011)

The premise is familiar: Subhamoy (Prosenjit Chatterjee) pressures his son, Gourav (Debdan Bhowmik), to forego his cricketing dreams and pursue studies instead. However, the plotline takes an outlandish turn with Subhamoy tying a bomb to his body and meeting the chief minister, but Chatterjee's screen presence makes the movie work.

FERRARI KI SAWARI (2012)

Sleek, witty and very human, *Ferrari ki Sawari* features outstanding performances from the three lead actors (Boman Irani, Sharman Joshi and Ritwik Sahore) as grandfather, father and son. Cricket makes relevant, convincing appearances. A poignant tale, beautifully told. Sachin Tendulkar does not make an appearance, but his Ferrari does.

KANAA (2018)

When Kowsi (Aishwarya Rajesh) sees her father break down after India's early exit from the 2007 World Cup, she vows to help India win the coveted prize, and goes on to do exactly that with her off-breaks. The route, as expected, is not easy for a rural woman who battles challenges as her father—a farmer—struggles to pay off his bank loan.

JERSEY (2019)

Jersey won two national awards, and deservedly so, for few Indian movies have dealt with failed cricketers with such empathy. The story revolves around Arjun (Nani), a Hyderabad Ranji Trophy player who quits cricket after being unable to break into the Indian side. Many years and incidents later, a near-broken Arjun earns a comeback to the Ranji Trophy side, and finally ends his career on a high. The climax alone makes the movie worth a watch.

It was later remade into Hindi, with Shahid Kapur playing the role of Arjun.

> **HOWZZAT!**
>
> After Independence, the cap and blazer of the Indian Test cricketer featured the Asoka Stambha, the Indian national emblem. It was replaced with the BCCI logo only in the early 1960s.

Cricketers in Unusual Professions

Making money from playing cricket is a fairly recent concept, as is BCCI's pension scheme. Cricketers of yesteryear had little option but to take up day jobs to sustain themselves even during their playing days—and beyond. Both in the government and private sectors, popular cricketers were employed to represent office teams. Some contests, especially in the Times Shield, often featured a galaxy of Test cricketers. The Indian Railways and the Armed Services have their respective Ranji Trophy teams.

In the pre-Independence era, employment was usually provided by royal families—whether in their personal teams or in other positions. The Maharaja of Patiala and the Maharajkumar of Vizianagaram were the forerunners, with Holkar, Baroda and Cooch Behar not too far behind. And then, there were the royal families of Nawanagar and Pataudi, some of whose members were excellent cricketers themselves.

However, some cricketers took up professions one would not usually associate with those in the sport. D.B. Deodhar, the first Indian first-class cricketer to live past the age of hundred, played on either side of the two World Wars, scored a hundred in each innings in a Ranji Trophy match at the age of fifty-three, and—was a professor of Sanskrit in Poona College! Here are some of the other notables in this list, though it does not include honorary roles.

LALL SINGH (THEATRE AGENT, NIGHTCLUB OWNER)

Perhaps no Indian Test cricketer has led a life as eventful as the Kuala Lumpur-born Lall Singh, whose only Test match was also India's first ever. He scored 15 and 29 in that match, and ran out Frank Woolley.

Lall Singh married (some sources suggest they lived together) Mexican actor–singer Myrtle Watkins, and became her theatrical agent. The couple later ran a nightclub in Paris. While in the nation of his birth, Malaya, he was arrested by the Japanese during the Second World War. He somehow escaped, and eventually took up his first paying job—as ground staff at the Selangor Club in Kuala Lumpur.

JANARDAN NAVLE (SECURITY GUARD)

Navle, wicketkeeper in India's debut Test match, was also the team's first man to face a ball. He was recruited in the service of Gwalior, but in subsequent years, he worked as a security officer in a sugar mill, and lived in a two-bedroom apartment in Poona. Rumours of him having to beg on the Bombay–Poona Highway in later life were, thankfully, nothing more.

RUSI MODI (AIDE-DE-CAMP, GOVERNOR OF BOMBAY)

Throughout the 1940s, Modi competed with the Vijays—Merchant and Hazare—for the unofficial tag of the most voracious Indian run-glutton of the era. He was the first Indian to score 1,000 runs in a Ranji Trophy season as well as the first to score a double hundred for a representative Indian side. His Test career was brief but prolific, and he remains one of India's finest cricket writers.

Modi was also the aide-de-camp of the Governor of Bombay. In 1949/50, when Governor Raja Maharaj Singh became the oldest person to play first-class cricket (at seventy-two!), Modi featured alongside him in the team.

CHANDU SARWATE (FINGERPRINT EXPERT)

One of the giants of Indian domestic cricket, Sarwate played 9 Test matches between 1946 and 1951/52. His most celebrated first-class performance was the 124—while batting at No. 10—and 5–54 against Surrey in 1946. A fingerprint expert by profession, Sarwate was often called upon in important cases as an expert witness.

JUDAH REUBEN (FINGERPRINT EXPERT)

Like Sarwate, Reuben was a fingerprint expert as well—for the Bombay Police, no less. He umpired in 10 Tests, between 1969/70 and 1976/77. It was an eventful career: he witnessed a riot on Eden Gardens on debut, and signed off at Chepauk amidst controversies over John Lever and Vaseline.

GHULAM GUARD (POLICE SI-TURNED-SUPERINTENDENT)

The first left-arm seamer to open bowling for India in Test cricket, Guard once knocked the bat out of Garry Sobers's hands (and took the catch on rebound) in a Test match. His 9 wickets in the 1959/60 Ranji Trophy final against Mysore earned him an entry in *The Indian Police Journal* (it began with 'Ghulam Guard, Sub-Inspector in the Bombay State Police Force...'). Now that is something not many Test cricketers can boast of!

Guard's day job eventually took him away from Bombay. He became superintendent of police in Gujarat.

RUSI SURTI (FIRE BRIGADE EMPLOYEE)

Surti had five seasons with Queensland, during which he also took up employment at the Queensland Fire Department. The experience was far from pleasant. In 1993, he filed a lawsuit against the fire department, accusing them of calling him, among other things, a 'curry eater' and an 'Indian bastard'. He lost the case; the court dismissed most of the phrases as 'mere banter'.

M.S. DHONI (TRAVELLING TICKET EXECUTIVE, INDIAN RAILWAYS)

Dhoni's wicketkeeping skills helped him get a job as a ticket collector (TTE) with the Indian Railways at Kharagpur Junction. His days of balancing both roles were depicted with reasonable accuracy in his biopic, *M.S. Dhoni: The Untold Story*. As he grew in stature, Dhoni got invitations for more matches, and eventually quit his job.

JOGINDER SHARMA (DEPUTY SUPERINTENDENT OF POLICE)

Sharma did not play international cricket after bowling the last ball of India's triumphant 2007 T20 World Cup campaign. A nation with little clue about cricket's shortest format suddenly took interest. In another decade, cricket's economy changed, perhaps forever. Sharma had an outstanding domestic career on either side of a life-threatening head injury in 2011, while still serving in Haryana Police. A deputy superintendent at the time of writing, Sharma earned accolades for his stellar role during the pandemic-induced nationwide lockdown of 2020.

RANJIB BISWAL AND MANOJ TIWARY (POLITICIANS)

Over the years, Indian cricketers have contested political elections. Mansur Ali Khan Pataudi, Chetan Chauhan, Kirti Azad, Mohammad Azharuddin, Navjot Sidhu, Ashok Dinda—the list is long and diverse. Khandu Rangnekar's stint as Mayor of Thane perhaps surpassed his cricketing career in stature. Almost all of them, however, became active politicians only *after* their days of serious cricket were over. There are a couple of exceptions, though.

In 1996, Ranjib Biswal was elected to the Lok Sabha from Jagatsinghpur. Even after he had become a Member of Parliament, he led Orissa against Bengal in that winter's Ranji Trophy and Ranji Trophy One Day in which he returned figures of 10-4-18-2.

Manoj Tiwary won the West Bengal Vidhan Sabha Elections of 2021 from Shibpur, and was appointed a Minister of State for Affairs of Sports and Youth. A year later, he turned up in the Ranji Trophy. In the tally of Bengal cricketers, his 433 runs were next only to Shahbaz Ahmed's 482 that season. He also broke through to the top ten in the list of leading run-getters in the history of the tournament.

HOWZZAT!

India's first Test victory in England in 1971 brought to an end England's record run of 26 undefeated Tests.

Butterfly Effects
Off-the-Field Incidents that Changed Indian Cricket

In the early 1860s, two Melburnians, Felix William Spiers and Christopher Pond, tried to convince Charles Dickens to travel across Australia for a lecture tour. When Dickens showed little interest, they invited some of the best English cricketers. This cricketing tour, the first between England and Australia, was the forerunner of the Ashes, still the most high-profile bilateral Test series in the world.

Dickens's refusal helped cricket evolve from assorted local events to an organized international sport. There are similar examples in Indian cricket, too.

FAZAL ATTACKED ON TRAIN

India were to visit Australia in late 1947 for their first cricketing tour after Independence. The pre-tour camp was held in Poona from 15 August 1947. Fazal Mahmood, twenty, was supposed to attend the camp, but a full-fledged curfew had been imposed at Lahore in the aftermath of religious riots. He travelled to Karachi by road before flying out to Bombay. He made it to Poona.

The camp concluded without much fuss. The cricketers took the train back to Bombay. A mob attacked this train with the intention of lynching the Muslim cricketers. C.K. Nayudu, then fifty-one, stood between the rioters and Fazal with a cricket bat. Fazal reached Bombay safely, abandoned his original itinerary (via Delhi), and flew straight back to Karachi.

He did not tour Australia with India. Instead, he became Pakistan's first great fast bowler. It took him five years to return to India—as the spearhead of the opposition's attack. He took 12–94 to help Pakistan win the second Test match ever at Lucknow.

Indian cricket of the 1930s was mostly dominated by pace, with Mohammad Nissar, Amar Singh, Jahangir Khan and even an ageing Ladha Ramji calling the shots. Fazal would not only have carried on that legacy but also inspired a generation after him, like Kapil Dev did in the 1980s.

As things turned out, no Indian fast bowler was able to take 100 Test wickets until Kapil in 1979/80, and the lack of fast bowlers meant that India seldom won Test matches outside the subcontinent.

SOFTBALL PLAYERS GET BORED

Softball used to be a popular sport in India in the early 1970s. In 1972, two sports organizers—Narendra Nikam and Dileep Chinchore—accompanied a team of female multi-sport athletes on a train journey. While proficient in basketball and hockey, the women were actually travelling for a softball tournament.

Bored of the long train journey, the women decided to play cricket inside the compartment using softball bats and balls. Nikam and Chinchore noticed how they were playing cricket with a straight bat.

Mahendra Kumar Sharma used to organize softball and handball for girls in Uttar Pradesh. He already knew several female cricketers across the country, particularly in the large cities, and that there was no central umbrella under which they could play.

When he met Sharma, Nikam told him about the authentic brand of cricket played by the softball players. Until then, Sharma had had ideas, but Nikam's inputs motivated him to not only found the Women's Cricket Association of India but also get it registered under the Societies Act of Lucknow.

Women's cricket took off in India.

WADEKAR GETS NEW SHOES

By the early 1970s, Bombay winning the Ranji Trophy every year was as inevitable as death and taxes. Having won fifteen titles in a row, they were set for a sixteenth when they met Karnataka in the semi-final of the 1973/74 season. Karnataka made 385 in the first innings, but Bombay cruised to 179/2 by stumps on Day 2 with Ashok Mankad and Ajit Wadekar at the crease.

Wadekar was wearing new rubber-soled shoes. He had been comfortable in them while batting in the nets—but net practice does not involve running between the wickets. Soon after play began on the third morning, Mankad played Karnataka captain E.A.S. Prasanna to point. As Sudhakar Rao sprinted in to pick up the ball, Wadekar called for a run, but Mankad sent him back. Wadekar had an eternity to return to the crease, but the new shoes let him down. He slipped, and could not make it back in time. Prasanna did the rest. Bombay collapsed to 307. Karnataka won on first-innings lead and advanced to the final. Bombay's streak had come to an end.

A vengeful Bombay won the next three seasons, but Prasanna's Karnataka had shown the rest of India that Bombay were not invincible. Every now and then Karnataka posed a threat, and by the end of the decade Delhi too became a force to reckon with. Bombay remained the best side, but it was no longer a monopoly.

KAPIL DENIED FOOD

In 1975, a young Kapil Dev was attending a camp for budding cricketers at the Cricket Club of India in Bombay. After a gruelling session in sultry heat, the youngsters were served a meal of two dry chapatis and vegetables.

A famished Kapil demanded more. When he was told that the instructions had come from Keki Tarapore, administrator of the camp, Kapil led a small group to Tarapore's office. Kapil was blunt: 'Nobody can fill his belly with such a small serving, and I am a fast bowler. I practise a lot and really sweat it out. That's the reason—'

Kapil never forgot Tarapore's response. 'Young man, India has been playing international cricket for over forty years, but till date

India hasn't produced a single fast bowler. Fast bowler … that's the best joke I've heard in years!'

The man who led India to their first World Cup victory, broke the stereotype of Indian cricket being dependent on batting and spin bowling forever and inspired generations of fast bowlers, has always cited Tarapore's reaction as a motivation behind his cricketing career.

SALVE DENIED PASSES

Two significant events at Lord's in June 1983 changed the course of Indian cricket forever. While the more famous one took place on the field—India beat West Indies in the final to win the World Cup—what happened just outside was no less significant.

N.K.P. Salve, BCCI President at that time, had requested the authorities for two extra passes for the final. When that was denied, a humiliated Salve vowed to bring the World Cup Championship out of England. Until then, England had hosted all three editions of the tournament: Salve set out to change that.

Along with representatives from Pakistan, Sri Lanka, Bangladesh, Singapore and Malaysia, Salve founded the Asian Cricket Council, and in 1984, the ACC hosted the inaugural Asia Cup, thus becoming the first regional organization to host international cricket and generate profit. Unlike Kerry Packer's World Series or the Rebel Test matches in South Africa, the Asia Cup was an official competition in which cricketers could participate without fear of being banned.

That same year, in the ICC meeting, Jagmohan Dalmiya and I.S. Bindra secured enough votes to fulfil Salve's vow: India and Pakistan co-hosted the next World Cup in 1987, thereby laying the first stone towards India's dominance in world cricket off the field.

DOORDARSHAN TELECASTS *GUIDE*

One Sunday evening in 1984, Doordarshan telecast the classic Dev Anand–starrer *Guide*. While the residents of Sahitya Sahawas Colony, Bandra, Bombay, sat glued to their television sets, three boys—Sunil Harshe, Avinash Gowariker and Sachin Tendulkar—climbed a mango tree. During their pursuit, a branch gave way and all three fell with a crash.

The boys received some 'treatment', but the Tendulkar household went a step further. The family decided that something had to be done about young Sachin's pent-up energy, especially during the long summer vacations. Ajit Tendulkar, his brother, recommended Ramakant Achrekar's cricket coaching camp. The rest is history.

LAMBA'S INJURY

The Karachi Test match of 1989/90 boasts two of the most significant incidents in the history of Indian cricket. One was Sachin Tendulkar's debut. The other took place not too long before the toss.

By the late 1990s, much of Mohammad Azharuddin's initial shine had worn off. Having gone almost three years without scoring a Test hundred, he was on the verge of being dropped from the side. In the Karachi squad Azharuddin would be the 12th man.

Just before the toss, Raman Lamba, who had scored the most runs for India in the recently concluded Nehru Cup, reported a finger injury. Azharuddin played instead, scored 35 in each innings, and took five catches, some of them spectacular. In the next Test match, he scored a 109. He was back. Lamba would never play Test cricket again.

India drew the series 0-0. A few days after the squad returned, Raj Singh Dungarpur, then chair of selectors, approached Azharuddin during a domestic match: *'Miyan, kaptaan banoge?'*

Azharuddin had led only four times in first-class cricket until then, two of these were after the Pakistan tour. He agreed, and went on to become one of India's longest-standing, as well as controversial, captains.

Indian cricket in the 1990s was, thus, shaped by the injury of a man who did not play for India in the 1990s.

SOUTH AFRICA RETURNS

South Africa's apartheid policies had earned them a ban from international cricket for almost two decades. However, throughout the 1980s, Ali Bacher—the last man to lead South Africa before the ban—tirelessly tried to arrange 'rebel' tours, inviting teams to South Africa, luring them with enough money to forego their international careers.

South Africa's first international series after the ban was in India, in 1991/92. Bacher, manager of this team, asked the BCCI about the formalities regarding broadcasting rights of the series in South Africa. This seemingly normal request left the BCCI authorities confused, for never in their history had anyone offered them money to telecast live cricket. BCCI's revenue from cricket matches in India came only from a share of stadium tickets and advertisements *inside the stadium*. If anything, at times they had had to pay Doordarshan to cover live cricket (and not the other way round).

After a frantic discussion, the BCCI got back to Bacher with an offer of USD 10,000 per match for the three ODIs. Bacher offered USD 40,000 per match (in other words, four times what the BCCI wanted *for the entire series*). South Africa's return to international cricket mattered to the people back home, whose future leader

Nelson Mandela would later say, 'Sport has the power to change the world.'

This sum of USD 120,000 for a high-profile series was the BCCI's first income from selling television rights. For perspective, the BCCI sold the IPL rights for five years to Disney Star and Viacom for USD 6.2 billion in 2022.

SIDHU HAS A STIFF NECK

On the morning of 27 March 1994, Navjot Sidhu woke up with a stiff neck in his hotel room in Auckland. India had an ODI that day against New Zealand, but now Sidhu was ruled out.

Who would replace Sidhu as Ajay Jadeja's opening partner? There was no reserve opener. A young Sachin Tendulkar volunteered. He even promised coach Ajit Wadekar that he would never repeat the request if he failed. He slammed a 49-ball 82 and never looked back.

Until that point, Tendulkar had scored 1,758 runs at an average of 30.84 with a highest score of 84. He would amass another 16,586 at 46.98 with 49 hundreds to finish as the most prolific run-scorer in ODI history.

Tendulkar the opener was born, and he grew with satellite television in India. So prolific would his run-scoring be that by the end of the decade he would earn the moniker 'God'.

ZEE LOSES BATTLE FOR TELEVISION RIGHTS

In the 1970s, Kerry Packer was denied broadcasting rights for cricket in Australia. He responded by launching World Series Cricket, a rebel league. He lured many underpaid cricketers from Australia and beyond, including the banned South Africans. The Australian and West Indian boards banned their cricketers, but so popular was the WSC that the Australian board gave in. Packer got the rights. And the Australian cricketers got paid substantially more than they used to.

Nearly three decades later, Subhash Chandra attempted something similar after losing at the bidding for the broadcasting rights several times. He launched the Indian Cricket League, where the teams were named after cities, and every team featured a mix of overseas stars and capped and uncapped Indian cricketers.

The BCCI responded by banning the Indian participants, and announcing the *official* Indian Premier League, an idea they had shelved over a decade ago. The ICL failed to take off: unlike the WSC, the ICL was unable to get the biggest local names on board. It was impossible for a tournament without Tendulkar or Kumble or Dhoni or Ganguly or Dravid or Sehwag or Yuvraj to compete against one with them.

While Subhash Chandra never got the rights he wanted, he inadvertently accelerated the advent of the IPL, triggering an irreversible change to the economics of cricket. Additionally, to prevent future rebel leagues from taking place, the BCCI increased the daily fees of the domestic cricketers by more than twice the existing amount.

AND FINALLY ... THE ONE THAT COULD HAVE, BUT DIDN'T!

On 10 July 1949, Narayan Masurekar was visiting a Bombay hospital to meet his nephew, who was born earlier that day. He noticed a tiny hole near the top of the left earlobe of the baby. When he returned next day, to his horror, the hole was no longer there!

Upon a frantic search, the infant Sunil Gavaskar was found 'sleeping blissfully' next to a fisherwoman. The babies had been swapped accidentally when they were being bathed. Had Masurekar not noticed, India might not have got their first legendary batter—at one point Gavaskar had the most Test runs and hundreds in the world—for decades. Worse, generations of batters would probably not have been inspired by a living legend.

Although, given Gavaskar's dedication, determination and discipline, India might have become the global leader in fishing!

HOWZZAT!

In 2003, Ramanlal Pathak, a Sanskrit scholar from Vadodara, recommended cricket commentary in the language. It had taken him seven years to create a dictionary. The jargon included *bat-dhar* (batter), *gachha* or *dhavan* (runs), *nivruttaha* (a dismissal), and so on. Unfortunately, the broadcasters were not too keen to say '*sahatu chowkaa, sarvatra prekshaka mandalie anandasya vatavaranam*' (another four, the crowd is ecstatic).

The Real Stakeholders
Iconic Indian Cricket Fans

'They throng to the grounds in their thousands and, over a full Test match, in their hundreds of thousands, cheerfully sitting in cramped space having bought legitimate and at times non-existent tickets after months of saving for the great day.'—Richie Benaud.

Of the hundreds of thousands—and, indeed, millions, thanks to television and online streaming of matches—some Indian cricket fans attained cult status.

BABU TANGEWALA

A Poona *tanga*-driver of humble means, Babu Tangewala began garlanding cricketers when they reached hundreds as early as in 1915. Such was his fame that the Maharashtra Ranji Trophy team considered him their mascot, and he enjoyed certain privileges such as the occasional ride in the team coach. Babu's legacy spread even beyond the local cricket grounds. In 1948, he sent Don Bradman a trophy through D.B. Deodhar, and corresponded with Bradman as well as Richie Benaud and Peter May in later years. He used to be a favourite of lawyer-author-politician N.C. Kelkar, who specifically booked Babu's *tanga* for cricket conversations, and chronicled his life in his works.

He continued garlanding cricketers until 1960, when the authorities put an end to the practice. His house was destroyed in a flood, but compensation arrived when the public raised INR 2,000 towards its restoration.

DULAN MEHTA

At Bombay in 1933/34, Lala Amarnath became the first Indian to score a Test hundred, and famously received lavish gifts from fans. After the Test match, Dulan Mehta, the daughter of a local jeweller, showed up at his room with 'a bag full of diamond jewellery' and asked Amarnath to elope with her. With no intention of agreeing, Amarnath asked her to wait until the end of the series!

Decades later, Rahul Dravid did not find things as simple: a female fan from Hyderabad arrived at his residence in Bangalore. She claimed to have left home and showed no inclination to leave his house.

CHARLIE

Charlie was probably not the real name of the short but ample Parsee fan at the Bombay Quadrangular and Pentangular in pre-Independence India. He earned that nickname for his ability to imitate Charlie Chaplin. One of the first popular Indian cricket fans, Charlie made wisecracks, garlanded cricketers and once ran *between the legs of* the Maharaja of Patiala.

SETH HIRALAL

Denis Compton was posted in MHOW during the Second World War. Holkar captain C.K. Nayudu got news and immediately poached Compton to play for them. Holkar reached the final of the 1944/45 Ranji Trophy at Brabourne Stadium. Here, after securing a 102-run first-innings lead, Bombay piled up 764, leaving Holkar to chase a mammoth 867.

They were 177/2 at stumps on the fifth day of the timeless match, with Mushtaq Ali on 106 and Compton on 55. Now Hiralal Seth, a local businessman, approached Compton: 'Mister Compton, this is a very important match for the whole locality. It is very necessary that we win, so for every single run you make after passing your century I will give you a hundred rupees.'

Compton was eventually left stranded on 249 as Holkar were bowled out for 492. On his way back, he calculated his potential earnings of around GBP 1,300—a substantial amount in the era. However, all he received was a note: 'Sorry, have been called to Calcutta on very urgent business.'

Compton never got the money, though Mushtaq claimed that *he* was paid for the 9 runs *he* had scored after reaching hundred.

AN UNNAMED LETTER-WRITER

A fan once wrote to Don Bradman, thanking him for signing an autograph. The letter ran: 'I thank you from the bottom of my heart for your kind reply. Oh how nice of you. How my heart is leaping for joy. Words refuse to come and I must stop here. I thank you once again. Many thanks—truly thanks. I beg to remain dear Don, a lingering memory at least.'

Bradman believed that words portray the personal attributes and qualities of their author. For the writer in question, the Don correctly surmised that he 'didn't need to see his signature—it is quite obvious he was from India.'

DEVDAS GANDHI

The youngest son of the Mahatma did something that even the most passionate cricket fans are unlikely to contemplate.

Gandhi was in England in 1948 when Don Bradman's Invincibles were on tour. Although the first Test match, at Trent Bridge, was sold out, Gandhi used his contacts in the press to obtain a ticket. However, he encountered a new problem in Nottingham: every hotel was fully booked. He somehow convinced the warden and acquired a bed in the Nottingham County Jail. It was ironic, for he had been arrested by the British before, during the Salt March. He broke his fast with the convicts the next morning. It was worth it: Bradman was at 130 by stumps.

SUDHIR KUMAR GAUTAM

Between 2002 and the outbreak of COVID-19, Sudhir Gautam had attended every match played by India at home, and had even cycled to Pakistan and Bangladesh for the away matches. He is easily recognizable in the stands, with the Indian tricolour and the words 'Tendulkar 10' (he added 'Miss U' after his favourite cricketer's retirement) painted across his torso and face, a map of India atop his head. There is also his famous conch that he blows to herald the team's arrival on the field …

So devoted is Gautam that he once cycled from Muzaffarpur to Mumbai to visit Tendulkar. After India won the World Cup in 2011, Tendulkar invited Gautam to lift the trophy and pose alongside. And during the 2019 World Cup, the Indian Sports Fan honoured him with the Global Sports Fan Award.

RAM BABU

Ram Babu is to M.S. Dhoni what Sudhir Gautam is to Sachin Tendulkar. A local of Mohali, Ram Babu also paints the tricolour on his person, though the words read 'Dhoni 7'. He changes his hairdo to match Dhoni's, and is gifted with the enviable ability to chant and wave the Indian flag all day.

He was in Bangladesh for the 2014 T20 World Cup. When he fell ill, the Indian team physiotherapist attended to him. When he did not improve, Dhoni sponsored an air ticket to send him back home. When he had to spend a month in hospital upon his return, Dhoni sponsored that too.

SARUN SHARMA

Ahead of the 2007 World Cup, Sarun Sharma, a salesperson in a shop in Sakchi, Jamshedpur, put up one of his kidneys for sale to be able to afford the trip to the West Indies: 'Anybody can survive with one kidney, but you will never get the opportunity to watch India win the cup in the West Indies.'

The police pointed out that it was an illegal sale. A dejected Sharma told media that he would jump off the nearby Mango Bridge. The police detained him but released him after a few hours.

India were eliminated in the first round.

RAVINDRA SAINI—OR PERHAPS SONIA

In 2009, one Ravindra Kumar Saini of Saharanpur, Uttar Pradesh, sold his shop of audio and video CDs to fund his trip to Ranchi, where he survived for thirty-five days in spartan conditions, even skipping meals and sleeping on the pavement, awaiting a chance to be photographed with M.S. Dhoni. The news reached Gautam Gupta, who informed his famous brother-in-law. Dhoni shook hands with Saini, while the cameras clicked.

What sets Saini apart from other fans was the reason behind his desperate act. His fiancée, Sonia, had agreed to marry him only if he got photographed with Dhoni.

GUWAHATI INMATES

During the 2015 World Cup, Doordarshan telecast only India's matches, but six inmates of Guwahati Central Jail wanted to watch every match. They filed a public interest litigation, demanding satellite television inside the prison. Cricket 'cannot be said to be out of the purview of Article 21 of the Constitution of India,' argued senior counsel Ashok Saraf on their behalf.

'Prisoners need recreation for a healthy mind,' read Justice Arup Kumar's verdict. He ordered the prison to arrange for cable television within five days.

CHARULATA PATEL

Charulata Patel was eighty-seven when the television cameras spotted her at Birmingham during the 2019 India against Bangladesh World Cup match. Tricolour scarf around her neck and vuvuzela in hand, Patel cheered for India with a vigour rarely seen even in fans decades younger than her. Indian captain Virat Kohli and vice-captain Rohit Sharma both met her after the match.

BHARAT ARMY AND SWAMI ARMY

The Bharat Army, 'founded' by four Indian fans based in England during the 1999 World Cup between India and Pakistan, has now expanded to a reasonable size. They coordinate to show up and cheer for the Indian team around the world, and are almost certainly the largest organized group of fans of the Indian cricket team.

In 2019/20, India won their first Test series on Australian soil. Over the course of the series, the Bharat Army came up with the song *'I just don't think you understand/he'll hit you for a six/he'll babysit your kids/we got Rishabh Pant'* to celebrate one of India's heroes.

The Swami Army was founded on similar lines during India's 2003/04 tour of Australia.

MOHAMMAD BASHIR BOZAI

Popularly known as Chacha Chicago—he runs a restaurant there—Bashir was struggling to find a ticket for the India–Pakistan semi-final of the 2011 World Cup in Mohali. M.S. Dhoni obtained one for him. The moment converted Bashir, who hails from Karachi, into a Dhoni fan.

Three heart attacks failed to prevent Bashir from travelling across the world to watch Dhoni in action. Nor did abuse from fellow Pakistan fans stop him for cheering for India. However, when Dhoni announced retirement from international cricket in 2019, Bashir decided to stop watching India–Pakistan matches at ICC events.

HOWZZAT!

In 2004, a group of boys playing cricket on the Naroda–Thakkarnagar Road in Gujarat spotted some unusual objects. One of the boys pulled what he thought was a string, resulting in an explosion. The police arrived to find twenty-three signal rockets.

Against All Odds
Indian Cricketers Who Overcame Pain

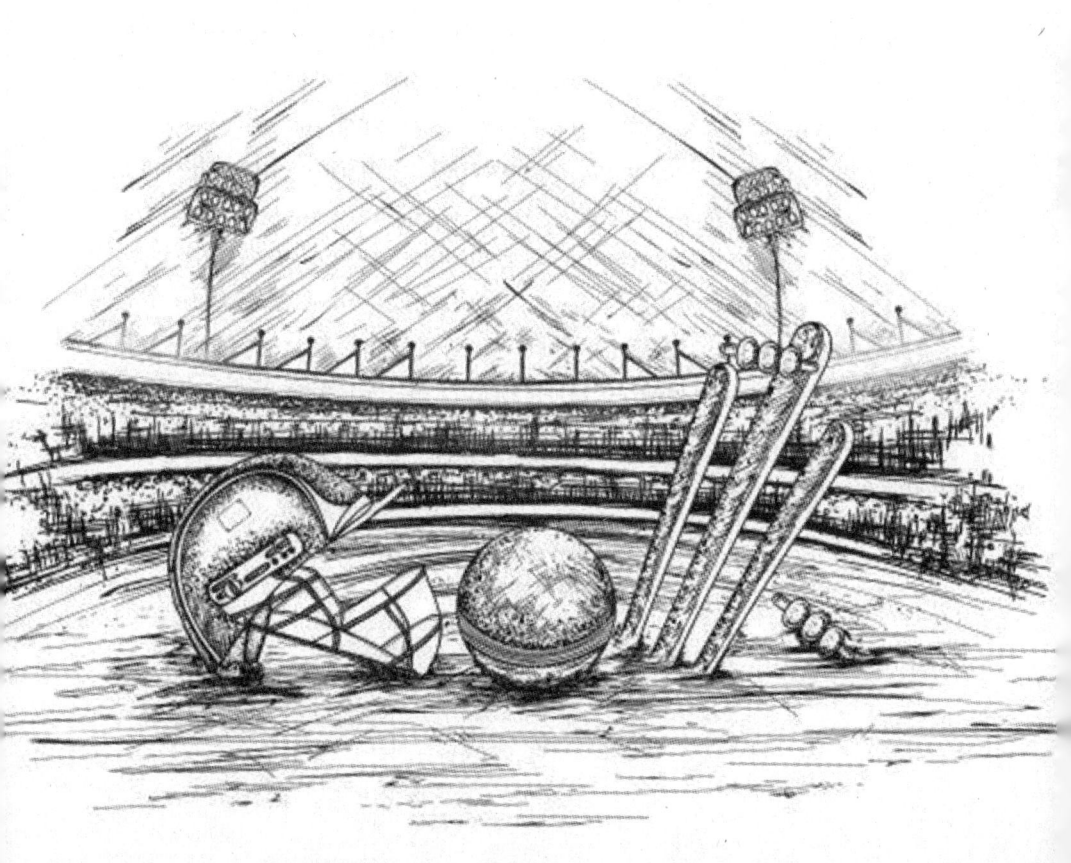

It is not easy for us, ordinary individuals, to fathom the pain threshold of top-level athletes. From time to time, cricketers have emerged triumphant in the battle against injuries, illnesses and other physical discomfort and pulled off heroic performances.

Mansur Ali Khan Pataudi lost his right eye in a car accident in 1961 even before he played Test cricket. When 'Gubby' Allen asked Pataudi why he took the bold decision to continue to play cricket with a glass eye, the latter responded, 'When I saw the English attack.' In 46 Test matches, Pataudi scored 2,793 runs at an average of 35: how many more he might have scored, one cannot help but wonder.

Bhagwat Chandrasekhar contracted polio at six, which restricted the use of his right hand. He recovered enough to play cricket from ten, and used his thin hand to add extra sting to his top spinner. Batters were often deceived by his faster ball, most famously John Edrich by his Mill Reef, discussed elsewhere in the book. So inept was Chandrasekhar with the bat—he sometimes had to support his right hand with his left, and when fielding, he threw with his left hand—that he had more wickets than runs in Test cricket. Yet his 242 Test wickets came at under 30 apiece, and some of his spells remain the greatest in the history of Indian cricket.

However, we shall discuss only performances—not careers in their entirety—in this section.

DILAWAR HUSSAIN AND OTHER BODYLINE WARRIORS

India hosted Test cricket for the first time in 1933/34, less than a year after Douglas Jardine had unleashed Bodyline to retrieve the Ashes from Australia. Though the team were missing Harold Larwood and Bill Voce, Jardine had 'Nobby' Clark and Stan Nichols, both genuinely quick and without qualms about bowling to a Bodyline field. The series became a 'bumper war', with the Indians, especially Mohammad Nissar, bowling to a similar field and hitting several batters.

The first Test passed peacefully, but Clark hit Dilawar Hussain—protected by neither headgear nor hair—on the head in India's first innings of the second match, in Calcutta. He had to be carried off the field. Dilawar, on 11 at this point, returned with a bandaged head to top-score 59 the next day. India followed on, and once again Dilawar top-scored, this time with 54. He had to retire midway, this time after Clark hit him on the thumb. He helped India draw the Test match.

In the third Test, in Madras, Naoomal Jaoomal tried to hook Clark, was hit above the eye, and had to be stretchered off. Yadavindra Singh, the Yuvraj of Patiala, took a few balls from Clark on his turban, while Merchant needed four stitches after Nichols hit him on the chin. Jaoomal did not return, but Yadavindra Singh got 24 and 60, and Merchant 26 and 28.

MANSUR ALI KHAN PATAUDI

Having pulled a hamstring, Mansur Ali Khan Pataudi had sat out of the first Test match of India's 1967/68 tour of Australia. He announced himself available only on the morning of the second Test match, at Melbourne, despite not having recovered. When he came to bat on the first morning, India had been reduced to 25/5 on a green wicket, Rusi Surti had retired hurt, and it was drizzling...

Pataudi's one-legged, counterattacking 75 was so spectacular that Lindsay Hassett compared him to Don Bradman. Robert Menzies, former Australian prime minister, was left wondering what Pataudi might have done with 'two eyes and two good legs.'

Pataudi added 85 in the second innings for good measure.

RAMAKANT DESAI

After being bowled out for 350 at Dunedin in 1967/68, New Zealand reduced India to 302/9. Dick Motz fractured Ramakant Desai's jaw with a bouncer, but Desai stayed put, adding 57 with Bishan Bedi for the last wicket to help India secure a 9-run lead. He remained unbeaten on 32.

Desai even bowled 7 overs in the second innings before the spinners took over. India won the match to create history: it was their first triumph away from home.

SUNIL GAVASKAR

India were leading 1–0 on their 1971 tour of the West Indies ahead of the final Test, a six-day match at Port of Spain. After a net session, a thirsty Sunil Gavaskar—who had debuted in that series—requested Ashok Mankad to pour cold water from a pitcher into his mouth. As Mankad obliged, a tiny piece of ice got stuck inside a tooth cavity that had been causing Gavaskar trouble for some time.

Problems began when the ice melted. The pain became excruciating. After a sleepless night, Gavaskar battled severe toothache for a further six and a half hours to score 124, but his struggle was far from over. West Indies raked up a lead of 166, and Gavaskar, deprived of sleep and solid food, again came to bat on the fourth afternoon. He finished the day on 57.

Manager Keki Tarapore had refused to take him to the dentist or avail painkillers or injections ('they'll only make you drowsy'). When Gavaskar got to his second hundred on the fifth day, non-striker Dilip Sardesai congratulated him with, 'I know you are not sleeping well, so go to sleep at the wicket and don't get out.'

Gavaskar took Sardesai seriously. He batted all of the fifth day to finish on 180, and eventually fell for 220 on the sixth morning, having batted for almost 9 hours (over 15 hours in the match). It was only then that he went to the dentist. To add a postscript, he did not follow Gundappa Viswanath's advice of keeping the tooth as a souvenir.

ANSHUMAN GAEKWAD

There was little doubt over Clive Lloyd's intentions at the Kingston Test of 1975/76. In the previous match, at Port of Spain, three West Indies spinners had failed to prevent India from chasing a then world record target of 403. Following heavy criticism, Lloyd fielded a four-pronged pace attack, consisting of Michael Holding, Wayne Daniel, Bernard Julien and Vanburn Holder on an undulating pitch with a prominent ridge.

Led by Holding, the fast bowlers deliberately aimed for the bodies of the Indian batters as cries of 'kill him, maan' reverberated around Sabina Park Cricket Ground. The umpires made no attempt to control the short-pitched bowling. India still managed to reach 178/1 on the first day. Soon after West Indies claimed the new ball the next morning, Gundappa Viswanath was caught off a ball which broke one of his fingers.

Anshuman Gaekwad was hit thrice on the gloves. His finger was split, and he was hit all over the body, but he batted for almost four sessions for a courageous 81 (he 'represented the splendid fighting spirit of the team,' Sunil Gavaskar would later write). Gaekwad continued until a searing bouncer hit him on the left ear and knocked his spectacles off at the stroke of lunch on the second day. The local authorities showed little urgency in rushing him to the hospital.

Brijesh Patel's lips were cut open by a bouncer. Bishan Bedi declared the first innings at 306/6. In the second innings, India ran out of batters at 97/5. The innings had to be closed.

KAPIL DEV, DILIP DOSHI, SHIVLAL YADAV

At the start of play on the fourth day of the Melbourne Test match of 1980/81, Australia needed to score only 143 to win.

Of the four specialist Indian bowlers, Shivlal Yadav, despite having his toe fractured by a yorker from Len Pascoe, had bowled 32 overs for his 2–100 in the first innings. He could neither bat nor bowl for the rest of the match. Kapil Dev had pulled a thigh muscle earlier in the match, had batted with a runner, and did not take field on the fourth evening. That left only Karsan Ghavri and Dilip Doshi.

Six days before the Test began, Doshi's left foot was fractured by a yorker during a tour match. He was advised to not walk for three weeks, but Doshi insisted on playing. He bowled 12 balls to prove he was match fit ('I learnt how not to put weight on my left foot'). Doshi had bowled 52 overs in the first innings to take 3–109. Now, in the second, he took out Graeme Wood before stumps.

Ghavri struck twice (including bowling Greg Chappell round his legs first ball), and Australia were 24/3 by stumps.

The next morning, Doshi claimed Kim Hughes early. He bowled unchanged for 22 overs with that broken foot to finish with 2–33.

At the other end, Kapil, fortified by painkillers, bowled unchanged as well to finish with figures of 16.4–4–28–5. Australia were bowled out for 83.

MOHINDER AMARNATH

Mohinder Amarnath had already scored 91 out of India's first-innings total of 209 in the Bridgetown Test match of 1982/83. After West Indies responded with 486, Amarnath missed a hook off Malcolm Marshall, was hit on the face, lost a couple of teeth and left the ground with a bloodstained shirt.

He returned a little later in a pristine white shirt—according to legend, he had washed the shirt himself in the dressing room—and counterattacked with an array of hooks and pulls against a phalanx of formidable fast bowlers. He was the last to be dismissed for 80. West Indies won by 10 wickets, but Amarnath was named Player of the Match.

MOHAMMAD AZHARUDDIN

South Africa scored 428 in the Calcutta Test match of 1996/97, and reduced India to 152/6 by stumps on the second day. That afternoon, Brian McMillan had hit Mohammad Azharuddin on the elbow, forcing him to retire for the first time in international cricket.

Azhar returned next morning with the score on 161/7 to launch an onslaught of savagery one hardly associated with him at that point. He blasted a hundred in 74 balls—the fastest by an Indian—hitting Lance Klusener for 5 consecutive fours en route. He eventually fell for a 77-ball 109. The follow-on had been averted.

SACHIN TENDULKAR

India needed 271 to win the Madras Test match of 1998/99. Sachin Tendulkar walked out to face Wasim Akram and Waqar Younis at a not-too-unfamiliar 6/2. By lunch the next day India were 86/5, virtually out of the match. But with Nayan Mongia refusing to get out, Tendulkar continued.

As the runs piled up for Tendulkar, he felt a shooting pain in his lower back. The pain flared up in Madras's heat and humidity. 'I knew it was going to be really difficult to bat for two more hours,' he said later. Realizing the futility of staying at the crease, he had little option but to go after the bowling.

He played some exquisite shots, taking India closer to the target. When the pain became unbearable and his back had 'all but given up', Tendulkar began taking his risks and eventually fell for 136—rated by some as his finest innings—while trying to loft one off Saqlain Mushtaq. India, left to score 17 with 3 wickets in hand, could add just 4.

ANIL KUMBLE

Mervyn Dillon hit Anil Kumble on the jaw in the second afternoon of the Antigua Test match of 2002. X-rays revealed a crack, and Kumble prepared to return home for surgery the next evening. However, realizing that Sachin Tendulkar was the lone Indian spinner on a pitch that yielded some turn, Kumble decided to bowl on the third evening before leaving for home.

The plan was set. Kumble would bowl with a bandaged jaw. Between his overs, he would field next to the boundary line where team physiotherapist Andrew Leipus would 'strap him up'. Kumble bowled unchanged for 14 overs, conceding 29 and trapping Brian Lara leg before.

MAMATHA MABEN

Indian captain Mamatha Maben wanted to opt out of India's match against Sri Lanka in Kandy in 2004. Her period pain had put her in 'deep discomfort', but coach Sudha Shah was adamant: 'You go for the toss and come, field for half an hour and sit, but you have to play.'

Thus, Maben played. The Sri Lankan openers had added 31 by the time Maben brought herself on. Nooshin Al Khadeer ran out Inoka Ranaweera before Maben struck thrice in quick succession and took herself off. She returned to strike thrice more and finish with 6.2–3–10–6—still the best figures for India in Women's ODIs. She required no assistance from her teammates for these dismissals (four bowled, two leg before).

Sri Lanka collapsed for 66. India won by 10 wickets.

MITHALI RAJ, NEETU DAVID

Until 2005, India had never reached the final of the Women's World Cup. In the previous edition, they had lost to New Zealand in the semi-final. In 2005, they had lost only once in the league stage—against New Zealand. The odds were against India.

Ahead of the tournament, captain Mithali Raj had torn a ligament in her right knee while fielding. Over the years, she would train herself to play with the injury, but at this point the injury was fresh, barely a month old. Despite that, she walked out at 38/2 and batted through the innings to finish with 91 not out off 104 balls. India finished on 204/6, winning by 40 runs, and reached the final for the first time.

Neetu David, who took 2–28 that day, was easily the best bowler of the tournament. She took 20 wickets (at a ridiculous 8.35 apiece). No other bowler took more than 14 wickets, and no non-Indian took more than 11.

Like Raj, David, too, played the matches with an injury she had noticed in a training camp just before the tournament. The medical team had first diagnosed a torn ligament. A second opinion recommended surgery (and subsequent rest). David chose to play the World Cup instead.

YUVRAJ SINGH

Even without his physical agony, Yuvraj Singh's performance in the 2011 World Cup—362 runs at 90.50, 15 wickets at 25.13, 4 Player of the Match awards—is arguably the greatest in the history of the tournament.

Throughout the tournament, however, he felt symptoms, including breathlessness and severe weakness and—especially in the match against West Indies—coughed blood.

A few months after India's triumph, he was diagnosed with a tumour in one of his lungs. It turned out to be mediastinal seminoma cancer, and he flew to the USA for treatment. He underwent three cycles of chemotherapy before returning to India in April 2012.

HARMANPREET KAUR

Harmanpreet Kaur had torn a ligament in her right wrist in the 2017 World Cup Qualifiers. In the World Cup, she dislocated her left ring finger while fielding against West Indies. This prevented her from gripping the bat properly, but it did not matter: she played every match in the tournament, batting with a strapped hand to score 359 runs at 59.83, and picking up 5 wickets.

During India's last league match, a must-win affair against New Zealand, physiotherapist Tracy Fernandes had to rush out to use the 'magic spray'. The finger had become 'lifeless', Harmanpreet would later admit. There was also an old shoulder injury.

It was under these circumstances that Harmanpreet took on the Australians in the semi-final in Derby. Her 115-ball unbeaten 171 that day—including 20 fours, 7 sixes—helped India reach the World Cup final for the second time, and is often hailed as one of the greatest innings of all time.

THE BATCH OF 2020/21

One of India's greatest triumphs came on India's 2020/21 tour of Australia, where they won the series 2–1 against all odds. Injuries (and other reasons) forced India to play 20 cricketers, a world record for a touring team in a single Test series. Several Indian cricketers braved injuries to leave a mark in the series, particularly in the third Test match, in Sydney, where Australia set India a target of 407 in four sessions.

In India's first innings, Pat Cummins had hit Rishabh Pant on the elbow, and Mitchell Starc had hit Ravindra Jadeja on the thumb. Neither batter took field when Australia batted. India were 98/2 by stumps on the fourth day. After scoring only 7 off the first 36 balls, Pant raced to his fifty in 64 balls next morning. He eventually fell for 97 in 118 balls, while braving severe pain—he needed help holding the water bottle properly at the drinks break.

India lost Cheteshwar Pujara early. At the crease were Hanuma Vihari, who had pulled a hamstring and was virtually unable to run, and R. Ashwin, whose back pain was so bad that he had refused to sit all morning for fear of being unable to stand up. None of the batters to follow had any batting credentials, though Jadeja was padded up, ready to bat if the situation demanded. India needed to bat a full session, and more.

The Australians tried their hardest, bowling short-pitched balls indiscriminately (perhaps going overboard occasionally), at times sledging the batters brutally. Vihari—unable to stretch—and

Ashwin—unable to bend—batted for 190 minutes and 42.4 overs to save the Test match.

In the last Test match in Brisbane, Pujara made 56 runs. He had sustained a finger injury in Melbourne, but decided to play anyway. He took eleven hits—on the helmet, ribs, shoulders, fingers (including the same finger injured by Josh Hazlewood)—but refused to bring his bat near the ball when the fast bowlers bounced. India successfully chased 328 to script history, winning the match and clinching the series.

HONOURABLE MENTIONS

Two incidents from domestic cricket are worth mentioning.

C.K. Nayudu was leading Holkar in the final of the 1951/52 Ranji Trophy at the Brabourne Stadium. Hosts Bombay included Vinoo Mankad, who had opted out of the upcoming England tour following a disagreement with Nayudu, then chair of selectors. Their relationship was not great at this point.

According to some versions, Mankad apparently asked Dattu Phadkar, then the leading Indian pacer, to bounce at 56-year-old Nayudu. Whatever his intentions might have been, Phadkar hit Nayudu on the mouth. Nayudu lost blood and a few teeth. The medical staff rushed out on to the ground, but Nayudu was not one for all this. He spat out his teeth and swept them off the pitch. Then he told Phadkar to not show any leniency. That done, he scored 66.

Over six decades later, Services bowled out Uttar Pradesh for 134 in the 2012/13 Ranji Trophy semi-final in Indore. Services then reached 263/9 when captain Soumik Chatterjee braved a bad knee and limped to the pitch. He had risked further clotting of blood, but it did not matter ('even if I lose my life, I will always be there for team'). It was a scene so moving that even the Uttar Pradesh fielders patted his back.

Unfortunately, Chatterjee fell leg before to the first ball he faced, off Ankit Rajpoot. *Uttar Pradesh coach* Venkatesh Prasad walked up to him, took the bat from Chatterjee, and helped him return to the dressing room.

Services were 54/5, chasing 113, when Chatterjee dragged himself to the middle a second time. Unable to run, he played some incredible strokes on one leg, including 5 fours and 2 sixes. In between, he hopped for singles, both for himself and Rajat Paliwal. Services did not lose another wicket to win the match.

As Services manager Deepak Bhaskar summed up, 'We are soldiers first, players later.'

HOWZZAT!

Shortly after the 2008 IPL, the Eden Gardens ground staff threatened to die by suicide if their financial demands were not met.

Parallel Universe
You Didn't Know They Were Cricketers

It is difficult to grow up in India and not play the game. And some Indians—renowned in other fields—had reasonable cricketing abilities. Here is a list of people who you probably did not know were also decent cricketers.

SWAMI VIVEKANANDA

Back in 1881, Hemachandra Bose spotted a strapping youth during a practice session of the Town Club in Calcutta. Bose trained this man to bowl overarm. The boy, Narendranath Datta, took 7–20 against the Calcutta Cricket Club. Bose told the impressed British that Datta would end the British supremacy at cricket someday.

Datta, however, chose not Lord's but Chicago as the starting point of his incredible journey. We know him as Swami Vivekananda.

SATYAJIT RAY

Ray's great-uncle Sarada Ranjan Ray—a W.G. Grace doppelganger—was one of the early great cricketers of India, and is often considered the founder of the game in Bengal. Ray's uncle Nripendra Mohan 'Kartick' Bose was a member of the first Bengal team that won the Ranji Trophy in 1938/39.

Ray himself bowled spin for Calcutta University, as did Feluda, the famous detective he created. Cricket kept featuring in Ray's works, from a story on a miraculous bat that belonged to Ranjitsinhji to a long monologue by Indranath Roy (played by Chhabi Biswas) in *Kanchenjunga*.

RAJDEEP SARDESAI

Sardesai's 7-match first-class career, all of which was for Oxford University, was full of curiosities. He scored only 2 fifties but, to be fair, four of his eight dismissals were off Derek Underwood (who had also dismissed Dilip Sardesai in a Test match), Eddie Hemmings, Allan Donald and Abdul Qadir. In his last innings he fell to, of all people, Michael Atherton.

Sardesai also tried his hand at a mind sport, quizzing, reaching the West Zone final of Siddhartha Basu's *Quiz Time* in 1985 before finally going to AFMC Pune.

PIYUSH PANDEY

India's most famous adman originally wanted a life in cricket. Captain of the Under-22 Rajasthan team, Pijush (that was how he spelt his name back then) took a few years to make it to the senior side, but played some important knocks by the 1976/77 season, most notably against the Railways.

Pandey was also a part of a very strong St. Stephen's cricket team led by Arun Lal and a Delhi University team that won multiple titles in the 1970s. He then ventured into the tea industry, as did Arun Lal, before finally trying a hand at advertising.

NASEERUDDIN SHAH

A regular cricketer at school, Shah dreamt of becoming a professional but decided that acting was easier ('cricket is a heartless mistress and much tougher than acting'). But he managed to continue his cricket with Match Cut XI, a team put together along with fellow cricket nut, Tom Alter. He was also a part of at least three movies involving cricket: as a ghost helping Shah Rukh Khan in *Chamatkar* (1992); playing against Gavaskar in *Maalamaal* (1988); and as Shreyas Talpade's coach in *Iqbal* (2005).

His nephew Owais Shah played international cricket, but for England, not India. Owais even played a couple of match-winning innings in the IPL, not Naseeruddin's favourite format!

ANGAD BEDI

The son of former India captain Bishan Singh Bedi, actor Angad was also—to nobody's surprise—a graceful left-arm spinner who played at the Under-16 and Under-19 levels for Delhi. With future international left-arm spinner Rahul Sanghvi also in the Ranji Trophy squad, Angad did not get his break at the senior level and decided to get into modelling and, subsequently, acting.

He did end up playing an international cricketer in Abhishek Sharma's *The Zoya Factor* (2019) and the captain of two franchises (in different seasons) in the 'Powerplay League' in Karan Anshuman's *Inside Edge* (2017–present).

CHUNI GOSWAMI

One of the finest attacking footballers of his era, Subimal 'Chuni' Goswami was the captain of the Indian team that won the Asian Games Gold medal at Djakarta in 1962. He was also a serious cricketer who focussed on the sport after he retired from football in 1968.

A competent batter, he debuted against the fearsome Roy Gilchrist of the West Indies, who was representing Hyderabad at the time. Chuni later captained Bengal in a Ranji Trophy final against Bombay. Before that, in the 1968/69 final, he scored 96 and 84 against Bombay but could not get Bengal the lead in a match decided on first-innings score.

Chuni once played for a combined East and Central zones team against the visiting West Indians. Given the new ball, he picked up 5–47 and 3–40, and scored 25 runs for good measure. He also appeared in Manu Sen's movie *Mohunbaganer Meye* (1976); was a more than competent tennis player; and was appointed the Sheriff of Kolkata. Quite the man for all seasons.

ASHWINI KUMAR CHOPRA

Decades before he became the editor of *Punjab Kesari* and an MP from Karnal, Chopra took 73 first-class wickets with his leg-breaks. He used to be Ashwini Minna in those days. His most famous match was, somewhat unusually, his debut, in the Irani Cup of 1975/76.

Along with Bishan Singh Bedi and E.A.S. Prasanna, the selectors picked him, instead of Bhagwat Chandrasekhar, for the Rest of India side as a leg-spinner. By then, Minna had earned a repute in age-level cricket. The match is immortalized by Dilip Vengsarkar's 6-studded 110 against Bedi and Prasanna, though he was kinder on the third spinner. Minna got just 1 wicket—the first of his career—but that was of a certain Sunil Gavaskar.

HARDAVINDER 'HARRDY' SINGH SANDHU

Hardavinder Singh Sandhu played only 3 first-class matches, all for Punjab, and was good enough to play an Under-19 Test match against England in 2004/05. An elbow injury ended his career in 2007. He soon re-emerged as a singer–actor, won multiple awards for his song 'Soch', and portrayed Madan Lal in Kabir Khan's *83* (2021).

HOWZZAT!

Ravi Shastri has a 100 per cent record as Test captain. He led India to victory in the only Test match he captained against Viv Richards's West Indies at Madras in 1987/88.

Unusual Scorecards

The most basic cricket scorecard consists of batting and bowling sheets and fall of wickets, but even that ranks among the most complicated, most informative match summaries across sports. A cricket fan may be a staunch supporter of the 'numbers do not mean anything' school of thought, but they will still refuse to follow a cricket match without a scorecard.

Some scorecards have stood the test of time—not because they chronicle historic matches, but because they have entries that are singular, even unique. Here is a compilation.

SINGLE-DIGIT SURRENDER, 1915/16

The early matches on Indian soil produced some incredible scorecards. Consider the Bombay Quadrangular match from 1915/16, where the Europeans declared on 201/5 and still won by a colossal margin.

They bowled out the Muslims for 21 and 39, but what made it even more spectacular was the fact that there was not a single double-digit score in either of the Muslims innings. The individual scores read 0-0-0-8-4-0-0-0-0-0-0 and 0-0-5-4-5-7-0-3-0-0-0. Thankfully, they were aided by 24 extras across innings.

BE-NAZIR SHOW, 1932

The brothers Wazir Ali and Nazir Ali had featured in India's first ever Test match at Lord's in 1932. Less than a month later, the Indians were playing Yorkshire at Harrogate, where Nazir played one of his most famous innings.

In their second innings, the Indians were bowled out for only 66 by George Macaulay (8–21) and Hedley Verity (2–40). Of these 5 were extras, and ten of eleven Indians scored 3 runs or fewer. The sequence of 1-1-1-0-2-0-0-0-3-1 was broken only by Nazir Ali's 52. Till date, the 66 by the Indians remains the lowest first-class total to include a half-century.

THE HAZARE DOMINATION, 1943/44

In the first half of the 1940s, when the Second World War was ripping Europe apart, the two Vijays—Merchant and Hazare—

engaged in a bloodless duel of their own, breaking each other's record for the highest score on Indian soil.

Things reached an absurd level in the Bombay Pentangular final of 1943/44. Merchant made 250 before declaring the Hindus innings closed at 581/5. The Rest were bowled out for 133, and Merchant enforced the follow on. The Rest fared better in the second innings, putting up 387—though they still lost by an innings. That does not sound unusual, unless one takes into account the fact that Vijay Hazare alone got 309 of these runs, and his brother Vivek another 21. The brothers added 300 runs for the sixth wicket. Their teammates got 1-5-0-3-6-8-2-1-0.

WINNING WITHOUT LOSING, 1960/61 AND 1977/78

At Srinagar in 1960/61, openers Vijay Mehra (107*) and Budhi Kunderan (116*) made an unbroken 236 before captain Lala Amarnath declared the Railways innings closed. Jammu and Kashmir were bowled out for 92 and 159, which meant that Railways had *won a match without losing a wicket*.

In 1977/78 in Chikmagalur, Karnataka's Sanjay Desai (218*) and Roger Binny (211*) put up 451 for the first wicket, Sudhakar Rao declared on 451/0, and Kerala managed only 141 and 124.

CHAMUNDESWARANATH C BALASUBRAMANIAM B ANANTHAPADMANABHAN AT VISAKHAPATNAM, 1990/91

Imagine having to fit all these names in a single row on a scoreboard!

Kerala might have produced several international cricketers, but their diehard supporters often rate K.N. Ananthapadmanabhan as their greatest cricketer. A leg-spinner whose career clashed with Narendra Hirwani's and Anil Kumble's, Ananthapadmanabhan never played for India, though he is now an international umpire.

Ananthapadmanabhan had Andhra captain V. Chamundeswaranath out, caught during the 1990/91 Ranji Trophy for 2. The fielder was K.N. Balasubramaniam, elder brother of Ananthapadmanabhan. Fittingly, it happened in Visakhapatnam.

A disgruntled Brian Levison would later comment, 'All that for 2!' Too harsh, perhaps, for even 2,000 runs would have been too few.

THE MAJITHIA SHOW, 1999/2000

The scoreline 'Madhya Pradesh 538/7 declared, Railways 216 and 86/5' does not make for remarkable reading, but it involved a mind-boggling feat.

On the last day, Railways, trying to save the match, batted 104 overs for only 83 runs—at that point the fewest runs in a single completed day's cricket. However, the world record features merely as a footnote in the match scorecard—that too only the remarkable figures of Madhya Pradesh left-arm spinner Manish Majithia. Not content with 12.3-9-3-1 in the first innings, Majithia improved on that with an astonishing 20-20-0-1 in the second. Never in the history of first-class cricket has anyone bowled so many balls (120) in an innings without conceding a run.

THE NAME IS NEHRA. ASHISH NEHRA., 2002/03

In 2002/03, India were playing New Zealand in a Test match in Hamilton. Ashish Nehra (not yet Nehra *ji*) edged Shane Bond to slip, where Stephen Fleming took the catch. It does not take a hardcore James Bond fans to connect the dots. But then, 'caught Fleming bowled Bond' happened seventeen times across formats in international cricket.

What made this particular entry unique was Nehra's score: c Fleming b Bond 007.

DUAL ACT, SAME INNINGS: PANDEY AND APARAJITH, 2013/14

Two hundred-run partnerships in the same innings are common—but *between the same pair*?

Playing for South Zone, Manish Pandey and Baba Aparajith added 190 for the fourth wicket in a Duleep Trophy 2013/14 match at Chepauk against West Zone. Then Pandey retired hurt. He was replaced by C.M. Gautam, who got out soon, but P. Rohan Prem helped Aparajith add 91 for the fifth wicket. By the time Rohan Prem got out, Pandey had recovered enough to resume batting. He and Aparajith then added another 140—a total of 330 runs between the same pair in the same innings, but in instalments!

BINARY BRIGADE, 2013/14

Three months after the Pandey–Aparajith brace, Karnataka put up one of the most bizarre top six entries in the history of first-class cricket: Robin Uthappa 100, K.L. Rahul 0, Ravikumar Samarth 0, Manish Pandey 0, Karun Nair 100, C.M. Gautam 100. In other words, anyone who got off the mark went on to score 100—no more, no less!

Down the order, Shreyas Gopal and H.S. Sharath also scored 0, but there were no more 100s.

THE DHANAWADE MILLENNIUM, 2015/16

In 2015/16, Pranav Dhanawade of K.C. Gandhi English School shattered records by becoming the first batter to slam an innings of a *decuple* century in organized cricket. Dhanawade faced 327 balls for his 1,009 runs, which included 129 fours and 59 sixes in a Bhandari Cup match.

K.C. Gandhi declared on 1465/3, and Arya Gurukul (CBSE) were bowled out for 31 and 52. Much has been written about the depleted Arya Gurukul side, but Dhanawade's feat is likely to stand the test of time.

The innings caused a stir in unexpected ways, not the least of which was ESPNCricinfo having to rewrite their scorecard script to accommodate a four-digit individual score!

TWO ALL OUT, 2017/18

It is difficult to say what was more remarkable that day at Guntur—the Nagaland Under-19 Women's total of 2 all out against Kerala, or that they took 17 overs for that. Kerala captain Minnu Mani had figures of 4-4-0-4. Opener Menka Muru scored 1 run for Nagaland, while Aleena Surendran bowled a wide. Both runs came before Nagaland lost their first wicket, so they technically lost all 10 wickets on the same team score.

Deepika Kaintura then opened bowling for Nagaland. She began with a wide, Kerala wicketkeeper Ansu Susan Raju hit the next ball for 4, and that was that. It took Kerala one legal delivery to win the match.

SIX AND OUT, 2000

In 2000, not one out of eleven Cuddalore Women managed to score a single run against Chennai 2nd XI. In fact, Balasoundari of Cuddalore hit a ball that *almost* reached the boundary but did not quite make it. Unfortunately, Balasoundari could not run—for she was down with cramps. However, Cuddalore were saved from utter ignominy by the six wides bowled by Chennai 2nd XI.

> **HOWZZAT!**
>
> Neetu David's 8–53 against England at Jamshedpur in 1995/96 is still the best bowling figures in women's Test cricket.

Numbers Game
Indian Cricketers and Music Albums

While hostile fast bowlers often dish out chin music to hapless batters, most cricketers typically limit their musical inclination to listening. A devoted fan of Mukesh, B.S. Chandrasekhar managed to convert several teammates into fans. When he bowled, Sunil Gavaskar would sometimes hum a Mukesh number to motivate him.

Some cricketers, however, took things a step further, even launching full-fledged albums.

PADMAKAR SHIVALKAR AND SUNIL GAVASKAR

The 1979 album *Marathi Geete* featured four songs, composed by Gautam Girish and written by Shantaram Nandgaonkar. Shivalkar recorded '*Ha chendu daiva*' and '*Kashasathi vedya*', while Gavaskar sang '*He jeevan majhe cricket*' and '*Mitra tula*'.

In later years, Shivalkar went on to become an accomplished singer, performing in shows. Gavaskar largely restricted his use of the microphones to cricket commentary.

SANJAY MANJREKAR

Vijay Manjrekar was an excellent singer, a talent his son, Sanjay, inherited. Soon after his retirement from cricket, in the late 1990s, Manjrekar recorded an album titled *Rest Day*, featuring his favourite Hindi songs as well as those of Mohammad Azharuddin, Sachin Tendulkar, Anil Kumble and Javagal Srinath.

In 2016, he returned with *Amar Bela Je Jaay*, an album featuring six Rabindra Sangeets, all of which had been previously recorded by Kishore Kumar. Manjrekar did not know Bengali, but trained himself by listening to Kishore's versions, and was guided by singer Sraboni Sen.

VINOD KAMBLI

While *Rest Day* was publicized as a Sanjay Manjrekar album, it also featured Kambli. He sang '*Tumse achha kaun hai*', a solo, and collaborated with Manjrekar and Arvinder Singh for '*Hum kasam khayenge*'.

S. SREESANTH

Sreesanth famously held the catch that helped India clinch the 2007 T20 World Cup in South Africa. Ahead of the tournament, however, he had penned four songs that became part of an album, *Desh*. These included the title track, 'Desh', and the more popular 'Jaago re'. In 2010, he launched a band, S-36 (to match his 'luckiest shirt number'), with his family members and friends.

HONOURABLE MENTION: JOHN WRIGHT

The former Indian coach used to sing in the choir in his school days. After a successful career as player and coach, Wright launched a musical career. His debut album, *Red Skies*, a folk blues mix with country flavours with eleven tracks, came out in late 2016. He has subsequently released two more albums, *Jump the Sun* (2019) and *Walking Tracks* (2021).

HOWZZAT!

In 2007, Abhijit Majumder, Animangsu Ghatak and Ashutosh Sharma of IIT Kanpur suggested that a 'super-adhesive tape' made of the pads of the feet of tree frogs, lizards, spiders and some insects be used to assist cricketers 'keep their gloves on'.

The Diaspora
Indians Playing Domestic Cricket outside India and England

In 1893, K.S. Ranjitsinhji played for Cambridge University. Two years later, he became the first Indian to feature in the County Championship. M.E. Pavri became the second in less than a month. Pavri caught Ranji during the match. K.S. Duleepsinhji and Iftikhar Ali Khan Pataudi, too, played Test cricket for England before Independence. Ranji, Duleep and Pataudi, all got hundreds in their maiden Test appearances against Australia. From Ranji and Pavri in 1895 to Cheteshwar Pujara in 2019, there has been no dearth of Indian cricketers in the English domestic circuit, including Scotland and Ireland.

While playing in the British domestic circuit is common among Indians, some have played in other countries as well.

SUBHASH GUPTE (TRINIDAD, 1962/63—1963/64)

Gupte was infamously dropped from the Indian Test match side after his roommate Kripal Singh asked the hotel receptionist out for drinks.

A disgruntled Gupte settled down in Trinidad with his wife, Carol, a local he had met on India's 1952/53 tour of the West Indies. He also played once for Trinidad and Tobago and twice for South Trinidad, taking 11 wickets at a shade over 20 apiece.

RUSI SURTI (QUEENSLAND, 1968/69—1972/73)

India were whitewashed 0–4 in Australia in 1967/68, but Surti impressed the locals. He scored runs; picked up wickets, bowling both pace and spin; and was so prolific on the field that the local crowd challenged the Australian batters to 'hit a ball past Surti'.

His performance on the tour helped him earn a contract with Queensland. In his fifth match, Surti became the first ever Queensland bowler to take a hat-trick. He played 35 first-class matches for Queensland, scoring 1,859 runs and taking 51 wickets. Unfortunately, he also faced racism severe enough for him to file a lawsuit.

EMMANUEL BENJAMIN (TASMANIA, 1981/82)

Good enough to play for India Schools, Benjamin played Ranji Trophy for Punjab. He then had a stint with Bedfordshire in the Minor Counties before settling down in Tasmania. There, he played his first first-class match in four years—and the last of his career—for the state team. He scored 6 runs and did not take a wicket.

'Benji' resurfaced in 2014, when he contested the Tasmanian State Elections. He got only 507 votes.

ROBIN SINGH (SOUTH AND CENTRAL TRINIDAD, 1982/83)

A bit of cheating here, for the Trinidad-born Robin Singh actually made his first-class debut for South and Central Trinidad in the 1982/83 Beaumont Cup, six seasons *before* he played for India. His next match was for Tamil Nadu, almost three years later.

Robin made his international debut in Port of Spain in 1988/89. The local crowd greeted him with tumultuous applause as he walked out to bat. It did not matter to them that he was playing *against* the West Indies.

PRAVIN AMRE (BOLAND, 1999/2000)

Amre's eight-month, 11-match Test career lasted until 1993. Six seasons later, he spent a season with Boland. There were some expectations, for he had scored a fifty on his ODI debut and a hundred on his Test debut—both *against* South Africa—but his 7 matches for Boland fetched him just 244 runs.

VINOD KAMBLI (BOLAND, 2002/03)

Three years after Amre, Boland got another student of Ramakant Achrekar's on board. Vinod Kambli, put out of contention for a spot in the Indian national side by a strong middle order, did a decent job. His 356 runs came at 35.60, and included 4 fifties.

DIGVIJAY AMARNATH (SRI LANKA, 2012/13—2014/15)

Son of Surinder Amarnath, and nephew of Mohinder Amarnath, Digvijay was approached by Darshana Gamage in the MRF Pace

Academy. He played 4 matches for the Badureliya Sports Club in 2012/13, and once for the Sri Lanka Air Force Sports Club two years later. His entire first-class career was, thus, in Sri Lankan domestic cricket. While he is only in his late twenties, a comeback seems unlikely.

RAHUL DRAVID, V.V.S. LAXMAN, L. BALAJI, AMIT MISHRA, DHAWAL KULKARNI, M. VIJAY (NEW ZEALAND, 2008/09)

India's 2008/09 tour of New Zealand started with the limited-overs leg. The Test matches followed, but no tour match was scheduled in between. For match practice, India's Test match specialists featured in the New Zealand State Championship (now Plunket Shield). Rahul Dravid played for Canterbury, Amit Mishra and M. Vijay for Northern Districts, V.V.S. Laxman for Otago and L. Balaji and Dhawal Kulkarni for Wellington.

THE T20 STARS

In its initial days, the BCCI did not object to Indian cricketers playing franchise-based T20 cricket outside India. This enabled the likes of Murali Kartik to play in the IPL as well as in overseas leagues. Then came the embargo on foreign leagues.

The rule did not apply to women, however. In 2016/17, Harmanpreet Kaur and Smriti Mandhana became the first Indians to play in the Women's Big Bash League. Veda Krishnamurthy followed suit a year later, as did Shafali Verma, Radha Yadav, Jemimah Rodrigues, Poonam Yadav, Richa Ghosh and Deepti Sharma in 2021/22.

The men joined soon, though they had to say goodbye to Indian cricket to obtain a no-objection certificate from the BCCI. Yuvraj Singh and Manpreet Gony both played for the Toronto Nationals in the Global T20 Canada; Pravin Tambe for the Trinbago Knight Riders in the Caribbean Premier League; and Irfan Pathan for the Kandy Tuskers in the Lanka Premier League.

Unmukt Chand—who never made it to the senior team despite having led India to the Under-19 World Cup title in 2012—played for the Silicon Valley Strikers in Minor League Cricket, USA before becoming the first Indian to feature in the Big Bash League as one of the Melbourne Renegades. A trend has been set.

BONUS ENTRY: THE EXPORTS

Not quite domestic cricket, but at the World Cup, for another team.

When the 1982 Women's World Cup was reduced to four teams, the organizers formed a fifth side—the International XI, with cricketers from Australia, England, India, New Zealand and the Netherlands.

The two Indians, Renuka Majumder and Sandra Braganza, had never played for their country before, but they now debuted for the International XI. While Majumder never played international cricket again, Braganza went on to represent India with distinction until 1993.

HOWZZAT!

Between July 1986 and January 1991, India Women did not play a single international match.

The Reverse Diaspora
Non-Indians Playing in Indian Domestic Cricket

The British brought cricket to India, and were obviously the first to play the sport in the country. The first major annual contest—the Bombay Presidency Match—was between the Parsees and the Europeans. The latter consisted of mostly British cricketers. This contest, played entirely on religious lines, later evolved into the Bombay Triangular (as the Hindus joined in), the Quadrangular (Muslims) and, finally, the Pentangular (the Rest).

The tournament drew several English Test cricketers, including all-time greats like C.B. Fry, Wilfred Rhodes, George Hirst, Harold Larwood and Denis Compton.

The pre-Independence Ranji Trophy teams often featured British and Indian cricketers alongside each other. The most famous 'acquisition' was Compton, who was posted in Mhow as a sergeant-major during the Second World War, only to be recruited by Holkar captain C.K. Nayudu. Among others, Albert Wensley, T.C. Longfield and Herbert Barritt led Nawanagar, Bengal and Western India, respectively, to Ranji Trophy titles.

After Independence, however, the trend died out—until the T20 arrived. The advent of the Indian Cricket League, the Indian Premier League, the Women's T20 Challenge and the Women's Premier League was accompanied by an influx of overseas cricketers that is likely to continue. But there were some players who came long before all this … and this doesn't include the ones who moved base to Pakistan.

ROY GILCHRIST (HYDERABAD), CHARLIE STAYERS (BOMBAY), LESTER KING (BENGAL), CHESTER WATSON (DELHI), 1962/63

To equip the Indian batters against fast bowling, the BCCI invited four pacemen from the West Indies for the 1962/63 Ranji Trophy, a tournament played against the backdrop of the Sino-Indian War. The four men were allotted to four teams, one in each zone: Gilchrist to Hyderabad, Stayers to Bombay, King to Bengal, and Watson to Delhi.

Three of these teams reached the semi-final, but the most famous clash involving these sides occurred in the quarter-final when Gilchrist and Pankaj Roy got involved in a duel. The experiment was not repeated.

DULEEP TROPHY TEAMS (2003/04—2007/08)

Between 2003/04 and 2007/08, the BCCI added an overseas team to the Duleep Trophy every year along with the usual five that represent geopolitical zones. This allowed the tournament to be split into two groups and pitted Indian domestic cricketers against some international stars.

The five teams in this short-lived experiment, in chronological order, were England A, Bangladesh Cricket Board XI, Zimbabwe Cricket Union President's XI, Sri Lanka A and England Lions. Several overseas Test cricketers also featured in these matches. Sri Lanka A finished runners-up in 2006/07.

VIKRAM SOLANKI AND KABIR ALI (RAJASTHAN, 2006/07)

When the BCCI allowed the Ranji Trophy teams to hire three professional cricketers, they did not restrict these recruitments to Indian cricketers.

Taking a cue, Rajasthan roped in Vikram Solanki, the first Supersub in international cricket, and his Worcestershire and England teammate Kabir Ali. Solanki was, in a way, a local—he was born in Udaipur.

ENAMUL HAQUE JR (MAHARASHTRA, 2008/09)

Haque made his Test debut at only sixteen. At eighteen years and forty days old, he set a world record by becoming the youngest player to take 10 wickets in a Test match—a record that still stands. He also became the first Bangladeshi to play in the Lancashire League. In 2008/09, he played 4 matches for Maharashtra as an overseas professional.

TANMAY MISHRA (TRIPURA, 2019/20)

Mumbai-born Mishra played for Kenya in the 2007 and 2011 World Cups, and even a solitary IPL match for the Deccan Chargers in 2012. In 2019/20, just before the pandemic clamped down on the world, Mishra played a full season for Tripura in all three formats.

ANSHUMAN RATH (ODISHA, 2021/22)

'Anshy' Rath has captained Hong Kong in ODIs. However, he holds an Indian passport, for his father hails from Bhubaneshwar.

Rath played club cricket in Nagpur and tried his luck for Vidarbha. When that did not work out, he switched to Odisha for the 2021/22 season. Unlike the others on this list, he wants to play Test cricket *for India*.

HOWZZAT!

Virat Kohli has over 50 million followers on Twitter and over 200 million followers on Instagram. He was the first cricketer in the world to reach either milestone.

All-Rounders
Indian Cricketers Representing Their Country at Another Sport

Structured sports training is not part of growing up for the average Indian, and thus it is hardly surprising that we have not produced many double internationals. However, when cricket was still played at an amateur or semi-amateur level in India, cricketers often tried their hand at other sports. Rusi Modi represented Maharashtra at table tennis and was excellent in both tennis and badminton. One of the best left-handed batters of his time, Khandu Rangnekar was a national champion at badminton before he turned to cricket. Bapu Nadkarni, a state champion at badminton, was persuaded by D.B. Deodhar to switch to cricket. Shubhangi Kulkarni played hockey for Maharashtra. Madhusudan Rege led his school at football. Pankaj Roy played for Sporting Union, while Kapil Dev made an appearance for East Bengal. Dilip Sardesai played mostly football while growing up in Goa, and took up serious cricket only during his days at Wilson College in Bombay. Jahangir Khan was a renowned discus thrower. Umesh Kulkarni represented Maharashtra in kho-kho. Even in the recent, more professional era, Jemimah Rodrigues made it to the Maharashtra Under-17 and Under-19 hockey teams, and played basketball to boot, and Yuvraj Singh was a champion skater. The list is long.

However, the rigours of cricket increased as the sport became more professional. Today, it is virtually impossible for the best contemporary Indian cricketers, after being identified at a young age, to focus on a second sport.

Amidst all these, there have been some true all-rounders who have represented India in cricket and at least one more sport.

IFTIKHAR ALI KHAN PATAUDI (CRICKET AND HOCKEY)

Pataudi played Test cricket for England and led India, but he was also excellent at field hockey. He was studying at, and playing cricket for, Oxford in 1928 when the Indian Olympics contingent arrived in England en route to Amsterdam. At the Folkestone Festival—a fairly popular hockey carnival in England—the Indian team beat an English side with nine international players. Pataudi was part of that Indian side. However, he did not travel with the team to Amsterdam. India went on to win their first ever gold medal at the Games that year.

Pataudi was also a talented billiards player, and died of a heart attack while playing polo.

M.J. GOPALAN (CRICKET AND HOCKEY)

Gopalan, the man who bowled the first ball in the history of the Ranji Trophy, also claimed the first first-class hat-trick at Chepauk, *and* dismissed Jack Hobbs, no less, in three consecutive innings. The third of these deliveries was pitched on leg and kissed the off bail, and remained his most celebrated moment in cricketing whites. The M.J. Gopalan Trophy, a now-defunct annual contest between the state of Madras and nation of Ceylon, was named after him.

Like Pataudi, Gopalan was skilled enough to play hockey for India in their pre-War period of invincibility, as a half-back. He was even selected for the Indian squad that went to the 1936 Berlin Olympics, one of the greatest teams of all time. But Gopalan chose to tour England with the cricket team. He could have come back an

Olympics gold medallist, instead he returned from the tour without adding to his career total of 1 Test match.

COTAR RAMASWAMI (CRICKET AND TENNIS)

Ramaswami was more fortunate than Gopalan in 1936, for he played 2 Test matches on that tour. At forty years and thirty-nine days, he remains the second-oldest Indian Test debutant. Not counting active cricketers, his batting average of 56.67 is the second-highest among Indian Test players, albeit over a small sample.

But before that, he had represented India in the International Lawn Tennis Challenge (now the Davis Cup) in 1922 and 1923. He had partnered Dr Hassan-Ali Fyzee in the Men's Doubles, and won his respective match on both occasions. He also took part in the 1922 Wimbledon Championship.

On 15 October 1985, he left his residence at Adyar and never returned. He was presumed dead a few years later. Curiously, Ralph Legall of the West Indies, the second person to play in both Test cricket and the Davis Cup, also went missing and is presumed dead.

SYED MOHAMMAD HADI (CRICKET AND TENNIS)

Like Gopalan and Ramaswami, Hadi, too, went on that 1936 tour of England. The first man to score a hundred in the Ranji Trophy, he never got a Test cap—but he did play an unofficial Test match against Jack Ryder's touring Australians in 1935/36.

Hadi represented India at the Davis Cup (in 1924 and 1925) as well as the 1924 Paris Olympics. In the latter, he partnered Mohammed Sleem to reach the quarter-finals in the Men's Doubles. In the 1922 Wimbledon, he reached the third round in both Men's Singles and Men's Doubles.

He also aced hockey, football, table tennis, chess and polo. His dominance over seven sports earned him the nickname 'Rainbow Hadi'.

SHIREEN KIASH (CRICKET, BASKETBALL AND HOCKEY)

More versatile than most cricketers, Kiash could bat, catch, throw and dribble with either hand, and played in 3 of the earliest cricket matches played by India Women, all against Australia in 1974/75. However, since Australia had sent Under-25 cricketers, these matches did not get international status.

Before that, in 1970, she played for India in the Asian Basketball Championship in Kuala Lumpur, and in 1967, she was part of the Indian hockey side that won the bronze medal at the Asian Women's Championship in New Delhi.

She later moved to Australia, where she tried her hand at netball.

YUZVENDRA CHAHAL (CHESS AND CRICKET)

An Under-12 national champion in chess, Chahal represented India at the Asian Youth Championship in Kozhikode and the World Youth Chess Championship in Greece. However, chess was expensive, and he had to quit when he could not find a sponsor. His FIDE rating (standard) is 1956.

HOWZZAT!

Narendra Hirwani has the best ever figures by any bowler on Test debut: 16–136 against Madras in 1987/88.

Tournaments
Iconic, Unusual and Forgotten

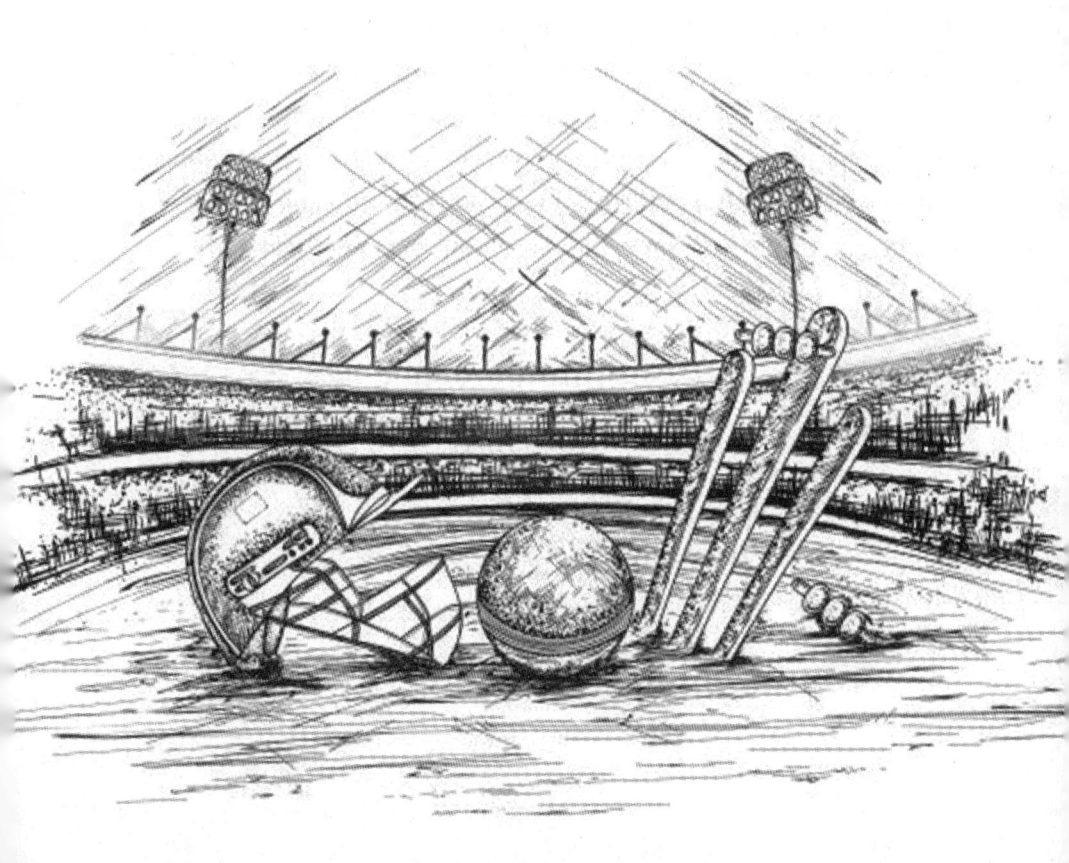

The Bombay Presidency Match—later the Triangular, Quadrangular and Pentangular—was the first cricket tournament in India that truly attracted following from every stratum of the population. Until it was abolished in the aftermath of the religious riots of the late 1940s, the Ranji Trophy always took a backseat. The Duleep Trophy (originally inter-zonal) and the Irani Cup (previously the Irani Trophy, an annual one-off match between the Ranji Trophy champions and the Rest of India) featured the cream of the Ranji Trophy. As limited-overs cricket came into vogue, more tournaments came into being, some of which were extremely popular (though none more so than the IPL); some others, not so much; some were of great historical significance; and some were just downright quirky.

AN UNUSUAL TRIANGULAR

Months before the First World War, in the winter of 1913/14, Calcutta hosted a triangular tournament, where the other two teams were Rangoon Gymkhana and Ceylon Europeans. Each team played the other two once. Rangoon lost both matches, while 'Calcutta' drew with Ceylon.

INTER-FAITH TOURNAMENTS OUTSIDE BOMBAY

The immense success of the Bombay Pentangular led to similar religion-based contests around the country, though not necessarily of five teams. Pune, Nagpur, Karachi, Lahore, Sind, Indore, Secunderabad, Surat, all hosted tournaments of various magnitudes drawn on religious lines. However, none of them attained the popularity of the Bombay Pentangular.

MOIN-UD-DOWLAH GOLD CUP TOURNAMENT

It will not be an exaggeration to call the early days of the Moin-ud-Dowlah Gold Cup a forerunner of the IPL—for they featured contests between privately owned teams that boasted the best Indian cricketers as well as overseas stars. In the 1930s, matches between the Freelooters (owned by Vizzy) and the Retrievers (owned by Patiala) attracted packed houses.

The tournament was not held between 1937/38 and 1962/63, at which time the BCCI revived it. The new-era teams to look out for were the State Bank of India and the Associated Cement Company. These were star-studded affairs. The 1971/72 final, for example, featured fourteen cricketers who had either played or would go on to play for India.

B. SUBRAMANIAM MEMORIAL TOURNAMENT

The first limited-overs tournament on Indian soil is often a matter of debate among cricket historians. The All-India Pooja Cricket Tournament (Thrippunithura, Kerala) and the Buchi Babu Trophy (Madras) are both contenders. However, neither is as old as the 55-overs-a-side B. Subramaniam Memorial Tournament, conducted by the Madras Cricket Association, which started in January 1944—nineteen years before the Gillette Cup in England, often considered the first limited-overs tournament in the world.

ROHINTON BARIA TROPHY

In 1935, Ardeshir Dadabhoy Baria donated a trophy—dedicated to the memory of his son Rohinton—for an inter-university cricket tournament in India. In 1940/41, the tournament came under the aegis of the Inter-University Sports Board of India. Many of the student participants—Sunil Gavaskar being the most significant—went on to play for, and even lead, India.

Over the years, the Rohinton Baria Trophy has evolved into one of the most keenly contested cricket tournaments in India. Between 1947/48 and 1970/71, even Ceylon University participated in the tournament.

M.J. GOPALAN TROPHY

One of cricket's most unusual contests was initiated to celebrate twenty-five years of the career of M.J. Gopalan, who played both cricket and hockey for India. This most singular duel, between the state of Madras (later Tamil Nadu) and the nation of Ceylon (later Sri Lanka), continued from 1952/53 to 1982/83 with the odd missing year in between.

The contest fizzled out as Sri Lanka grew in stature as an international side. An attempt to revive the trophy in the twenty-first century did not work.

RAGHURAMAIAH TROPHY

Elected representatives to the two houses of Parliament get a chance to play a game of cricket regardless of whether they have played serious cricket in their lifetime. The winner of the match between the members of the Lok Sabha and the Rajya Sabha receives a trophy named after Kotha Raghuramaiah, Union Cabinet Minister of Defence, Civil Supplies, Petroleum and Chemicals and Parliamentary Affairs.

SIR TERENCE SHONE TROPHY

The annual contest between the Roshanara Ladies club and the British High Commission ran from 1953 to 1972, and is acknowledged as the first major organized women's cricket series on Indian soil. Meena Talwar Khanna of Roshanara, whose pace earned her the moniker 'Demon Meena', was one of the superstars in these clashes.

H.D. KANGA MEMORIAL CRICKET LEAGUE

Cricket during peak monsoon in Mumbai may seem a preposterous idea, but the Kanga League was founded in 1948 with the intention of playing matches during a season that mimics a wet English summer in the city. As the season proceeded, the wickets deteriorated. The ability to survive on such wickets has often been cited as a cornerstone of the famous Bombay School of Batting.

In fact, batting here can be so difficult that, reportedly, no one had scored a double hundred in the tournament until Aditya Tare (much to his own surprise!) in 2013. This, despite the likes of Sunil Gavaskar and Sachin Tendulkar featuring in the league.

HOT WEATHER TOURNAMENT

If you can play cricket in the Mumbai rain, why not in Delhi's summer? And if you decide to host a tournament, why be subtle about the name?

The purpose of the Hot Weather Tournament is to make young cricketers endure the harshest of conditions. The timing is also convenient, for when else is there a two-month window when every school and college is closed? Of course, the organizers have to stock water and glucose in abundance for emergencies…

THE FIVE TROPHIES INSIDE THE RANJI TROPHY

For a long time, the teams in the Ranji Trophy were divided into groups based on zones. While multiple teams qualified for the next round from each group, there was also an award for the group topper for every zone.

However, the groups have not been zone-specific since 2002 and the Mona Mitter Memorial Trophy (winner from the East Zone), the Devraj Puri Trophy (North Zone), the M.D. Sounderrajan Trophy (South Zone), the Talim Shield (West Zone) and the Mewar Trophy (Central Zone) are all defunct now.

MOHAMMAD NISSAR TROPHY

Back in 2006, when India and Pakistan used to play bilateral cricket series, the BCCI and the PCB announced an annual four-day match between the champions of the Ranji Trophy and the Quaid-i-Azam Trophy, the premier first-class domestic tournaments of the two nations. The trophy was named after Mohammad Nissar, who was born in Hoshiarpur, India; died in Lahore, Pakistan; and bowled the first ball for undivided India in Test cricket.

Uttar Pradesh beat Sialkot by 316 runs in the first edition, in Dharamsala. Next season, Mumbai beat Karachi Urban on first-innings lead, in Karachi, while Sui Northern Gas Pipelines beat Delhi in 2008, at the Feroz Shah Kotla. The 26/11 attacks happened the same year, and brought the curtains down on what could have been a keenly awaited clash today.

INDIAN CRICKET LEAGUE

The Indian Cricket League did not last long, but it left an indelible impact on Indian cricket.

By the time India won the 2007 World T20 Cup, Subhash Chandra of Zee had already planned the ICL, a Twenty20 league with city-based teams, which was launched a few months later.

The high amounts of money lured many Indian cricketers, particularly the ones with little or no chance of playing international cricket otherwise. The BCCI refused to recognize the ICL; it promptly banned players from joining the league and sacked Kapil Dev, head of the executive board of the ICL, from the National Cricket Academy.

Unfazed, the ICL expanded beyond national borders. Soon enough, the league came to feature the Lahore Badshahs and the Dhaka Warriors, teams of almost international standards from Pakistan and Bangladesh, alongside Indian teams that boasted players such as Chris Cairns, Shane Bond, Lance Klusener, Nathan Astle and Jason Gillespie. Unfortunately, the ICL could not lure the Indian stars. After the IPL—the BCCI's official T20 League—was launched in 2007, the ICL faded away. However, as a result, the daily match fees of Indian domestic cricketers increased from INR 16,000 to INR 35,000 per day.

THE CELEBRITY CRICKET LEAGUE

If cricketers can act in movies, why can't things happen the other way round? Where else will you find Mohanlal batting or Kiccha Sudeep keeping wickets or Bobby Deol steaming in to bowl? Or teams with names as exotic as the Bhojpuri Dabbangs or Punjab De Sher?

The Celebrity Cricket League, a tournament featuring India's most prominent film industries, was launched in 2011. The Chennai Rhinos beat the Karnataka Bulldozers in the finals of the first two editions, but the Bulldozers won the next two. This was followed by a hat-trick from the Telugu Warriors, a win for the Mumbai Heroes in 2019 and another for the Warriors in the most recent edition in 2023. The 2018 edition was cancelled.

MASTERS CUP AND ROAD SAFETY WORLD SERIES

In March 1995, Brabourne Stadium, Bombay, hosted a Masters Cup featuring former cricketers from India, Australia, England, West Indies, South Africa and Sri Lanka. A star-studded Indian team, featuring Sunil Gavaskar, Gundappa Viswanath, Dilip Vengsarkar and Kapil Dev, lost to the West Indies, who used the same eleven players throughout the tournament, in the final.

The South Africans piqued some interest, for it was the first time Indian fans got to see stars of the 1970s and 1980s—Barry Richards, Graeme Pollock, Garth le Roux, Vintcent van der Bijl, Ken McEwan, Baboo Ebrahim, Henry Fotheringham—in action.

In 2020, Ravi Gaikwad, chief of the Regional Transport Office, Thane, launched the Road Safety World Series, a seven-nation tournament on the same lines as the Masters Cup, with Gavaskar as commissioner and Sachin Tendulkar as brand ambassador. Thousands sat glued to their screens to watch the likes of Tendulkar, Virender Sehwag and Yuvraj Singh, as well as former overseas stars, in action years after they had hung up their boots.

The tournament had to be postponed when the second wave of COVID-19 broke out in India. When play was resumed in 2021, the Australia Legends—all teams bore the 'Legends' suffix—opted out. India won the tournament, beating Sri Lanka in the final.

SIACHEN CRICKET LEAGUE

During the War of 1971, the Indian army captured a strategic area of Turtuk, one of the northernmost villages of India and among the gateways to the Siachen Glacier. To celebrate the Golden Jubilee of the victory, the Siachen Brigade, 'under the aegis of' the Fire and Fury Corps, organized the Siachen Cricket League.

The Twenty20 tournament featured eight local teams: Turtuk, Panamic, Sumur, Diskit, Thang, Bogdang, Tyakshi and Pratappur. Panamic won the final, scoring 155 and restricting Turtuk to 152.

THE ONE THAT DID NOT HAPPEN

By the mid-1990s, the popularity of cricket under floodlights was apparent to television advertisers. Lalit Modi, whose Modi

Entertainment Networks was already the official distributor of ESPN in India, had just returned from the USA. He wanted an NBA-style cricket league in India—city-based teams owned by franchises, featuring both Indian and foreign cricketers. There would be television coverage to surpass international cricket, both in glamour and entertainment value. Modi had conceived of the IPL, albeit in the fifty-over format.

The team—Modi himself, Amrit Mathur, Piyush Pandey and Arun Lal—wrote a proposal, identified coaches, venues and office spaces, and even talked to local associations. But the BCCI rejected the proposal, for they found the amounts in Modi's proposal unrealistic, and did not want to sell cricket to private organizations.

The BCCI finally launched the IPL only after Subhash Chandra announced the abovementioned Indian Cricket League.

THE ONE THAT DID HAPPEN, YET DID NOT

Molipur, a village in Mehsana district, Gujarat, hosted the Century Hitters T20 in 2022. It featured teams from around India, like the Chennai Fighters, Gandhinagar Challengers, Maharashtra Rangers, Haryana Warriors and Palanpur Sports Kings.

Unlike other similar cricket tournaments, this one was streamed on YouTube using high-definition cameras, complete with crowd noises and a commentating voice that sounded like—but was not quite—Harsha Bhogle's.

But that was far from being the most singular aspect of the Century Hitters T20. The tournament featured about twenty-five cricketers—who took turns to play for all the teams. They were locals who showed up for INR 400 a day. They were fake cricketers, just like the cricket.

Molipur was home to perhaps the greatest scam tournament in cricketing history. Its sole purpose was to provide betting opportunities to Russians, based mostly out of Moscow, Voronezh and Tver. The bets were accepted through Telegram, the social media app. The umpires communicated with both the organizers and 'cricketers' real-time throughout the match for best possible results.

The organizers—one of whom was the Bhogle impersonator—were arrested.

HOWZZAT!

In June 2006, a few months after Sourav Ganguly was sacked as captain and dropped from the Indian side, his family sought the help of a tantrik. The man travelled from Lucknow to Kolkata, performed the rites, and predicted a comeback for Ganguly. By December, Ganguly was playing for India again.

Indian Derbies
Famous Rivalries

The first major rivalry in Indian cricket was seen during the Bombay Presidency match between the Europeans (almost always entirely British) and the Indian Parsees. The annual contest continued for fifteen years before the Hindus, Muslims and a fifth team called The Rest joined—in that order—to create the Bombay Pentangular. The contests were hard-fought but never caustic. Despite the teams being drawn on religious lines, there was virtually no instance of a riot on a cricket field—even in the troubled 1940s. By then, however, a bitter rivalry had taken off elsewhere...

PATIALA VS VIZIANAGARAM

Despite not quite mastering the sport, members of Indian royal families considered personal teams as a means to rise up the social ranks and establish themselves as 'equals' of the British. While the clans of Nawanagar and Cooch Behar were patrons of renown, it was the rivalry between Patiala and Vizianagaram that defined Indian cricket in the 1920s and 1930s.

Rajinder Singh, the Maharaja of Patiala, formed his personal team (including three or four overseas players!) in the 1890s. In 1926/27, his son Bhupinder Singh invited an MCC side, led by Arthur Gilligan, to India. He hosted matches on his personal ground.

Around 1930, Vizzy set out to match Patiala. He too owned an excellent ground in his family estate in Banaras. He wanted Don Bradman (!) for his personal side. When Bradman did not agree, the royal used his purse generously to ensure Jack Hobbs and Herbert Sutcliffe—arguably the greatest opening pair of all time—overcame their reservations and played for his team.

The Moin-ud-Dowlah Gold Cup Tournament began in 1930/31. Although there were multiple teams on the roster—Hyderabad Remnants, Nizam's State Railway, Young Diehards, Crescent Club of Lahore, to name a few—the contest was marked by the intense rivalry between the Freelooters, owned by Vizzy, and the Retrievers, owned by Patiala. Both teams featured the finest talent in India as well as overseas superstars. When the two teams clashed in the final, in 1934/35, about fifteen thousand spectators watched the Retrievers beat the Freelooters by 3 wickets at the Gymkhana Ground in Secunderabad.

RAILWAYS VS AIR INDIA

In 1985/86, Railways first fielded a women's team in the national championships. The team consisted of cricketers recruited by the Indian Railways under their sports quota. The players worked until three, and practised after that. With the finances taken care of, they—unlike their counterparts in other teams—could focus solely on cricket. That, combined with aggressive hiring from other states, made Railways the strongest women's team in Indian domestic cricket. The facilities were top-notch. For example, they travelled in air-conditioned coaches when other teams were only entitled to second-class compartments.

Air India entered the fray in 1992/93, and emulated Railways' policies. The facilities were probably superior (air travel!). By the end of the millennium, Railways versus Air India became the national derby. Between 2000 and 2006, the two teams were involved in numerous pitched battles.

The rivalry ended in 2006 when the BCCI took over women's cricket in India. Unlike Railways, Air India were not a registered member of the BCCI, and were not allowed to participate in domestic tournaments. Thus, while Mithali Raj continued to play for Railways, Jhulan Goswami had little option but to represent Bengal.

The healthy two-team contest had led to both teams trying to beat each other. As a collateral, Indian women's cricket benefitted like never before. The disbanding of the Air India team reduced Indian cricket to a Railways monopoly. Despite the occasional upset, it continues to remain that way.

DADAR UNION VS SHIVAJI PARK

Of the eighty-six editions of the Ranji Trophy, Bombay have won forty-one—a feat often attributed to club cricket. And while rivalry among Bombay clubs is fierce, nothing quite matches the intensity of Dadar Union versus Shivaji Park Gymkhana.

Founded in 1927, Dadar Union became a force in the 1950s under Madhav Mantri, who led and mentored the side into becoming the most feared in the city. Naren Tamhane, Ramnath Kenny, Sunil Gavaskar, Dilip Vengsarkar, Sanjay Manjrekar—Dadar Union used to be a roll call of greats. Gavaskar, the most illustrious of them, would return from an international tour in the wee hours of the morning and be on the ground by nine to play for Dadar Union.

Their strongest competition came from Shivaji Park Gymkhana, just across Tilak Bridge. Over the years, Shivaji Park has given Bombay—and India—stalwarts like Ramakant Desai, Vijay Manjrekar, Ajit Wadekar, Sandeep Patil, Sachin Tendulkar, Vinod Kambli, Pravin Amre and Ajit Agarkar.

In 2008, Tendulkar famously carried soil from Shivaji Park to add to a mixture and smear on the foreheads of his Mumbai Indians teammates.

SONNET VS NIS

The National Institute of Sport, Delhi, has produced some famous players like Kirti Azad, Gursharan Singh, Maninder Singh and Vivek Razdan. Run by the government, the NIS boasted excellent facilities, and were obviously one of the strongest sides in the national capital. However, they would often attract the children of government officials and politicians, or—as the locals called them—the 'hi-fi people'.

In 1969, Tarak Sinha decided to set up a training centre for children from lower-middle-class families—and the Sonnet Cricket Club was formed. For years, Sonnet did not have a ground of their own—and even new balls for practice were not something they could take for granted. The stark difference made them natural rivals of the NIS, though, as senior sports journalist Vijay Lokapally would say, the NIS cricketers were seldom condescending to Sonnet.

Surinder Khanna, Sanjeev Sharma, Manoj Prabhakar, Anjum Chopra, Raman Lamba, Ajay Sharma, Atul Wassan, Aakash Chopra, Ashish Nehra, Shikhar Dhawan, Rishabh Pant—if you were a Sonnet star, you were almost certain to be a Delhi regular. They went on to compete with, defeat and surpass the NIS as the strongest club in Delhi cricket.

MOHUN BAGAN VS EAST BENGAL

Kolkata is one of a handful of major cities where football giants—in this case, Mohun Bagan and East Bengal—clash in the city cricket derby as well. The most famous club football rivalry in India may date back a century, but the cricket contest grew in intensity only in the 1970s when a group of cricketers—Gopal Bose, Subrata Guha, Raja Venkat, among others—moved from Mohun Bagan to East Bengal.

Many local stars turned out (and switched allegiances) for one of the two clubs. And, as in the Lancashire League, both clubs had non-local professionals showing up for them. While East Bengal had giants like Kapil Dev, Sachin Tendulkar and Anil Kumble, Mohun Bagan recruited Lala Amarnath, Vijay Hazare, M.S. Dhoni, Virat Kohli and even Chaminda Vaas.

The rivalry intensified in the 1980s and 1990s, spilling over into the first decade of the new millennium. Some contests in the P. Sen Memorial Trophy—the most high-profile of the Kolkata tournaments—featured crowds large enough to draw comparisons with the famed football clashes between the two clubs, and attracted media from across the country.

MUMBAI INDIANS VS CHENNAI SUPER KINGS

Between them, the Mumbai Indians and the Chennai Super Kings have won ten of the first sixteen editions of the IPL, making them the two most successful teams in the history of the league. And when the two teams clash, the viewership often reaches unbelievable highs.

A 2021 league-stage clash between Mumbai and Chennai had a viewership of 367 million, making it the most-viewed IPL league-stage match. For perspective, the T20 World Cup final—the most high-profile international cricket match—attracted 167 million viewers in 2021, while the Day/Night Test match of the 2021/22 Ashes in Adelaide was watched by a mere 440,000. The number bears testimony to the volume of the gargantuan cricket fanbase in India—something that is often acknowledged but seldom understood.

HOWZZAT!

Mohammad Azharuddin began his career with centuries in his first 3 Test matches—110 at Calcutta, 48 and 105 at Madras and 122 and 54 not out at Kanpur, all against England. This remains a world record.

It's a Match!
Unusual Cricket Contests

Every now and then, one comes across an unusual cricket match, played for a cause, for pure fun, or perhaps to mark a historic moment. Here are a few that may not qualify as classics, but are certainly singular.

DELHI LADIES STUN MCC

While English teams have toured India before, Arthur Gilligan's Englishmen of 1926/27 were the first team of serious strength to come to this part of the world. True to their reputation, they completed their four-month tour of India, Ceylon and Burma losing just one match.

The lone defeat came against the Delhi Ladies Cricket Club, who put up 124 ('Ladies first, please,' said Gilligan at the toss) and bowled out the Marylebone Cricket Club for 69. It was not a serious match—George Brown of the MCC took field in a clown's outfit, complete with the nose—but history will perhaps acknowledge Delhi Ladies as the first Indian team to beat a strong touring side.

NEIGHBOURS UNITE

A Commonwealth XI, led by Jock Livingston and featuring Frank Worrell, John Holt, George Tribe and Bill Alley, among others, toured the Indian subcontinent in 1949/50. One of their matches, in Colombo, was against a Ceylon, India and Pakistan Combined XI—where India's Vinoo Mankad and Dattu Phadkar played alongside Munawwar Ali Khan and Rusi Dinshaw from Pakistan and Mahadevan Sathasivan and Stanley Jayasinghe from Sri Lanka.

The three nations reunited for a match in Colombo a year later, when a different Commonwealth XI (led by Les Ames, featuring Worrell, Sonny Ramadhin, Eddie Paynter, Harold Gimblett, and Jim Laker) toured. This time India was represented by Vijay Hazare, C.D. Gopinath and Shute Banerjee.

Decades later, in 1996, India, Pakistan and Sri Lanka hosted the sixth edition of the World Cup. Australia and West Indies refused to tour Sri Lanka for their matches, citing security concerns in the wake of the Colombo bombing. As a gesture of solidarity, co-hosts India and Pakistan, who had not played a bilateral series since 1989/90, fielded a *combined* team, the Wills India and Pakistan Combined XI led by Mohammad Azharuddin, in a 40-over warm-up match against Sri Lanka, in Colombo, ahead of the World Cup.

Romesh Kaluwitharana of Sri Lanka fell early. His mode of dismissal—c. Tendulkar; b. Akram—was something cricket fans of the subcontinent had dreamt of for years but never imagined would come true. The combined XI won easily—the match, and much more.

Even after this, Australia and West Indies refused to tour Sri Lanka, and opted to forfeit their points instead.

GENERATIONS COME TOGETHER

While common in college events, (mis)matches between former and contemporary international cricketers is a rarity.

In 1957/58, however, a team of retired cricketers brought their kits out to take on a full-strength Indian squad. After C.S. Nayudu, almost forty-four, bowled 28 overs to take 5–146, forty-three year-old Vijay Hazare lit up Feroz Shah Kotla with his 167. The 'Present' cricketers took a 133-run lead and reduced the 'Past' to 124/5, but the senior men saved the match. C.K. Nayudu, then sixty-two, hit 4 sixes in his fourth-innings effort of 60. The BCCI had originally intended this as an annual fixture, but they did not host it again.

Ahead of the 1999 World Cup, the selected Indian squad played against the World Cup winners of 1983. There was much hype around the 35-over match, billed as the Good Luck India Match, but it turned out to be a far from serious affair. While Sachin Tendulkar got his obligatory hundred, the match ended in a farce, with Dilip Vengsarkar and Madan Lal slogging merrily against Rahul Dravid.

But then, a match between the best in contemporary India and champions who had retired years ago was not expected to be a serious affair.

IN THE DARK, IN EVERY SENSE

By the mid-1990s, the BCCI had figured out the magnitude of the Indian cricketing fanbase, and the rapidly increasing reach of satellite television. Inspired, they tried an experiment that was far ahead of the times. The Ranji Trophy final of 1996/97, between Mumbai and Delhi in Gwalior, was telecast all over India—and played under lights.

The initial idea was to paint the red SG balls white, but the BCCI later decided on using the white Kookaburra balls that were in vogue everywhere outside England and India at that point. A new ball was used every 40 overs. A not-so-delightful feature of the match were the insects that came out after sundown. One of them flew inside Vinod Kambli's ear, forcing him to rush off the ground.

The experiment was never repeated. Interestingly, India was one of the last ICC Full Members to start playing Test matches under lights.

A 'GRUDGE' MATCH

Ashutosh Gowariker's *Lagaan* is about a team of Indian villagers defeating a team of British soldiers in cricket in 1893. Tired of filming their on-field loss, the British cast of *Lagaan* challenged their Indian counterparts to a *real* cricket match. 'This has injured their vanity,' wrote Satyajit Bhatkal in *The Spirit of Lagaan*.

Aamir Khan put together a team largely made of technicians. When the British camp, hit by injuries, reported a man short, Aditya Lakhia (who played Kachra in the movie) played for the British. The Indian camp taunted Lakhia with calls of 'Traitor, traitor...'

Chris England (Yardley in the movie) led the British against Aamir Khan's Indians on 26 March 2000. It turned out to be an anti-climax. Despite their on-screen prowess (and cricketing experience of varying levels), the Indians were no match for the British, several of whom were serious cricketers.

The British won without breaking a sweat. Fortunately, this time, no *lagaan* had to be paid.

CEASEFIRE CRICKET

The Hizbul Mujahideen, a militant group that operated in Jammu and Kashmir, obviously never enjoyed a cordial relationship with the Indian Army. However, in August 2000, they played a friendly match against the Army at Kupwara in front of a large crowd.

The Hizbul won, but their commander left as soon as the match was over to avoid being arrested.

A TALE OF PATELS

The match in question took place at Bradford, but few cricket matches have been as Indian in flavour.

There was nothing unusual in the cricketing sense when Yorkshire LPS beat Amarmilan by 31 runs in this Sunday League match. What made it remarkable was the fact all twenty-two cricketers involved in the match shared the same surname: Patel.

While Amarmilan often fielded all-Patel XIs, Yorkshire LPS used to go in with ten of them. However, ahead of the match in question, their wicketkeeper (the only non-Patel) got injured. The replacement was, of course, a Patel.

Thankfully, one of the scorers was on first-name terms with the cricketers. One wonders how they would have coped otherwise.

BEATING ENGLAND AT NORTH POLE

In 2008, a team from the Indian Navy completed the three-pole challenge. Having already reached the South Pole and Mount Everest, they conquered the North Pole—and were in no mood to rest on their laurels.

They then beat a British team by 1 run in a cricket match played at -40°C. There was no cricketing gear, so the teams strapped up socks to manufacture a ball, and used a shovel for a bat and ski poles for stumps.

SUITS

In a 2013/14 Dr D.Y. Patil Cup match, the Comptroller and Auditor General team met Customs and Central Excise in what was expected to be a clash of stiff-upper-lipped executives in crisp grey suits.

In reality, the Comptroller and Auditor General boasted of top domestic cricketers like Jalaj Saxena, Biplab Samantray, Sachin Baby, Basant Mohanty and—Virender Sehwag. One wonders whether they audited the scoresheets after the match, which ended in a tie.

HOWZZAT!

In 1993/94, Kapil Dev went past Richard Hadlee's world record for most wickets in Test cricket. Among the many congratulatory messages, there was a cardboard cricket ball that expanded to 90 feet, signed by 13,000 students and staff of South Point High School, Calcutta. Between 1984 and 1992, the school used to hold a world record as well—for most students.

Ranji Trophy Remix
Defunct, Modified, Renamed, and Returning Teams

The Ranji Trophy began in 1934/35, with fifteen teams. By 2022/23—the most recent season—the tournament had expanded to thirty-eight teams. These include thirty-two teams from twenty-eight states (Maharashtra and Gujarat have three teams each), four (out of eight) Union Territories, Railways and Services.

    The teams, mostly drawn on geopolitical lines, have changed over time in response to the Partition and the abolition of the princely states. Some teams have merged, some split, some been renamed, while some have ceased to exist. Here is a list.

THE ERSTWHILE

Both Northern India and Sind featured in the inaugural edition of the Ranji Trophy, while the North-West Frontier Province first played in 1937/38. Much of these regions became part of Pakistan after Partition.

AT THE CENTRE OF IT ALL

The central Indian states have undergone numerous changes over the years, as have their Ranji Trophy teams. Central India was split into Holkar and Gwalior. Holkar played from 1941/42, while Gwalior entered as a separate team from 1943/44.

Although the state of Madhya Bharat came into being in 1948, the Central Provinces and Berar team continued until 1949/50, and Holkar until 1954/55. It was only in 1955/56 that Madhya Bharat first played as a team. In 1956, Madhya Pradesh was formed, combining Madhya Bharat, Bhopal and Vindhya Pradesh. The team changed name accordingly.

Berar, meanwhile, went to Maharashtra, and participated as a separate team in 1957/58, under the name of Vidarbha.

The state of Chhattisgarh was created in 2000, but they became a Ranji Trophy team only in 2016/17.

THE LAND OF FIVE WATERS

Southern Punjab played in the first edition of the Ranji Trophy, and remained the only team from the state even after Partition, until 1951/52. Patiala joined as a separate team in 1948/49 and Eastern Punjab in 1950/51.

In 1956/57, Patiala and Eastern Punjab States Union (PEPSU) participated as a team for the only time. Eastern Punjab was also there, though Patiala was not. Patiala featured sporadically until 1958/59 and Eastern Punjab until in 1959/60—the season in which Southern Punjab reappeared. Northern Punjab entered the fray in 1960/61, and coexisted with Southern Punjab until 1967/68.

In 1968/69, the two Punjabs combined to form one team called Punjab for the first time in the history of the Ranji Trophy. Meanwhile, the Punjab Reorganisation Act of 1966 led to the creation of Haryana, who became a Ranji Trophy team in 1979/80.

In 2019/20, Chandigarh—a Union Territory and the shared capital of Punjab and Haryana—became the third team from erstwhile Punjab to play in the Ranji Trophy.

TRAVANCORE–COCHIN

After Independence, the princely states of Travancore and Cochin were merged to form a single state. Travancore–Cochin played in the Ranji Trophy until the state was merged with Malabar and Kasaragod to form Kerala in 1956. Since 1957/58, the team has played as Kerala.

RANJI'S MEN, RANJI'S TROPHY

Ranjitsinhji was the Jam Saheb of Nawanagar, which made the Nawanagar team the cynosure of all eyes in a tournament named after him. Nawanagar played in the Ranji Trophy from 1936/37 until they signed the Instrument of Accession in 1948. Another team, Western India, based out of Rajkot, played from 1934/35 to 1945/46.

Western India were replaced by Kathiawar in 1946/47. They played alongside Nawanagar for two seasons before the latter stopped featuring. Saurashtra finally began playing as a team in 1950/51.

LOST AND FOUND

Bihar played in the Ranji Trophy from 1936/37 to 2003/04. Jharkhand became a separate state in 2000, and took most of Bihar's cricketing infrastructure with it. While the Bihar Cricket Association remained, the Ranji Trophy team was replaced by Jharkhand. It is only since 2018/19 that both Bihar and Jharkhand have participated in the Ranji Trophy.

INITIAL RETENTION

United Provinces were one of the teams in the first edition of the Ranji Trophy in 1934/35. In 1950/51, when the state changed its name (while retaining the initials 'U.P.'), to Uttar Pradesh, so did the team. The state of Uttarakhand, carved out of Uttar Pradesh in 2000, became a Ranji Trophy team from 2018/19.

WHAT'S IN A NAME?

Several Ranji Trophy teams followed suit when the entities they were named after changed their names. These include Uttar Pradesh (erstwhile United Provinces), Services (Army), Rajasthan (Rajputana), Tamil Nadu (Madras), Karnataka (Mysore), Mumbai (Bombay) and Odisha (Orissa).

On the other hand, Bengal never changed its name to West Bengal, the name the state acquired after it lost its eastern part during Partition. A similar example is of the Baroda team, who have not adopted the city's new name, Vadodara.

HOWZZAT!

Off spinner Neha Tanwar played 5 ODIs and 2 T20 Internationals for India, all in 2011. She played domestic cricket until 2014, took time off cricket, and made a successful comeback for Delhi after giving birth to a son.

PETA on the Pitch
Indian Cricket and Fauna

Despite the dignified presence of Tiger Pataudi, it can be safely assumed that cricket—Indian or otherwise—is restricted to the homo sapiens. However, local fauna have occasionally graced the sport with their presence, often of their own accord. The list does not include famous pets of cricketers, like Ranjitsinhji's parrot or Ravindra Jadeja's horses.

ELEPHANT, NEVER FORGOTTEN

For centuries, the West has used the elephant as a cliché to describe India even beyond cricket. As late as in 1992/93, Phil Tufnell's 'I've done the elephants, I've done the poverty, it's time to go home', said during England's disastrous tour of India, caused quite a stir.

Indian royal families put the majestic creature to extensive use. For the early English touring teams, royal treatment often involved getting to ride an elephant for *shikar*. Bhupinder Singh, the Maharaja of Patiala, went a step further: the roller on his personal cricket ground was pulled by an elephant.

The most famous elephant appearance, however, was on the ground on the fourth day of the Oval Test match of 1971, which coincided with Ganesh Chaturthi. As a good omen, the local Indian fans had arranged to lease Bella, a three-year old elephant, from Chessington Zoo. During the lunch interval, Bella, suitably bedecked in headgear, paraded across the ground … and into history. (The first chapter of Mihir Bose's *A History of Indian Cricket* is fittingly titled 'The Day the Elephant Came to the Oval'. Bella also features on the cover of Arunabha Sengupta's *Elephant in the Stadium*.) India famously went on to win the Test match—their first on English soil—and with that, the series.

MONKEY BUSINESS

On their 1951/52 tour of India, while the Englishmen were playing a tour match against Maharashtra in Poona, a monkey took up position at mid-wicket. It was later identified as Jaico, a local favourite.

In 2012/13, when England (again!) were playing Haryana in Ahmedabad, another money paid a visit. No direct relationship has been established between these simian cricket afficionados.

MAN'S BEST FRIEND

Unlike, say, England, Ireland and Australia, Indian cricket grounds typically do not allow pets, but it is difficult to keep strays away. There have been numerous instances of them invading the ground. The most famous of them was in Chennai, during the 2011 World Cup match between India and West Indies. Fortunately, this dog left on its own—unlike some others.

In 2009, when the IPL had to be moved to South Africa, a black foxhound—in a red collar, too—took field in Newlands to interrupt a match between the Chennai Super Kings and the Mumbai Indians. M.S. Dhoni tried to convince it to leave and Manpreet Gony tempted it with the ball, but to no avail. It left when it wanted to—after holding up the match for ten minutes.

'Play was delayed for 20 minutes by a mad dog on the field,' was how *Wisden* described a similar halt on the third day of a Ranji Trophy match between Uttar Pradesh and Vidarbha in Nagpur in 2000/01.

A RACEHORSE

After winning the Epsom Derby in 1971, Mill Reef became the symbol of speed in Britain. England were in control at that year's historic Oval Test. They had taken a lead of 71, and were 24/1 in the second innings.

As Bhagwat Chandrasekhar strode in to bowl the last over before lunch to John Edrich, Dilip Sardesai prompted, 'Mill Reef,' from mid-off. Chandrasekhar had contemplated bowling a googly, but he changed his mind midway, trusted Sardesai's judgement, and bowled his famous quicker ball. Edrich was bowled before he could complete his back lift.

Chandrasekhar finished with 6–38, England were bowled out for 101, and India pulled off a historic win.

A DEAD HORSE

In a local match in 2007 in Lalru (near Chandigarh), a batter hit a six that soared outside the ground and hit a horse, of Amritsari breed, on the head. The animal died after running around in agony for twenty minutes.

The blow also cost Paramjeet Singh, the owner, his livelihood. The cricketers never apologized, though a 'confused police department' filed criminal charges against 'unidentified cricketers'.

THE OTHER MONGOOSE

The two semi-finals and the final of the Cricket Association of Bengal Diamond Jubilee Tournament (Hero Cup) 1993 were the first floodlit international matches played at the Eden Gardens. On all three nights, a packed stadium saw a mongoose scamper across the ground—and gave it a standing ovation on the last two.

It was scant consolation for the poor creature, whose nocturnal abode had probably been usurped for a game of cricket.

THE OTHER HAWKEYE

On their 1949/50 tour, the touring Commonwealth XI were playing the Raja of Jath's XI at the Club of Maharashtra in Poona. Just when Jim Laker was about to bowl, he spotted a rat 'almost as large as a terrier' on the pitch. Moments later, just when the rat arrived at 'the good-length spot', a kite swooped—successfully—and left with its dinner between its talons.

Laker's accuracy was legendary; he would do great things on the cricket field, especially against the Australians, but this incident shocked him. His next ball bounced twice and was dispatched for four.

TO KILL A BIRD ... OR TWO

Jahangir Khan played 4 Test matches for India, but on this occasion in 1936, he was playing for Cambridge University against the MCC at Lord's. He bowled, Tom Pearce played forward, and realized that something—not the ball—had hit the stumps. It was a dead sparrow. The sparrow was stuffed and mounted on the ball responsible for its demise, and together they rest at the Memorial Gallery in Lord's. In 2006, it visited The Grand House Sparrow Exhibition in Rotterdam.

Nearly half a century later, India were playing Australia in a Test match at Adelaide when Kapil Dev hit a cracking drive. It claimed the life of a seagull, a species whose presence is guaranteed wherever there is a cricket match in that country. A visibly upset Kapil asked for a glass of water to recover but Australian captain Allan Border turned down his request.

SERPENTINE THREAT

When Pakistan were supposed to play India in 1998/99, the Shiv Sena threatened to release venomous snakes in the outfield during the Test match at Feroz Shah Kotla. Whether it was a genuine threat is unknown, but the organizers were prepared. The best snake-charmers of Delhi were placed at strategic points in the stands. Thankfully, the threat was never made good on.

However, a year later, a Ranji Trophy quarter-final between Punjab and Tamil Nadu at Chepauk had a delayed start because there was a snake in the outfield.

APIAN ATTACK

In 1981, some children in Bangalore were throwing stones at a beehive. The angry bees swarmed onto the playing ground during a cricket match and took it out on the players. Play had to be abandoned, and six cricketers and an umpire had to be treated in a hospital.

A less impactful bee invasion took place in the same city at the M. Chinnaswamy Stadium during the 1979/80 Test match between India and Pakistan. No major harm was done, but play was held up as the cricketers and umpires flung themselves on the ground. The Bangalore bees were back at Chinnaswamy during India's 1999/2000 Test match against South Africa as well.

A month after this incident, bees invaded Chepauk during a Ranji Trophy match between Tamil Nadu and Punjab (the same quarter-final where a snake held up play) when a beehive on the terrace was disturbed. The cricketers were unharmed, but some spectators and media personnel were not as fortunate.

The active interest of Indian bees in cricket was in evidence throughout the twenty-first century. Bees invaded an India–Pakistan ODI at Visakhapatnam in 2005, an India–Australia Test match at Delhi in 2008 and a match between India A and England Lions at Thiruvananthapuram in 2018/19. During this last incident five spectators were stung, and India A coach Rahul Dravid, usually an unfazed man, was seen running for safety.

TRAPPED

In the era of social media, fans know that M.S. Dhoni, Yuvraj Singh, Virat Kohli, Rohit Sharma, Hardik Pandya and Bhuvneshwar Kumar are dog lovers. Ravi Shastri's quintet—Bouncer, Beamer, Flipper, Yorker, Skipper—is no less famous than their doting owner.

One former cricketer whose heart does not melt at the sight of man's best friend is Sunil Gavaskar, who, in fact, continues to be scared of Bouncer and Beamer, indeed of any dog. During his stint with Somerset, Gavaskar was once trapped inside a telephone booth because Ian Botham, perfectly aware of Gavaskar's phobia of canines, waited outside with an Alsatian!

HOWZZAT!

In 2013, shaadi.com shared a study that revealed a steep rise in the number of people who wanted a cricket-loving spouse since the advent of the IPL. It held for both women (pre-IPL 11.4 per cent, post-IPL 23.1 per cent) and men (20.2 per cent to 32.8 per cent).

Family Matters
Related Indian International Cricketers

The first All-India side toured England in 1911. They were led by Bhupinder Singh, the Maharaja of Patiala and one of the greatest patrons of cricket in pre-Independence India. His son Yadavindra Singh played a Test match against England, at Madras in 1933/34, and was among the contenders for captaincy for the 1936 tour of England.

The 1911 tour also featured two of the four Palwankar brothers: Baloo—the first outstanding Indian cricketer—and Shivram. All four Palwankar brothers (Vithal and Ganpat were the others) played first-class cricket but Test cricket came too late for them. Thus, India had related cricketers in their XIs long before they played Test cricket.

C.K. Nayudu captained India in their first Test match at Lord's in 1932. But when the squad had left India, Nayudu was not captain, for such honours were reserved for members of the royal families. Natwarsinhji Bhavsinhji, the Maharaja of Porbandar, was named captain, while his brother-in-law Kumar Shri Ghanshyamsinhji Daulatsinhji Jhala of Limbdi was his deputy. Neither was a competent cricketer, and both stepped down to let Nayudu take charge in the Test match.

Here is a list of related Indian international cricketers, some of whom are related to international cricketers of other countries.

WAZIR ALI AND NAZIR ALI, AND KHALID WAZIR (PAKISTAN)

India's first Test match—Lord's, 1932—featured the brothers Wazir Ali, one of the country's finest pre-Independence batters, and Nazir Ali, the first Indian to dismiss Don Bradman. Both brothers moved to Pakistan after Independence. Khalid Wazir, son of Wazir, played 2 Test matches for Pakistan.

C.K. AND C.S. NAYUDU

Cottari Kanakaiya Nayudu, India's first Test captain, needs little introduction. His younger brother Cottari Sabbanna played 11 Test matches (four more than C.K.) on either side of Independence, and still holds the world record for bowling most balls in a first-class match (917 in the 1944/45 Ranji Trophy final).

LADHA RAMJI AND LADHA AMAR SINGH

Amar Singh, arguably India's best pre-Independence all-rounder, bowled the second over for India and scored their first ever Test match fifty in Test cricket. Ramji, ten years older, was acknowledged as India's quickest bowler of the 1920s. He played a Test match too, but being in his early thirties by then, he was not at his quickest. Unfortunately, both brothers died young, Ramji at forty-eight, Amar Singh at twenty-nine.

LALA, SURINDER AND MOHINDER AMARNATH

Lala Amarnath, the first Indian to score a Test hundred, and his elder son Surinder are the only father–son pair to score hundreds on Test debut. Lala also led Independent India in their first Test tour in Australia in 1947/48, and to their first Test series win against Pakistan in 1952/53. Surinder's brother Mohinder played 69 Test matches, and was Player of the Match in both the semi-final and final of the 1983 World Cup.

JAHANGIR KHAN, BAQA JILANI, KHAN-BURKI CLAN (PAKISTAN)

Jahangir Khan played 4 Test matches for India in the 1930s. His last Test was the only one for his brother-in-law Baqa Jilani, the first man to get a hat-trick in the Ranji Trophy. Jilani 'earned' his Test cap after insulting C.K. Nayudu, the great rival of Vizzy, the captain, at the breakfast table.

Jahangir moved to Pakistan after Partition. His son Majid led Pakistan, as did Majid's cousins, Javed Burki and Imran Khan. Majid's son Khan Bazid played Test cricket too, making it three generations of Test cricketers in the family.

DATTARAM HINDLEKAR, VIJAY AND SANJAY MANJREKAR

Wicketkeeper Dattaram Hindlekar toured England in 1936 and 1946 and played 4 Tests. Nephew Vijay Manjrekar, probably India's finest batter in the 1950s and early 1960s, scored 586 runs in India's first ever Test series win against England in 1961/62. Vijay's son Sanjay was renowned for his technique, particularly against pace. His greatest feat was the 569 runs in the 1989/90 tour of Pakistan. Father and son both scored over 2,000 Test runs and were occasional wicketkeepers.

IFTIKHAR ALI KHAN (ENGLAND AND INDIA) AND MANSUR ALI KHAN PATAUDI

Iftikhar Ali Khan, the eighth Nawab of Pataudi, played 3 Tests *for England* and got a hundred on Test debut, all in 1932/33. In 1946, he led India in 3 Tests in England, and remains the only person to play Test cricket for both England and India. The bilateral Test series played by India in England is fittingly named the Pataudi Trophy.

Mansur, who succeeded Iftikhar as the Nawab, became Test captain in 1962/63 (despite losing an eye in an accident)—the youngest in the world at that point. He was India's first long-serving captain, leading them almost throughout the 1960s and in 1974/75.

ABDUL HAFEEZ KARDAR (INDIA AND PAKISTAN) AND ZULFIQAR AHMED (PAKISTAN)

Abdul Hafeez played thrice for India on their 1946 tour of England. After Partition, he became Pakistan's first Test captain. Playing as Abdul Hafeez Kardar, he led them to famous wins in Lucknow (1952/53) and The Oval (1954). He married Shahzadi, sister of Zulfiqar Ahmed, who played 9 Test matches for Pakistan.

VINOO AND ASHOK MANKAD

The Second World War pushed Vinoo Mankad's Test debut to the age of twenty-nine. Even then, it took only 23 Test matches—then the fewest in the world—for him to achieve the 1,000 run–100 wicket double. The greatest Indian all-rounder before Kapil Dev, Mankad played a key role with the ball in each of India's early Test match wins; held the record for their highest individual score (231) for nearly three decades; and, along with Pankaj Roy, put on a first-wicket stand of 413 that remained a world record for over half a century.

His son Ashok, hailed by some as the greatest captain in the history of Bombay, played 22 Test matches.

MADHAV MANTRI, SUNIL AND ROHAN GAVASKAR, GUNDAPPA VISWANATH

Madhav Mantri played 4 Test matches in the 1950s. Among the many cricketers he mentored was his sister Meenal's son, Sunil Gavaskar. Sunil's sister Kavita married Gundappa Viswanath. Throughout the 1970s, Indian fans were divided over who was the greater of the two giants (the argument continues in some circles even today). Sunil's son, Rohan, played ODIs in 2004.

GHULAM AHMED, ASIF IQBAL (PAKISTAN), SHOAIB MALIK (PAKISTAN) AND MOHAMMAD AZHARUDDIN

India's first outstanding off-spinner, Ghulam Ahmed played 22 matches for India from 1948/49 to 1958/59 for his 68 wickets, including three times as captain. His nephew Asif Iqbal played for Hyderabad (India) in 1959/60 and 1960/61. He subsequently moved to Pakistan where he played from 1964/65 to 1979/80. Ghulam's wife's niece Sania Mirza, one of India's finest tennis players, married Shoaib Malik, who led Pakistan as well. Sania's sister Anam married Mohammad Azharuddin's son Asad, which makes Sania related to four Test captains.

PANKAJ, AMBAR AND PRANAB ROY

India's go-to opening batter in the 1950s, Pankaj Roy was the only Indian opener to score 2,000 Test runs before Sunil Gavaskar. Often remembered for the world-record opening partnership of 413 with Vinoo Mankad, Roy also led India once in 1959.

Pankaj's nephew Ambar—a flamboyant stroke player—played 4 Test matches in 1969/70, while Pankaj's son Pranab—a more conservative batter, like his father—played 2 Tests in 1981/82.

MADHAV AND ARVIND APTE

Despite averaging 49.27 in the early 1950s, Madhav Apte played only 7 Test matches before being dropped for controversial reasons discussed elsewhere in this book. His brother, Arvind, played once as well, at Leeds in 1959.

SUBHASH AND BALOO GUPTE

Hailed by Garry Sobers and Jim Laker, among others, as the greatest leg-spinner they had seen, Subhash Gupte picked up 149 wickets at 29.55, phenomenal numbers in an era when Indian close-in fielding was, at best, sub-par. A more telling statistic is his 12 5-wicket hauls in 36 Test matches. His brother Baloo, also a leg-spinner, played only 3 Test matches despite having an illustrious domestic career.

DATTA AND ANSHUMAN GAEKWAD

Datta Gaekwad played 11 Test matches and led India on the 1959 tour of England. Son Anshuman, one of Sunil Gavaskar's many opening partners, built a reputation for handling hostile pace. This resulted in him playing 22 of his 40 Tests against the West Indies. Anshuman's most famous innings was the 81 at Sabina Park in 1975/76, during which he took two blows, one split his finger and the other burst his eardrum.

K.S. RANJITSINHJI (ENGLAND), K.S. DULEEPSINHJI (ENGLAND), HANUMANT SINGH, K.S. INDRAJITSINHJI, AJAY JADEJA

Despite their stature, and the fact that two of India's most important domestic tournaments are named after them, both Ranjitsinhji and his nephew Duleepsinhji played for England, not India—though the latter did play in the Bombay Quadrangular.

Duleep's sister married the Maharawal of Banswara. Their son Hanumant Singh played 14 Test matches. Indrajitsinhji, grandson of Ranji's brother Mohansinhji, played 4 matches for India. Ranji's nephew Digvijaysinhji's son Y.S. Shatrushalyaji's cousin K.S. Chatrapalsinhji's nephew Ajay Jadeja played 15 Test matches, but was more renowned for his prowess in limited-overs cricket. He scored over 5,000 ODI runs and led India 15 times.

A.G. KRIPAL SINGH AND A.G. MILKHA SINGH

Amritsar Govindsingh Ram Singh, the patriarch of the Sikh family of cricketers of Madras, was the first to achieve the 1,000 run–100 wicket double in the Ranji Trophy. He did not play Test cricket, but two of his sons, Kripal and Milkha, did, even together once.

BEHROZE AND DIANA EDULJI

The Edulji sisters, Behroze and Diana, played in India's first Women's Test match against West Indies in Bangalore in 1976/77. Behroze did not get a wicket and never played for India again, but Diana became a cricketing legend. Her 63 Test wickets are the most by an Indian and the third-most of all time. She was India's first ODI captain, and led them in two World Cups, fifteen years apart, in 1978 and 1993. With her bowling, shrewd tactics and leadership skills, she virtually built the near-invincible Railways side.

SUSAN ITTICHERIA AND DINESH KARTHIK

Susan Itticheria played 7 Test matches (including India's first Women's Test match) and in the 1978 World Cup. Her daughter, Dipika Pallikal, a champion squash player, married Dinesh Karthik, who has kept wickets for India in all three formats. Karthik was the first Indian to win a Player of the Match award in a T20 International, and made a surprise comeback to the national side in 2022.

HEMANT AND HRISHIKESH KANITKAR

Hemant Kanitkar played 2 Tests against the West Indies in the 1970s. His son Hrishikesh, remembered merely—and unfairly—as the man who hit the boundary off Saqlain Mushtaq to help India win the 1998 Independence Cup in Bangladesh, played 2 Tests as well—to go with 34 ODIs. Hrishikesh's CV includes leading Rajasthan when they became only the fifth side to *defend* their Ranji Trophy title, and coaching India to their fifth Under-19 World Cup win in 2022.

SYED ABID ALI AND SYED KIRMANI

Abid Ali played 29 Test matches and some of India's early ODIs, and was at the crease during both of India's iconic wins in 1971 in the West Indies and England.

An integral part of the Indian side from the mid-1970s to the mid-1980s, Syed Kirmani was named Wicketkeeper of the Tournament when they won the World Cup in 1983. In 2002, Abid Ali's son, Faqeer, married Kirmani's daughter Nishad Fatima.

ROGER AND STUART BINNY

Roger Binny was the leading wicket-taker of the 1983 World Cup, and the coach of the Indian team that won the 2000 Under-19 World Cup. He played 27 Tests and 72 ODIs, and—remarkably—featured on a stamp of Bhutan. His son, Stuart, played for India between 2014 and 2016, and holds the best ODI figures (6–4) for an Indian.

YASHPAL AND CHETAN SHARMA

Yet another key member of the 1983 squad, Yashpal Sharma once batted through an entire day in Test cricket. Nephew Chetan took a 5-wicket haul in Lord's, was the first to get a hat-trick in a World Cup, scored an ODI hundred, and became the chair of selectors.

YOGRAJ AND YUVRAJ SINGH

One of Kapil Dev's new-ball partners, Yograj Singh played for India during the 1980/81 tour of Australia and New Zealand, but with little success. His son Yuvraj was one of India's finest middle-order batters in the shorter format. Prevented from taking up skating by his father, Yuvraj became a cricketer and was part of the champion Indian sides of the 2000 Under-19 World Cup, 2007 World T20, and 2011 World Cup.

VIKRAM RATHOUR AND ASHISH KAPOOR

Opening batter Vikram Rathour (6 Tests, 7 ODIs) and off-spinner Aashish Kapoor (4 Tests, 17 ODIs) had brief international careers in the mid-1990s, but reasonably long careers in domestic cricket. Rathour married Kapoor's sister.

YUSUF AND IRFAN PATHAN

A left-handed seam bowling all-rounder, Irfan Pathan is one of a handful of Indians to achieve the 1,000 run–100 wicket double in both Tests and ODIs. His half-brother Yusuf, two years older than Irfan, never played Test cricket, but was part of India's triumphant campaigns in the 2007 World T20 and the 2011 World Cup.

HARDIK AND KRUNAL PANDYA

Throughout his international career, Hardik Pandya has had to battle injuries and unfair comparisons with Kapil Dev. Living up to the tradition of Indian cricket, elder brother Krunal debuted later, and is trying hard to claw his way back to the national side.

Instrumental behind the success of the Mumbai Indians in their golden decade of the 2010s, both brothers moved on to other franchises. In 2022, Hardik led the Gujarat Titans to the IPL title in their debut season, and led India in the shortest format of the game.

DEEPAK AND RAHUL CHAHAR

A quality swing bowler who is more than handy with bat, Deepak Chahar held the best figures (6–7) in Men's T20 Internationals at one point. Rahul Chahar is a limited-over specialist as well, though he bowls leg breaks. Their fathers, Lokendra and Desraj, are brothers, while their mothers, Pushpa and Usha, are sisters, which makes Deepak and Rahul double cousins.

R.P. SINGH AND HARRY SINGH (ENGLAND UNDER-19S)

Two Uttar Pradesh seam bowlers called Rudra Pratap Singh have played for India. R.P. Singh, the Younger (and the more well-known), played on national side from 2005 to 2011. R.P. Singh, the Elder, played 2 ODIs against Australia in 1986/87. Over three decades later, in 2022, his son Harry—an opening batter—played Under-19 Test matches *for England*. He even scored a hundred in his second outing.

HOWZZAT!

Amitabh Thakur, an IPS officer, was a rare happy Indian when India lost the 2015 World Cup semi-final against Australia. He sent a cheque of INR 1,000 to Indian captain M.S. Dhoni, along with a note that mentioned how almost every government official 'was glued to the TV set, neglecting official work and even misbehaving with the occasional visitor who dropped in without appointment' during the semi-final.

Family beyond Cricket
Indian Cricketers Related to Famous Personalities

Jagaddipendra Narayan, the Maharaja of Cooch Behar and a first-class cricketer, defied his family to secretly marry American actor Nancy Valentine. The hush-hush marriage inspired Diana R. Chambers to pen The Star of India. Aryaman, son of Kumar Mangalam Birla, played for Madhya Pradesh and Rajasthan Royals.

While neither man played for India, here is a list of international cricketers and the famous people they are related to.

YADAVINDRA SINGH AND AMARINDER SINGH

Yadavindra Singh was the Yuvraj of Patiala when he scored 24 and 60 in his only Test match against England at Madras in 1933/34. In 1938, he succeeded his father, Bhupinder Singh, to the throne, becoming the only Indian Test cricketer to become a king.

His son, Captain Amarinder Singh, served in the Indian Army before serving Punjab as chief minister, from 2002 to 2007 and from 2017 to 2021.

LALL SINGH AND MYRTLE WATKINS

Perhaps the most exotic personality to play for India, Lall Singh played India's first ever Test match against England at Lord's in 1932. He was the third husband of Mexican actor–singer Myrtle Watkins (who later took the name Paquita Zarate). Lall Singh met Watkins at the Taj Mahal Hotel. They moved to Paris, got married (some sources mention 'lived together'), and ran a nightclub for a few years before they divorced.

SADU SHINDE AND SHARAD PAWAR

Shinde played 7 matches for India just after the Second World War, and holds the curious record of having a higher batting average (14.17) than career best score (14). He died of typhoid at only thirty-one. Twelve years after Shinde's death, his daughter Pratibha married Sharad Pawar, who, among other things, became the chief minister of Maharashtra, held multiple cabinets in the Government of India and was elected BCCI President.

KHERSHED MEHERHOMJI AND KERSI MEHERHOMJI

Wicketkeeper Khershed Meherhomji toured England in 1936, and played in the Old Trafford Test match when Dattaram Hindlekar opted out with an eye problem. Meherhomji's nephew Kersi, a reputed cricket writer and statistician, was honoured with the Medal of Order of Australia in 2022.

SANIA MIRZA, GHULAM AHMED AND MOHAMMAD AZHARUDDIN

We have discussed Ghulam Ahmed and his wife's niece Sania Mirza elsewhere in this book. She is also related to Mohammad Azharuddin through marriage: her sister is married to Azhar's son. Mirza attained doubles world no. 1 ranking in 2015—the year when she won the women's doubles at both Wimbledon and the US Open. In early 2016, she also won at the Australian Open. Having won three mixed doubles Grand Slams as well, Mirza is easily the greatest female Indian tennis player of all time.

MANSUR ALI KHAN PATAUDI, SHARMILA TAGORE, AND CHILDREN

Mansur Ali Khan Pataudi married Sharmila Tagore, at that point one of India's top actors, in 1968. Having started her career with Satyajit Ray's *Apur Sansar* (1959) and *Devi* (1960), Tagore made a seamless transition from Bengali to Hindi movies in the 1960s. She has won two National Awards, and was honoured with the Padma Bhushan in 2013.

Two of their children, Saif and Soha, are also actors, and the third, Saba, is a jewellery designer.

Sharmila is also a very distant relation of Rabindranath Tagore.

DILIP AND RAJDEEP SARDESAI

Rajdeep Sardesai's cricket career—all of 7 matches for Oxford—does not quite compare to that of his father, Dilip, hailed as Indian cricket's Renaissance Man. However, Rajdeep went on to become one of India's most prominent journalists and news anchors.

ASHOK MANKAD, NIRUPAMA VASANT, AND HARSH MANKAD

Ashok Mankad played 17 Test matches for India. His wife, Nirupama Vasant, was the top-ranked Indian tennis player for 13 years and won the Asian Women's Tennis Championship twice. She and Anand Amritraj reached the second round of the Wimbledon mixed doubles in 1971. Ashok and Nirupama's son, Harsh, played for India in the Davis Cup, and won the Manchester Challenger in 2006.

SUSAN ITTICHERIA, DIPIKA PALLIKAL, AND DINESH KARTHIK

Dipika Pallikal won the gold medal in squash at the 2014 Commonwealth Games in Glasgow and was honoured with the Padma Shri the same year. At the World Doubles Championships in 2022, she won the gold medal in both the women's doubles and mixed doubles categories.

Pallikal's mother, Susan Itticheria, and husband, Dinesh Karthik, have both played cricket for India.

BHARATH AND SRIYA REDDY

Bharath Reddy replaced Syed Kirmani as wicketkeeper on India's 1979 tour of England. His daughter Sriya (also spelled Shreya), an anchor and video jockey, has also acted in movies, mostly Tamil. She won accolades for her performance in Priyadarshan's *Kanchivaram* (2008).

SANDEEP AND CHIRAG PATIL

Two decades after winning the 1983 World Cup with India, Sandeep Patil coached underdogs Kenya to the 2003 World Cup semi-finals. Son Chirag has acted in both Hindi and Marathi movies; including playing his father in Kabir Khan's *83*.

MOHAMMAD AZHARUDDIN AND SANGEETA BIJLANI

One of the finest batters and fielders in the 1990s, Mohammad Azharuddin turned India into an invincible unit in the decade. His relationship with Sangeeta Bijlani—of *Tridev* (1989), *Yodha* (1991) and *Khoon ka Karz* (1991) fame—and their subsequent wedding in 1996 caused a stir in contemporary media.

SACHIN TENDULKAR AND ANAND MEHTA

Anand Mehta has won the Indian national bridge championship multiple times, but he could not convert, or even interest, his illustrious son-in-law: 'Sachin doesn't play bridge. He isn't even interested in learning the game. We usually do not have any interaction on bridge. I couldn't make him play bridge.'

SOURAV GANGULY AND DONA ROY

A student of both Amala Shankar and Kelucharan Mahapatra, Dona Roy—a leading Odissi dancer who runs the dance troupe Diksha Manjari—belonged to a family that was not on the greatest of terms with their neighbours, the Gangulys. She eloped and married their son Sourav, who would go on to become Indian captain and BCCI president.

HARBHAJAN SINGH AND GEETA BASRA

The third Indian to take 400 Test wickets and hero of several of India's famous wins, Harbhajan Singh married British actor Geeta Basra in 2015. Since her debut in Aditya Datt's *Dil Diya Hai* (2006), Basra has worked in both Hindi and Punjabi movies.

YUVRAJ SINGH AND HAZEL KEECH

Five years after being named Player of the Tournament in the 2011 World Cup, Yuvraj Singh married British actor–model Hazel Keech. After uncredited appearances in Harry Potter movies, Keech moved to India and acted in movies.

ZAHEER KHAN AND SAGARIKA GHATGE

In *Chak De! India* (2007), her debut film, Sagarika Ghatge played Preeti Sabarwal, the leading goal-scorer at the hockey World Cup who turns down an Indian international cricketer's marriage proposal. A national-level hockey player in real life, Ghatge is married to Zaheer Khan, the second Indian fast bowler to take 300 Test wickets.

TINU AND T.C. YOHANNAN

In 1973, T.C. Yohannan set a new national long jump record (7.78m) that stood for nearly three decades. In 1974, he set an Asian record (8.07m) at the Tehran Asian Games, winning a gold medal. He was also part of the Indian contingency in the 1976 Montreal Olympics.

In 2000/01, T.C.'s son Tinu became the first Kerala cricketer to play for India (the Kozhikode-born Narain Swamy never played for the state).

S. SREESANTH AND MADHU B.

A well-known singer, Madhu B. won the Kerala State Film Award for the song *Amme Amme* in 2002. Four years later, he won the corresponding award in Tamil Nadu for *Konja neram*. Madhu has also sung in Kannada and Telugu. He is married to Divya, elder sister of the mercurial Sreesanth—hero of India's first ever Test match win on South African soil.

VIRAT KOHLI AND ANUSHKA SHARMA

Just like Mansur Ali Khan Pataudi four decades before him, Virat Kohli, then Indian captain, married Anushka Sharma, one of Bollywood's leading actors, in 2017. Such was the hype around the couple that they needed a secret, closed wedding in Italy to escape the media. Their relationship with the Indian media and fans has had its highs and lows over time.

STUART BINNY AND MAYANTI LANGER

Despite playing only 6 Test matches and 14 ODIs, Binny holds the Indian record for the best bowling figures in ODIs (6–4). He married sports journalist–anchor Mayanti Langer, who has hosted various editions of the ICC World Cup, FIFA World Cup and the Commonwealth Games.

HARDIK PANDYA AND NATAŠA STANKOVIĆ

In 2022, Hardik Pandya led the Gujarat Titans to IPL triumph in their maiden season. At the time of writing this, he was on his way to reclaim the slot of the main all-rounder of the national side. In 2020, he married Serbian dancer–actor–model Nataša Stanković.

JAYANT AND YOGENDRA YADAV

When Jayant Yadav got a Test match hundred against England in Mumbai in 2016/17, politician–activist Yogendra Yadav, founding member of the Swaraj Abhiyan and Jan Kisan Andolan, surprised cricket fans by congratulating Jayant as a 'proud *chacha*'. The cricketer is the son of Jai Singh Yadav, Yogendra Yadav's cousin.

HOWZZAT!

India and Pakistan drew 13 consecutive Tests—the last 2 matches of 1952/53, all 5 matches in each of 1954/55 and 1960/61, and the first Test match of 1978/79.

Nominal List
Nicknames of Indian Cricketers

Indians love assigning monikers and adjective to cricketers. Thus, Sunil Gavaskar became Little Master, Kapil Dev became Haryana Hurricane, Sachin Tendulkar became God, Rahul Dravid became The Wall (thanks to a Reebok commercial), M.S. Dhoni became Captain Cool, Virat Kohli became King. Others, like 'Sir Ravindra Jadeja' and 'Lord Shardul Thakur', started off as ironic before attaining cult status.

Nicknames are different, and are perhaps more common. They can also be classified into several types.

DERIVED FROM ACTUAL NAMES

Abbreviating first names, especially long ones, is the commonest way to coin nicknames. Rusi (Rustomji) Modi, Ranga (Sriranga) Sohoni, Polly (Pahlan) Umrigar, Dattu (Dattatraya) Phadkar, Hemu (Hemchandra) Adhikari, Chandu (Chandrakant) Borde, Ravi (Ravishankar) Shastri and Robin (Robindra) Singh—only to name a few—became so popular that they appeared on official scorecards. The actual first names of these cricketers are all but forgotten.

On the other hand, Pat (Mansur Ali Khan Pataudi), Sunny (Sunil Gavaskar), Kaps (Kapil Dev), Maddi-pa (Madan Lal), Vishy (Gundappa Vishwanath and Sadanand Viswanath), Mithu (Mithali Raj), Jhulu (Jhulan Goswami), Mahi (M.S. Dhoni), Yuvi (Yuvraj Singh) and Zak (Zaheer Khan), while popular, did not attain 'official' status.

Nor have Jinks (Ajinkya Rahane), Jaddu (Ravindra Jadeja), Ash (Ravichandran Ashwin), Puji (Cheteshwar Pujara), Harry (Harmanpreet Kaur), Bhuvi (Bhuvneshwar Kumar), Boom (Jasprit Bumrah), Yuzi (Yuzvendra Chahal), Jemi (Jemimah Rodrigues) and Shifu (Shafali Verma).

Initials too qualify as nicknames. Laxman was often referred to as 'VVS'; and, despite his first name being one word on official scorecards, Surya Kumar Yadav has become a convenient 'Sky'.

ACTUAL NICKNAMES

As is often common in India, several cricketers have nicknames that have nothing to do with their full names or cricketing careers. Some, like Lala (Nanik Amarnath), Vinoo (Mulvantrai Mankad), Shute (Sarobindu Banerjee), Mantu (Sudangsu Banerjee), Nana (Padmanabha Joshi) and Bal (Hemchandra Dani), are considered 'official'. These players are seldom referred to by their actual first names.

Nicknames like Khokon (Probir Sen), Putu (Nirode Chowdhury), Jimmy (Mohinder Amarnath), Kaka (Ashok Mankad), Bobjee (M.V. Narasimha Rao), Cheeka (K. Srikkanth), Piggy (Arun Lal), Dolly (Preeti Dimri), Papali (Wriddhiman Saha), Chintu (Cheteshwar Pujara) and Charu (Sneh Rana), among others, have largely been restricted to dressing-rooms and fanbases.

Perhaps the most iconic of these is Tiger, a popular nickname Mansur Ali Khan Pataudi was known by. 'As an infant I had a tigerish propensity for crawling energetically about the floors on all fours,' he wrote in his autobiography, aptly titled *Tiger's Tale*.

ON-FIELD ACTS

Shantha Rangaswamy was a ferocious hitter, and would sometimes demand applause from the crowd after hitting a boundary. Her brutal stroke play earned her the nickname 'Bheem', something the fans would chant affectionately when she took strike.

Navjot Sidhu was fielding at mid-on when Anil Kumble bowled one of his famous faster balls. 'Jumbo Jet!' exclaimed an awestruck Sidhu. While 'Jet' dropped off from the nickname over time, the first part stayed on.

In his Ranji Trophy days, Shikhar Dhawan often fielded close to the bat. When a big partnership brewed, he would often mutter lines from *Sholay*—'Bahaut yaarana lagta hai', an iconic Gabbar Singh line, being among the politest of them. The name 'Gabbar' stuck.

THE GANDHI CONNECTION

Unlike his teammates who preferred the underwear, Rameshchandra Nadkarni preferred to wear the *langot*, the traditional Indian loincloth. This was a matter of great interest among his teammates, who coined the nickname 'Bapu', after Mahatma Gandhi, who also used to don the same. He appears as Bapu Nadkarni on official scorecards. Axar Patel is also called 'Bapu', but for a simpler, less interesting reason than Nadkarni's: like Gandhi, Patel hails from Gujarat.

One cricketer did get the nickname 'Gandhi' for his appearance, but Ian Redpath was Australian, not Indian.

FATHER'S WORKPLACE

Sharad Dravid worked for jam manufacturers Kissan, so it was perhaps inevitable that his son Rahul would be tagged 'Jammy'. Rahul Dravid appeared in several commercials for Kissan, where he was almost always addressed by the name.

So popular is the nickname that there is a Bengaluru cricket tournament called the Jammy Cup, where the Player of the Match is hailed as the 'Jammy of the Day'.

OTHER CRICKETERS

Madhav Mantri's nickname 'George', after George Headley, was almost certainly coined by Polly Umrigar, who had a penchant for assigning nicknames. Umrigar might have seen Headley in action when West Indies toured India in 1948/49, Headley's last series and Umrigar's first.

Wilf Ferguson was a leg-spinner who played 8 Test matches for the West Indies in the late 1940s and early 1950s. When India toured the West Indies in 1952/53, leg-spinner Subhash Gupte captured 50 wickets (27 of them in Test matches), met his future wife, Carol, and earned the nickname 'Fergie', after Ferguson. This, too, was probably coined by Umrigar.

Vijay Manjrekar seldom bowled in Test cricket, but he had always wanted to be an off-spinner. On his Test debut, in Calcutta in 1951/52, Manjrekar was dismissed by England off-spinner Roy Tattersall. The elusive science of nicknames meant that Manjrekar inherited Tattersall's nickname, 'Tatt'.

The tall Dilip Vengsarkar used to hit clean, enormous sixes in his early days, drawing obvious comparisons with Colonel C.K. Nayudu. Unfortunately, Vengsarkar never liked the nickname 'Colonel'. Sports writer Clayton Murzello observed that the Dadar Union, renowned for their discipline, boasted of cricketers with military nicknames: 'Colonel' Dilip Vengsarkar, 'Marshal' Vithal Patil, 'Major' Suresh Tigdi …

In his prime, Raju Kulkarni was one of the fastest bowlers in India, but lack of consistency at the highest level restricted his international career to 3 Test matches and 10 ODIs. He could generate pace and steep bounce from an unusual action, prompting teammates to address him as 'Thomson' after the Australian fast bowler.

Before he became arguably the greatest spinner in the history of Bengal, Utpal Chatterjee wanted to be a left-arm seamer. He modelled his action on that of legendary Australian all-rounder Alan Davidson. The nickname 'David' stuck. He played 3 ODIs, all in 1995.

Ashok Mankad's favourite actor, Rajesh Khanna, was affectionately called 'Kaka'. Sunil Gavaskar, with whom Mankad opened batting for both Bombay and India, coined the same name for Mankad. Of course, Khanna never played serious cricket.

APPEARANCES AND DEMEANOUR—IRONIC AND OTHERWISE

Deceptively fast for a five-foot-four man, Ramakant Desai toiled through the 1960s, often as the sole pacer in an era when India focused entirely on spin. 'Tiny' was an easy nickname for someone of his frame. The unusually long spells at sustained pace meant that he never played Test cricket after he turned twenty-eight.

Charming, both on and off the field, and handsome, Salim Durani acted opposite Parveen Babi in *her* debut movie, *Charitra*. The nickname 'Prince' would not have been as fitting for any other cricketer.

All-rounder Manohar Hardikar played for India twice in 1958/59, and is regarded by some as one of Bombay's finest captains. His perennial crew cut prompted Polly Umrigar to christen him 'German'.

Hanumant Singh made a hundred in the first of his 14 Test matches in the 1960s. His diminutive appearance earned him the nickname 'Chhotu'.

Roger Binny's nickname is inspired by his physique as well. Someone noticed the similarity between his posterior and a jackfruit, and Binny became 'Jackie'. While the nickname is not ironic, it is not clear whether he cherishes it.

One of the lankiest men to have played for India, Venkatapathy Raju was part of the Indian squad that toured South Africa in 1992/93. Brian McMillan, known to be a jokester, coined the ironic nickname 'Muscles'.

Jhulan Goswami's six-foot frame made her easily recognizable even in her early days of relative obscurity. It also earned her the nickname 'Taal Gachh' (palm tree) among Bengali teammates. Of course, the world knows her as 'Chakdaha Express'.

Virat Kohli once got a swanky haircut during a Ranji Trophy match in Mumbai, leading assistant coach Ajit Chowdhary to remark, 'Not bad, you look like a *cheeku*.' Ironic, perhaps, that a man that feisty would be named after a fruit as sweet as the sapota. Shikha Pandey shares the nickname, but that is probably derived from her first name.

THE ADOPTED

John Glennie Greig was born in India in 1871, grew up in England, played cricket in England in summer and in India in winter, mostly before the Wars, and is often acknowledged as the first outstanding cricketer to play regularly on Indian soil. The local Indians often struggled to pronounce his name. 'Jungly' Greig, they called him.

Like Greig, A.L. Hosie and T.C. Longfield also played in both England and India. Their initials paved way for the names 'Amrit Lal' and 'Tulsi Chand'.

ALCOHOLIC BEVERAGE

M. Vijay had travelled with the Under-16s to play in the bitter cold Delhi winter. Out exploring, he found a man who was drinking something from a glass. 'It keeps you warm,' the man explained, and the teenage Vijay took his first sip of Old Monk. He is still called 'The Monk'.

THE REVERSE-ADOPTED

In England, K.S. Ranjitsinhji's fate was similar to Greig's. His teammates at Sussex could not pronounce his name either. Nor did they try to come up a nickname that sounded remotely similar. Thus, Ranji became 'Smith', a nickname his nephew K.S. Duleepsinhji coincidentally acquired at Cambridge.

On a similar note, Ramesh Divecha, who was part of the first Indian team to win a Test match, became 'Buck' during his days at Oxford and Northamptonshire.

Manek Pallon Bajana became 'Pyjamas' at Somerset, where he played in the early 1910s. In Winchester (and later), they called Mansur Ali Khan Pataudi 'Noob', a take on his royal title, Nawab. And during his Derbyshire days, S. Venkataraghavan was sometimes 'Rent-a-Wagon' ('Rent-a-Caravan' was a variation).

Anil Kumble was the only bowler to take more than 100 wickets in the 1995 County Championship. For his Northamptonshire teammates, his name undertook the convoluted journey from Kumble to 'Crumble' to 'Apple Crumble' to merely 'Apple'.

When Yorkshire cricketers insisted on calling Cheteshwar Pujara 'Steve'—as they had been doing with many cricketers of colour for a long time—he took offence. In 2021, Pujara's former Yorkshire teammate Jack Brooks apologized to him.

THE ROCKSTAR

Vasudeo Paranjpe was—by most accounts—the first to use the nickname 'Sunny' for Sunil Gavaskar, who went on to call his first book *Sunny Days*. The sporting gear brand SG, whose initials match Gavaskar's, later named one of their bats 'Sunny Tonny'.

Around 2020, broadcasters added a 'G' to that nickname, probably to draw in the youngest generation, making it Sunny G. (like Jazzy B.). The phonetic similarity to Sunny-*Jee* appealed to the Indian audience as well.

ROYAL TITLES

Among the many oddities shared by members of royal families was the usage of titles, instead of names, even on scorecards.

While not strictly nicknames, the Maharaja of Patiala, the Maharaja of Porbandar, Kumar Shri Limbdi and the Nawabs of Pataudi were referred to by the names of their kingdoms. In fact, scorers used to list Mansur Ali Khan Pataudi ('Pat' to his teammates) as the Nawab of Pataudi or Mansur Ali Khan Pataudi until he lost the title after the 26th Amendment to the Indian Constitution, in 1971. Some subsequent scorecards had him as Mansur Ali Khan. Pusapati Vijay Ananda Gajapathi Raju, 'Vizzy' to many, also appeared on scorecards as the Maharajkumar of Vizianagaram.

However, this did not apply to all royalty. Ranjitsinhji, Duleepsinhji (both related to the Nawanagar royal family), Hanumant Singh (Banswara) and Yajurvindra Singh (Bilkha) were all referred to by their names.

Jayasinhrao Ghorpade was the maternal uncle, or Mamasaheb, to three first-class cricketers from the royal family of Baroda. The word, usually shortened to 'Mama', went on to become his nickname even in his days as a Test cricketer.

HOWZZAT!

In Durban, in 1992/93, Sachin Tendulkar became the first batter to be given out by the third umpire when he was caught short by a throw from Jonty Rhodes.

What's in a Name?
Cricketers Named after Other Cricketers

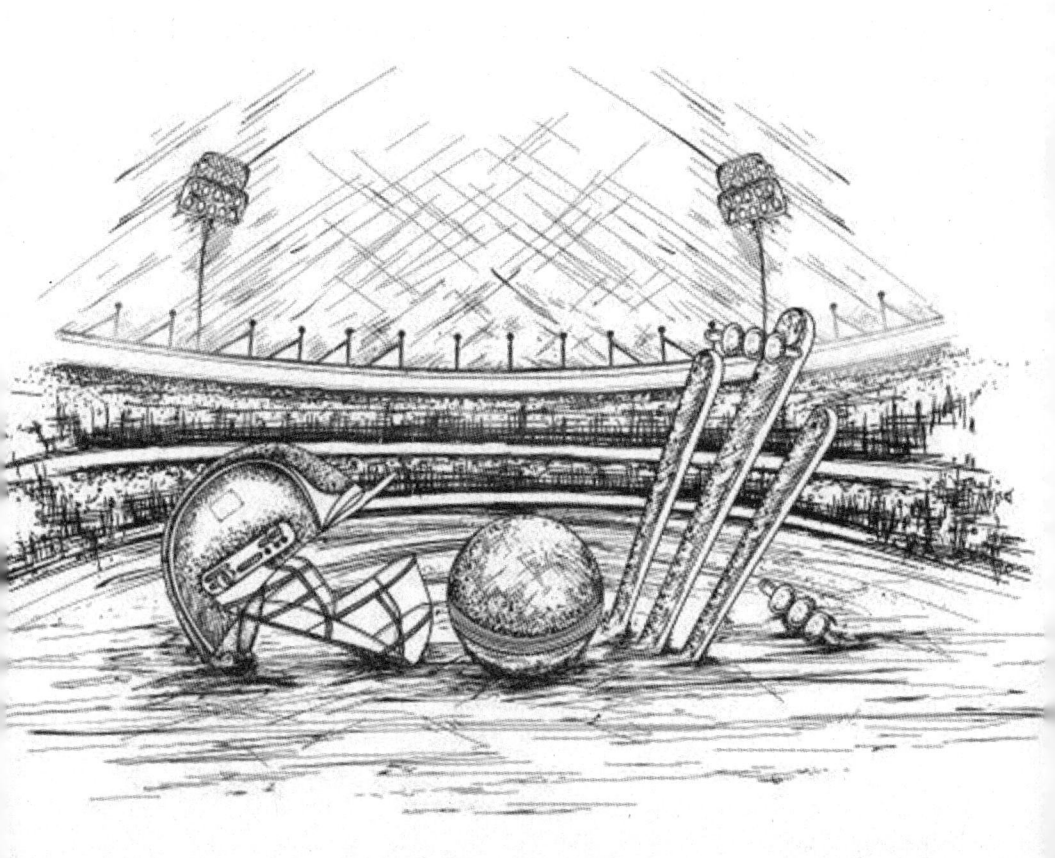

In India, naming a child is often a family effort where every member seems to have an opinion. Cricket fans, on the other hand, often try to keep things simple: why consider anyone else when there is a role model ready to lend their name? In this section, we shall find Indian cricketers named after foreign cricketers and vice versa.

SUNIL NARINE, AFTER SUNIL GAVASKAR

'I was named after you,' said Sunil Narine to Sunil Gavaskar during a post-match interview. Gavaskar jokingly told Narine that his father had named him well. Sunil Narine's father, Shadeed, was one of many Trinidadians who became Gavaskar fans, especially after his feats on his debut tour in 1970/71, and then again in 1975/76.

ROHAN JAIVISWA GAVASKAR, AFTER ROHAN KANHAI, M.L. JAISIMHA AND GUNDAPPA VISWANATH

Sunil Gavaskar named his son after not one but three of his favourite cricketers. Gavaskar had been a fan of West Indian legend Rohan Kanhai even before he went on his first tour—and his admiration only grew once he saw Kanhai's famous falling sweep shot.

Jaisimha, a flamboyant opening batter, was hero-worshipped by many contemporaries as well as subsequent generations.

Viswanath, the wristy stylist in the middle order, perfectly complemented Gavaskar's straight bat, often giving rise to heated discussions between fans and critics on which of the two players was greater. Sunil was not the only member of his family to be enamoured by 'Vishy': his sister Kavita married him in 1978.

DINESH KARTHIK, AFTER SUNIL GAVASKAR

Krishna Kumar is a fan of Sunil Gavaskar. There is nothing unusual in that: many people across the world are. Some, as we have seen, have even named their sons after him. Krishna Kumar, however, decided to do it differently. He named his son Dinesh, after the *suiting brand* Gavaskar used to endorse in the 1980s and 1990s. Now that Dinesh Karthik's shirts are attaining cult status, perhaps he deserves an apparel endorsement too ...

BARRINGTON ROWLAND, AFTER KEN BARRINGTON

Arguably the greatest-ever middle-order batter England has produced, Ken Barrington toured India twice in the 1960s, scoring runs like a glutton (674 runs at an average of 96) and earning numerous fans in the crowd with his on-field antics. One of them, Lincoln Rowland, named their son after him. Barrington Rowland played 68 first-class matches from 1999/2000 to 2007/08, mostly for Karnataka.

SACHIN BABY, AFTER SACHIN TENDULKAR

By 1988, a year before his international debut, Sachin Tendulkar was already being hailed as the next big thing in Indian cricket. On 11 December that year, he scored 100 not out on his first-class debut for Bombay against Gujarat at the Wankhede Stadium. Exactly a week after that, a boy was born in Thodupuzha, Kerala, and his father, P.C. Baby, decided to name him Sachin.

Sachin Baby made his debut in domestic cricket when Tendulkar was an active cricketer.

K.L. RAHUL, AFTER ... ROHAN GAVASKAR!

Prof. K.N. Lokesh wanted his son to have the same name as the son of his favourite cricketer, Sunil Gavaskar. But for some reason he was under the impression that Gavaskar had named his son 'Rahul', not Rohan. In an ideal world, K.L. Rahul might have grown up as K.L. Rohan.

YUZVENDRA CHAHAL, AFTER YAJURVINDRA SINGH

K.K. Chahal was an admirer of former Test cricketer Yajurvindra Singh who had equalled the world record for most catches in a Test innings (5) as well as in a match (7). He had initially decided to name his son Yuzvender before settling on Yuzvendra (it is not clear why he did not name him Yajurvindra). Aware of this, Yajurvindra Singh sent Chahal Jr a congratulatory text when the latter took 6 wickets against England.

RACHIN RAVINDRA, AFTER RAHUL DRAVID AND SACHIN TENDULKAR

Ravi Krishnamurthy used to play with the likes of Javagal Srinath during his days in Bangalore. He later moved to Wellington, New Zealand, where he had a son. Unable to choose between Rahul Dravid and Sachin Tendulkar, his two heroes, Krishnamurthy took one syllable from each name and called his son—a future New Zealand Test cricketer—Rachin.

HOWZZAT!

India was dismissed twice in a single day in Test cricket. England began the third day of the Old Trafford Test match of 1952 on 292–7. They declared on 347–9, and bowled out India twice, for 58 and 82, on the same day.

Why Me?
Cricket Venues Named after Unusual People

One would expect international cricket grounds to be named after international cricketers, but that is hardly the case in India. Political leaders (Jawaharlal Nehru alone has eight international grounds named after him) and cricket administrators are among the most common inspirations behind names, but venues have been named after some unexpected people too. For this list, we shall stick to venues on Indian soil where international cricket has been played.

AN AUTHOR AND NOVELIST

Emily Eden, an English writer of the early nineteenth century, visited India to meet her brother, George Eden, the governor general of India between 1836 and 1842. Her much-acclaimed memoirs, *Up the Country: Letters Written to Her Sister from the Upper Provinces of India*, were published in 1867. Eden Gardens, Kolkata is named after her.

A HORSE-RIDER

Green Park, Kanpur, is *supposedly* named after one Madam Green. Her full name is unknown, though some sources suggest the Greens were a British family that owned a hotel in Kanpur, while others mention military connections. Madam Green used to practise horse-riding on the grasslands where the stadium now exists.

The theory, however, has been disputed by some, who believe that the word 'green' refers to the grass in the park. But then, that holds true for most cricket grounds …

HOCKEY PLAYERS

Not one but two Indian grounds are named after hockey players. Captain Roop Singh famously scored 10 goals alone against USA in the 1932 Olympics, and was a member of the Indian sides that won the Olympic gold medals in 1932 and 1936. The hockey stadium in Gwalior, named after him, was later converted to a cricket stadium.

K.D. Singh ('Babu') was part of the Indian side that won the gold medal in hockey in the 1948 Olympics. He led the team to the same honours in 1952, and is sometimes compared with Dhyan Chand. He lent his name to one of several international venues in Lucknow.

GENERAL MANAGER, TATA STEEL

The city of Jamshedpur is named after Jamshedji Tata, while the railway junction is called Tatanagar. Surprisingly, the main cricketing venue in the city *does not* bear the name of the Tatas (though there is a Tata Digwadih Stadium in Dhanbad, in the same state of Jharkhand). Instead, it was named after John Lawrence Keenan, former general manager of Tata Steel. Keenan became the first American to lend his name to an international cricket venue.

CHAIR OF RAILWAY BOARD

Karnail Singh, former chair of the Railway Board, helped build the multi-sports venue named after him in Paharganj, Delhi. The home ground of the Railways cricket team, Karnail Singh Stadium was also witness to Paan Singh Tomar's steeplechase record, the 2008 National Kabaddi Championship, and a 1997 Women's World Cup match between Sri Lanka and West Indies, among other events.

FINALLY, A TEST CRICKETER

Gandhi Stadium, Jalandhar, is one of a handful of cricket venues where a wicket has fallen off the first ball (Kapil Dev trapped Mohsin Khan leg-before). The name was changed to B.S. Bedi Stadium, after one of the greatest cricketers to come from the state of Punjab (though Bedi played most of his cricket for Delhi).

There were also attempts to get the Sector 16 Stadium in Chandigarh named after Kapil Dev, but they were unsuccessful.

HOWZZAT!

On 1 September 2020, the Government of India added 'tennis ball cricket' to the list of 'sports disciplines for recruitment of sportsperson' for government jobs—a formal term for the 'sports quota'.

Remember My Last
Lesser-known Last Names of Indian Cricketers

The last name is often the official scorecard entry for most cricketers. This convention may or may not apply depending on one's faith or the region they belong to, such as certain parts of Tamil Nadu. Some Sikhs (Harbhajan Singh Plaha, Harmanpreet Kaur Bhullar) or Sindhis (Naoomal Jaoomal Makhija, Gogumal Kishenchand Harisinghani) too have chosen not to use their last names. Here are some other singular instances.

VIJAY MADHAV THACKERSEY

There are many versions of the story of how young Vijay Thackersey got his last name, but most of them agree on one thing. At school, when he was asked about his family name, Vijay mistook the question and responded with his family profession. The scion of the Thackersey group thus came to be known as Vijay Merchant.

NANIK AMARNATH BHARADWAJ

Lala Amarnath has the rare distinction of being known neither by his first name nor by his last. His full name, Nanik Amarnath Bharadwaj, is obscure enough to feature in quiz questions. Lala's sons, Surinder Amarnath and Mohinder Amarnath, both Test cricketers, did not use the full family name either.

ABDUL HAFEEZ KARDAR

Before becoming Pakistan's first Test captain, Kardar played 3 Test matches for India on their 1946 tour of England. For reasons not very clear, he did not use his last name while playing for India. Scorecards mention him as Abdul Hafeez.

SURENDRA NATH

A seamer who could toil for hours even on placid pitches, Surendra Nath played 11 Test matches between 1959 and 1961. He would have played more had India not switched to a spin-dominated attack in the 1960s. He went on to become a colonel in the Indian Army.

Surendra Nath appeared in most scorecards as one word, Surendranath, and even as Raman Surendranath on occasion. It was as late as 2020 that his son Shiven came forward to clarify the cricketer's name—and that there had never been a Raman in it.

HOWZZAT!

India's poor performance at the 2007 World Cup impacted the notebook and exercise book industry. Only 10 per cent of that summer's new books—mostly used by schoolchildren—featured cricketers on the cover. This was a steep drop from the usual 60–70 per cent.

Time Out
Abrupt Halts and Unexpected Endings in Indian Cricket

Cricket matches, and even entire tours, have been paused—or even called off—under unusual circumstances throughout the world. India have been in several such situations, some of these on home soil.

EARTHQUAKE

In 1937/38, Lionel Tennyson brought a reasonably strong team of English cricketers to India for a series of 5 unofficial 'Test' matches. During the first 'Test', in Lahore, an earthquake held up play for some time. When the pavilion clock fell with a crash, the panic-stricken crowd rushed onto the safest place: the cricket ground.

WORLD WAR

On 2 August 1939, England announced a sixteen-member squad for that winter's tour of India, one that would feature 26 matches including 3 Tests. However, on 1 September, Hitler attacked Poland. Cricket—and everything else—came to a halt.

FORFEITURE TO AVOID EMBARRASSMENT

In a Ranji Trophy match in Poona in 1948/49, Maharashtra bowled out Kathiawar for 238 and were 826/4 on tea on the final day. There was no question of an outright result, but B.B. Nimbalkar was on 443, a mere 10 runs behind Don Bradman's then world record first-class score.

At this point, Thakore Saheb of Rajkot, the captain of Kathiawar, gave Maharashtra an ultimatum: either declare the innings or Kathiawar would concede the match. The Maharashtra team—and even the umpires—requested for 2 overs of batting to achieve the world record, but to no avail. Kathiawar forfeited the match.

Nimbalkar's 443 is still the only quadruple hundred by an Indian, and he remains the only man to score a quadruple hundred but never play a Test match. Scant consolation arrived when Bradman sent a personal note, congratulating Nimbalkar.

A similar incident took place in a Times Shield match in 2005/06. Nandu Patil of P.D. Hinduja Hospital was on 403 when Central Excise, the opposition, conceded at tea on the final day. Patel had been eyeing Dadabhoy Havewala's record score of 515 in the Shield, set in 1933/34 for Bombay Baroda and Central India Railways against St Xavier's College, Mumbai.

MASS FOOD POISONING

West Indies had scored 366 in the Calcutta Test match of 1948/49, but India responded with 204/2 at stumps on the second day. Although a packed Eden Gardens waited on the third morning, the cricketers took their time. Umpire 'Bapu' Joshi and several cricketers had been facing the after-effects of fried prawns the night before.

Play eventually began fifteen minutes late. Clyde Walcott could not take field at all that day, leaving Robert Christiani to don the big gloves. After lunch, Balkrishna Mohoni, the other umpire, had to leave the field for ten minutes.

DEATH OF A KING

England were 224/5 at stumps on the first day of the Madras Test match of 1951/52. But by the time they left the ground, news arrived that King George VI had succumbed to coronary thrombosis. The organizers immediately rescheduled the following day as the rest day of the Test. Incidentally, this was India's first Test victory.

A CRICKETER'S HAIRCUT

During India's Old Trafford Test match of 1974, Sunil Gavaskar decided that his long hair was falling over his eyes, making batting difficult. He approached umpire Dickie Bird, who paused the game, procured a pair of scissors and gave Gavaskar an on-field haircut.

PARACHUTISTS

Nottinghamshire hosted the Indian team in 1974, at Trent Bridge. During the match, some amateur parachutists landed somewhere around fine leg. Play was held up until the ground could be cleared.

DELAYED KITS

India were scheduled to host Australia for 2 ODIs in 1984—in Trivandrum on 1 October and in Jamshedpur on 3 October. The landing strip in Jamshedpur was not designed for a large aircraft, so while the cricketers travelled by air, their kits came via road from Calcutta. The transport left too late—at four in the morning for a 300 km long journey and a match time of nine-thirty. The match finally got underway after a three-hour delay—and had to be called off due to rain after just 31 balls.

A decade later, India were supposed to host West Indies for a day match in Visakhapatnam on 7 November 1994, after playing a day–night match in Calcutta on 5 November. The Calcutta–Bhubaneswar–Madras Indian Airlines flight halted in Visakhapatnam. Players from both sides and the kits of the Indians got off the flight—but not the West Indian kits. The toss was delayed by an hour. Indian Airlines Managing Director P.C. Sen later ordered a probe.

ARREST OF A FORMER PRIME MINISTER

On 20 December 1978, former Prime Minister Indira Gandhi was expelled and sentenced to prison by the Lok Sabha for 'breach of privilege and contempt of the House'. She became the first Member of Parliament to suffer this ignominy.

Her arrest led to civil unrest throughout India, including in Bangalore, where a Test match was being played. Having secured a 66-run lead, West Indies were 200/8 at stumps on the fourth day—but the turmoil meant that the last day's play had to be called off in its entirety.

DEATH OF A PRIME MINISTER

India toured Pakistan in 1984/85 for 3 Test matches and 3 ODIs. They had already played 2 Tests and 1 ODI. In the second ODI, in Sialkot, India were 210/3 in 40 overs when news arrived that Indira Gandhi, the Indian Prime Minister, had been assassinated. Not only the match, but the entire tour was also called off.

UNDERPREPARED PITCH

On Christmas Day in 1997, India hosted Sri Lanka in Indore. The Indian team management had a look at the parched pitch and insisted the ground staff roll out a second strip. Sri Lankan captain Arjuna Ranatunga objected, and match referee Ahmed Ebrahim ordered that the match be played on the original pitch.

The first ball, from Javagal Srinath, landed and exploded. Nayan Mongia gathered a ball above his eyes and another near his ankles. The ball moved at absurd angles on a clearly underprepared pitch. Eventually, Srinath hit Roshan Mahanama on the glove. The umpires had a word with the captains and called off the match: the pitch was too dangerous.

However, the teams agreed to a 25-over exhibition match on the adjacent pitch for the crowd. Only spinners and slow medium pacers were allowed to bowl. Sri Lanka won by 2 runs. After the match, Ravi Shastri, one of the commentators, prodded the pitch softly with his shoe and managed to dig a small hole.

A few days later, a local lawyer demanded that Tendulkar, Ranatunga and Ebrahim be arrested for depriving the spectators of their right to watch the match they had paid for.

An encore took place in Delhi in 2009/10. Once again Sri Lanka batted first, though this time the match lasted 23.3 overs before the pitch was found to have 'extremely variable bounce' and be 'too dangerous for further play'. Feroz Shah Kotla got a one-year ban from hosting international matches.

DESERT STORM

A brief yet intense dust storm held up a Coca-Cola Cup match at Sharjah in 1998 for fifteen minutes. Once the storm subsided, another began as Sachin Tendulkar tore into the Australian bowlers, helping India qualify for the final with a 131-ball 143. A classic Tendulkar performance, this one is often affectionately referred to as the 'desert storm'.

ANGRY PARENTS

Pramod Doss was good enough to play for the Tamil Nadu Under-16s, and definitely old enough to qualify for the Under-14s. Yet, when the Under-14s team was announced, he had not been picked for the side. While this does not seem logical, most would have let it pass. Doss's parents were not as forgiving: they sat down on the pitch in protest during a match of the tournament, in Madras, holding up play for forty minutes.

INVADING JOURNALISTS

A group of journalists invaded the pitch during the 2000/01 Ranji Trophy quarter-final between Madhya Pradesh and Orissa in

Gwalior, demanding an apology from Madhya Pradesh cricketers Narendra Hirwani and J.P. Yadav. The players were accused of manhandling a journalist.

WELL, OF COURSE

During a match in Kolkata in 2006, the ball fell into a well, stopping play immediately. Alok Patra, among the more adventurous of the players, went down the well to retrieve the ball—and got stuck. The fire brigade had to be summoned to rescue him.

TERRORIST ATTACK

In 2008/09, India were leading the ODI series against England 5–0. The cricketers returned to their hotel rooms after the fifth ODI in Cuttack on 26 November, only to learn about the terrorist attacks in Mumbai. The remaining 2 ODIs were called off and England flew back home. However, they returned to play the 2 Test matches, which were moved from Mumbai and Ahmedabad to Chennai and Mohali.

HELICOPTER LANDING

A helicopter landed *on the pitch* during a Vijay Hazare Trophy match between Himachal Pradesh and Punjab in Dharamsala in 2008/09, sending the players running for cover. The helicopter flew away after half an hour.

Later, it was revealed that a fire had broken out near the ground, and the pilot had interpreted that as smoke signals. But what clinched it for him was the enormous H (for Himachal Pradesh) on the ground: it convinced him that it was a helipad.

COURT ORDER

The C.K. Nayudu Trophy Under-23 game between Jammu and Kashmir and Goa in 2016/17 was stopped indefinitely after an order was passed by the Jammu and Kashmir High Court. Hashim Saleem, a cricketer, had filed a petition with the court, accusing Jammu and Kashmir Cricket Association selector Mansur Ahmad of selecting his son Moomin Mansur. The BCCI postponed the match to avoid contempt of court charges. The match was later replayed in Sanguem, Goa.

NO RAIN

A stark departure from the age-old 'rain stopped play'.

The Kanga League is played in the Mumbai monsoon, and matches are often washouts. However, in 2017, the city received very little rain which kept the grass from growing and binding the soil, particularly in Matunga and Azad Maidan. The ground staff requested postponement of the first round of the league so they could prepare wickets to last all season.

CAR INVASION

Delhi and Uttar Pradesh were playing a 2017/18 Ranji Trophy match at the Palam A Ground in Delhi. How it happened is unknown, but about twenty minutes before stumps, one Girish Sharma drove a silver-grey WagonR onto the ground, and parked it in the middle of the pitch. He was stopped by security on his way out, but no formal complaint was lodged. Play continued after match referee Narayanan Kutty's 'playable' verdict.

POLLUTION

In 2017/18, a month after the WagonR incident, Sri Lanka were fielding against India in a Test match in Delhi when Lahiru Gamage experienced shortness of breath, while Dhananjaya de Silva and Suranga Lakmal vomited on the ground. The match was held up for twenty minutes. The cause for players' sudden illness was revealed to be the excessive smog conditions. Subsequent studies showed that the air pollution level was almost fifteen times the limit suggested by the World Health Organization.

THE SUN

After bowling out New Zealand for 156, India were 44/1 at the end of 10 overs in the Napier ODI of their 2018/19 tour. The pitch at McLean Park runs east to west, as a result of which the setting sun got into the eyes of the batters, Shikhar Dhawan and Virat Kohli. The match was held up long enough for an over to be deducted.

In the Jubilee Test match of 1979/80 at Wankhede Stadium, the rest day had to be scheduled after the first day. The sun played its part in this as well: the rest day coincided with a solar eclipse.

COVID-19

Halfway through the 2021 IPL tournament, the second wave of COVID-19 swept across India. Following the outbreak of

Coronavirus in multiple camps, the tournament was halted after 29 matches, on 2 May. The remaining matches were played in the UAE, from 19 September.

That same year, India left their five-match Test series in England unfinished after a COVID-19 outbreak was reported in the camp on the day of the last Test match. They returned in 2022 to finish the series.

HOWZZAT!

Mithali Raj and Reshma Gandhi debuted against Ireland at Milton Keynes in 1999. Both scored hundreds and batted through the 50 overs as India finished on 258-0.

Silver Screen
Cricketers Who Acted in Movies

Given the popularity of cricket in India, one can understand the eagerness of the makers to use cricketers for publicity. However, these roles have mostly been restricted to small cameos, where the cricketers played themselves—often during an on-screen cricket match.

The handsome Ranga Sohoni once turned down a role from V. Shantaram. However, some cricketers did take the next step, and had full-fledged roles in movies as bona fide actors.

SALIM DURANI

Durani's debonair appearance earned him more than the fitting nickname 'Prince'. He was almost certainly the first Indian Test cricketer to play the lead role in a feature film. B.R. Ishara's *Charitra* (1973) also marked the debut of Parveen Babi. Unfortunately, contemporary tabloids spread rumours about a non-existent relationship between the two lead actors, which did not go down well with him.

YOGRAJ (AND YUVRAJ) SINGH

It can be safely concluded that Yograj's career in Punjabi movies surpassed his cricketing achievements. *Batwara*, his first movie according to IMDb, was released in 1983, at a time when his international career—1 Test match, 6 ODIs—was over, and his domestic cricket days were on their last legs.

An active actor even as of 2022, Yograj has acted in almost a hundred movies, including Bollywood hits like *Bhaag Milkha Bhaag* (2013) and *Chandigarh Kare Aashiqui* (2021). The list includes *Mehndi Shagna Di* (1992), which had Yograj's pre-teen son Yuvraj as a child artist.

SUNIL GAVASKAR

Savli Premachi, Datta Keshav's 1980 Marathi movie, featured stars like Madhumati (as the female protagonist), Sulochana, Agha, Vikram Gokhale and Shreeram Lagoo. Piloo Reporter, international umpire and brother of Madhumati (whose real name was Hutoxi Reporter), convinced Sunil Gavaskar to play the lead opposite his sister. The song *'Hey dil kunacha'* became a superhit.

When Rajkumar Saxena (Naseeruddin Shah) must spend Rs 300 million in a month—with certain terms and conditions—in *Maalamaal* (1988), he hires Gavaskar to play for a local team. Gavaskar did play himself in the film, but the role was longer than the usual cricketer's cameo.

SANDEEP PATIL AND SYED KIRMANI (AND SACHIN TENDULKAR)

The hype around *Kabhie Ajnabi The* (1985) was tremendous, for it featured Sandeep Patil and Syed Kirmani, one of India's heroes from the 1983 World Cup. Unlike Patil, who was part of the plan from the beginning, Kirmani was included 'only because he was keen to perform some kind of role'. The makers promoted the movie around them, particularly an action scene featuring the two.

Tribune's verdict of Patil and Kirmani being 'clean bowled on the big screen' sums up the fate of the movie. However, Poonam Dhillon and Debashree Roy received plaudits, especially the latter.

The movie had a scene that required some young cricketers at the RCF Ground, Chembur. Among the twenty-one local boys, there was one Sachin Tendulkar, then barely ten.

VINOD KAMBLI

Ravi Dewan's *Annarth* (2002) was one of many gangster films made in Bollywood. The movie, starring Sanjay Dutt and Suniel Shetty in key roles, marked Vinod Kambli's acting debut. Kambli played Bandya, whose death was a key plot point. He later had a cameo in *Pal Pal Dil Ke Ssaat* (2009) in which former teammate Ajay Jadeja played the lead role.

AJAY JADEJA

In 2000, Ajay Jadeja was banned for five years from the sport in the aftermath of match-fixing scandals. The Supreme Court quashed the ban in 2003. In the interim period, Jadeja made his Bollywood debut in *Khel* (2003), starring Suniel Shetty, Sunny Deol and Celina Jaitley. He later played the lead role in *Pal Pal Dil Ke Ssaat* (2009) alongside Mahie Gill and Vinod Kambli.

SALIL ANKOLA

Salil Ankola and Sachin Tendulkar made their Test debuts together, but Ankola never played another Test match, though he did play 20 ODIs. After quitting cricket, he acted in several television serials, and played major roles in *Kurukshetra* (2000) and *Pitaah* (2002), both directed by Mahesh Manjrekar and featuring Sanjay Dutt in the lead role. Though the films he appeared in thereafter flopped, Ankola kept working in television serials.

In 2003, he turned down an offer to play a match-fixer on screen, saying it was 'against his principles'.

S. RAMESH

Ramesh took to the silver screen after his cricketing career faded away in the first decade of the new millennium. He debuted with M. Raja's *Santhosh Subramaniyam* (2008), and played the lead role—a cricketer-cum-coach—in Yuvaraj Dhayalan's hit movie, *Potta Potti* (2011). He also appeared in Sundar C.'s *Madha Gaja Raja* (completed in 2013), but has not been seen much of since then.

VARUN CHAKRAVARTHY

Unlike others on this list, Varun was an actor even before he played domestic cricket. He played a minor role, as a club cricketer, in Suseenthiran's 2014 movie *Jeeva*. At that point he was a club cricketer who had played a season in league cricket in England. His career graph saw a steep rise after the 2018 Tamil Nadu Premier League. By 2021, he was playing for India.

S. SREESANTH

After exploring dance—both on, in the face of Andre Nel, and off the field—and music, it was only natural that Sreesanth would take to acting at some point. When he did, he turned out to be as versatile as mainstream actors. His first six feature films—*Big Picture* (2015, Malayalam), *Team 5* (2017, Malayalam), *Aksar 2* (2017, Hindi), *Cabaret* (2019, Hindi), *Kempegowda 2* (2019, Kannada) and *Kaathuvaakula Rendu Kadhal* (2022, Tamil)—spanned four languages.

In between all this, he also participated in some of India's most popular reality shows—*Ek Khiladi Ek Haseena* (2008), *Jhalak Dikhla Jaa* (2014), *Bigg Boss* (2018) and *Khatron ke Khiladi* (2019). Now that he has retired from cricket, his acting career can only go uphill.

SUSHREE DIBYADARSHINI

Sushree Dibyadarshini Pradhan has not played international cricket at the time of writing this book, but she has impressed in the Women's T20 Challenge. In 2018, she acted in *Kanaa*, Arunraja Kamaraj's cricket-themed movie, where she played Deepika, an Indian cricketer. She later said in an interview that she might have been an actor.

MOHINDER AMARNATH

To add a realistic touch to the cricketing action, Kabir Khan's *83* featured some—Harrdy Sandhu and Tagenarine Chanderpaul, for example—who had played serious cricket. However, only one of them was an Indian Test cricketer. Mohinder Amarnath playing his father, Lala, an important figure in Indian cricket for several decades, was one of the most loved touches in the movie.

HONOURABLE MENTION 1: FRANK WORRELL

Around the World (1967) was the first Indian movie to be released in 70 mm. It featured Om Prakash asking a confused Frank Worrell utterly bizarre questions in a one-minute scene of little importance, clearly designed to somehow accommodate the legendary cricketer. Worrell died of leukaemia before the movie was released. The makers dedicated the movie to his memory.

HONOURABLE MENTION 2: MOHSIN KHAN

Mohsin Khan played 48 Test matches and 75 ODIs for Pakistan, and made his foray into Bollywood after marrying actor Reena Roy. He impressed in his debut film, J.P. Dutta's *Batwara* (1989), despite being part of an ensemble cast. Filmfare even nominated him in the Best Supporting Actor category. He acted in several movies in the 1990s, including Mahesh Bhatt's superhit *Saathi* (1991).

HONOURABLE MENTION 3: BRETT LEE

In 2007, Brett Lee recorded a duet, 'You're the one for me', with Asha Bhosle, where Lee's lines were in English and Bhosle's in Hindi. In 2015, Lee acted in Anupam Sharma's Australian movie

UNIndian alongside Tannishtha Chatterjee and Supriya Pathak. He played Will Henderson, who teaches English to Indian immigrants in Australia. The movie had an Indian release in 2016.

HOWZZAT!

In the 1932/33 Ashes—the Bodyline Series—Iftikhar Ali Khan Pataudi of England played against Victor Richardson of Australia. In 1969/70, Iftikhar's son Mansur led India against an Australian side that featured Richardson's grandson Ian Chappell.

Sharma Ji Ke Bachche
Highly Qualified International Cricketers

Sports and formal education seldom go hand in hand. Only the exceptional succeed at both. And yet, there have been Indians who earned enviable academic qualifications as well as the chance to represent their nation at cricket. And whose parents never got a chance to complain.

Of course, there are many similar examples in domestic cricket, particularly between 1947—when royal patronage began to dwindle—and the late twentieth century. Barring the very best, cricket was not a financially rewarding profession, and many players often had to fall back on their degrees to get day jobs. 'More than half the Indian players are graduates; and of them no less than thirteen have achieved a masters [sic] degree in arts, commerce, or science,' Richard Cashman wrote in his seminal work Patrons, Players and the Crowd in 1980.

In the era before structured age-group cricket, inter-university tournaments like the Rohinton Baria Trophy were covered extensively by the media and followed by the selectors. Schools and colleges sometimes aggressively 'recruited' cricketers to boost their teams. Madhav Apte, for example, demonstrated his googly to the principal of the Elphinstone College at his interview. Manohar Hardikar and Ramakant Desai were quite open about joining college to play cricket for the teams.

Over time, as cricket became more competitive, cricketers had to make their mark very early, often while at school. In India, higher education used to be the key to reasonable income for many. With cricket providing an equal amount of, if not more, money, a degree is no longer a necessity for a talented cricketer. Vinoo Mankad, Mantu Banerjee, Dilip Sardesai, Ajit Wadekar, Irfan Pathan and Parthiv Patel were among those who chose cricket when important matches coincided with exams. Shantha Rangaswamy, the first woman to lead India, famously admitted to being the least qualified of all her siblings (four of whom were engineers, one a PhD and another a double graduate).

The round-the-year matches schedule has not helped, either. In 2004, the Gujarat government refused to allow Parthiv Patel and Irfan Pathan to re-take their twelfth standard board examination when it coincided with India's tour of Pakistan, for which both were picked. Such clashes have become common over the years.

Of course, there are exceptions to this.

THE DOCTORATES

Jahangir Khan played in India's first ever Test match at Lord's in 1932. He stayed back in England to complete his doctorate at Cambridge, where he won the cricket blue all four years, and passed the final Bar from Middle Temple School. It was while playing for Cambridge that his ball accidentally killed a flying sparrow at Lord's. When India toured England again in 1936 he played in all 3 Test matches.

One of the most erudite people to have played international cricket, Dilawar Hussain was known for his encyclopaedic memory, and could recite scorecards at will. He held two master's degrees and a doctorate in philosophy, and became the principal at the Government College, London, and later at the Muslim Anglo-Oriental College in Lahore.

THE ENGINEERS

The list should begin with E.A.S. Prasanna. By the time he debuted in Test cricket in 1961/62, he was already being hailed as a special talent. He was selected for the West Indies tour that was to follow, but his father was not impressed. M. Chinnaswamy, then BCCI secretary, stepped in. He convinced Jayachamarajendra Wadiyar, the last Maharaja of Mysore and then governor of Mysore state, to talk to Prasanna senior. EAS only got permission when he promised to complete his engineering degree upon his return.

Prasanna kept his word. He spent close to five years in oblivion while he got his degree from the National Institute of Engineering, Mysore. He then took up a job at ITI for a monthly salary of

INR 300. Thankfully, ITI was a supportive organization, and Prasanna was back on the field.

S. Venkataraghavan had meanwhile established himself as the premier off spinner of the side in Prasanna's absence. Over the years, the two would fight for a place in the Test XI, but also play alongside each other from time to time. Venkat, too, was an engineer, from the College of Engineering, Guindy, Madras. His gift with numbers made him invaluable to the team from 1969, when prize money became a regular thing. 'He had the knack of dividing thousands by any number and arriving at an even figure,' his captain Mansur Ali Khan Pataudi once said.

Other Indian international cricketers who are also engineers include K. Srikkanth, Anil Kumble, Javagal Srinath and R. Ashwin.

OTHERS

No doctor has represented India at cricket, but some might have. Wicketkeeper Chandu Patankar played once for India, against New Zealand in Calcutta in 1955/56, in lieu of the injured Naren Tamhane. He wanted to be a doctor like his father, but for that he needed a first-class in his BSc, which he did not manage, and settled for an MSc in zoology instead. Decades later, V.V.S. Laxman—both of whose parents are doctors—opted out of a medical career to focus on cricket.

Seam-bowling all-rounder Ajit Pai's only Test match was also against New Zealand, though in Bombay in 1969/70. Pai did a 'government-approved course in architecture' from the Bandra School of Art (now Raheja School of Art), and went on to work as an architect at the Bank of Baroda.

The only Test cricketer born in Brazil, Ashok Gandotra was a champion in university cricket while he pursued his master's in economics from St Stephen's. He played 2 Tests, both in 1969/70, before being appointed 12th man for the next match against Australia in Delhi. He skipped the match because it coincided with his Rhodes Scholarship interview. Cricket was probably not a career he wanted to pursue.

The affluent could afford to send their children overseas for higher studies. The Pataudis (father and son), 'Buck' Divecha, Abdul Hafeez (Kardar) and Abbas Ali Baig all got their MAs from Oxford, while Jahangir Khan and Cotar Ramaswami went to Cambridge.

Among others, Chandu Sarwate was a law graduate; M. Vijay graduated with a degree in economics before going to the SRM University for his MBA; Anshuman Gaekwad did an MCom; and Sudhir Naik an MSc.

HONOURABLE MENTIONS

D.B. Deodhar was forty when India played their first Test match. He never got a Test cap, though he got first-class hundreds even in his fifties. However, he played for Indian representative sides multiple times. He was a professor of Sanskrit at the Poona College.

Anuradha Doddaballapur played age-group cricket for Karnataka, and is a postdoctoral research scientist at the Max Planck Institute for Heart and Lung Research in Bad Nauheim. She leads Germany, is an ECB Level 2 certified coach, and is the first woman to take 4 wickets in 4 balls in Twenty20 Internationals.

Saurabh Netravalkar played in the 2010 Under-19 World Cup, became a computer science engineer from the University of Mumbai, and played for Mumbai before acquiring a master's degree in computer science from Cornell University. He went on to lead USA, and took their first 5-wicket hauls in both ODIs and Twenty20 Internationals.

HOWZZAT!

L. Balaji became a sensation on the Pakistan tour of 2004/05. Fans in the stadium cheered every time he even touched the cricket ball on the ground, often singing *'Balaji, zara dheere chalo'* in chorus to the tune of *'Babuji...'*.

Early Prowlers
Outstanding Indian Fielders before the Modern Era

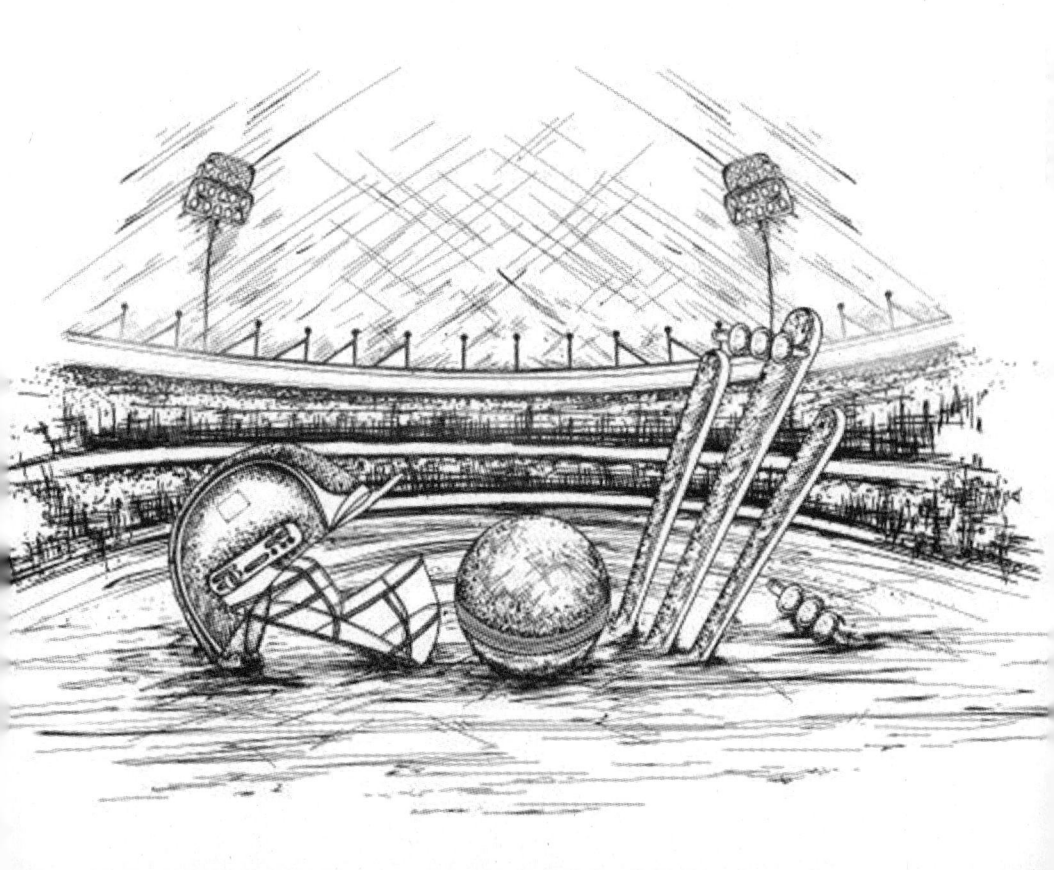

The nostalgic often emphasize on the superiority of the past. However, even the staunchest among them agree on the evolution of fielding. What used to be considered an outstanding catch even at the turn of the millennium is routine now. The ODI revolution in India in the 1980s changed fielding forever. The excellent Kapil Dev and Madan Lal were joined by the new generation: Mohammad Azharuddin, Raman Lamba, L. Sivaramakrishnan, Maninder Singh. Ajay Jadeja and Robin Singh followed them, and Yuvraj Singh and Mohammad Kaif arrived in the 2000s.

Some of the finest Indian bowlers—Vinoo Mankad, Ghulam Ahmed, Subhash Gupte—missed out on wickets because of ordinary close-in catching. For decades, Indian cricket used to have fielders who seldom charged for high catches in the deep; dives and slides were unheard of. And yet, even in that period, there were some who stood out.

LALL SINGH

In India's first ever Test match in 1932, Lall Singh did not bowl or keep wickets. A decent but unexceptional batter (he averaged below 25 in first-class cricket), he batted at number eight and seven in the match. He was, however, to quote *The Cricketer*, 'about the best fieldsman in an exceptionally good fielding side'. *Wisden* commented that he 'glided over the ground like a snake'.

He left a mark early in that Test match—his only one—sprinting from mid-on, swooping on the ball, and running out Frank Woolley.

HEMU ADHIKARI

India's fielding was lauded on their 1952/53 tour of West Indies. Madhav Apte, Polly Umrigar, Datta Gaekwad, 'Mamasaheb' Ghorpade and Chandrasekhar Gadkari were a formidable unit, particularly in the outfield. Later in the decade, G.S. Ramchand would earn a reputation for standing very close to the batters and plucking the ball virtually off the bat.

But the outstanding fielder of the Indian team of the era was Hemu Adhikari, who manned cover point with notable alacrity. Decades later, Raj Singh Dungarpur claimed to have been reminded of Adhikari when he saw South Africa's Jonty Rhodes field. Adhikari was also perhaps the first Indian cricketer to understand that fielding can be a leveller in cricket, that any side can match the even the finest sides in that one department. Under him, Services became the best fielding unit in the country. Perhaps the military discipline came in handy, for they reached the Ranji Trophy final twice, in 1956/57 and 1957/58—the only times in Services' history. The only cricketers from Services who made it to the Indian Test side—Gadkari, Narain Swamy, Surendra Nath, Apoorva Sengupta, V. Muddiah and Adhikari himself—were from Adhikari's team.

But Adhikari's role did not end there. He was manager of the Indian side that won their first Test series in England in 1971. The cricketers underwent rigorous training under Col. Adhikari. The umbrella of close-in fielders—Eknath Solkar at short leg; Abid Ali at backward short leg; Sunil Gavaskar, Ajit Wadekar, S. Venkataraghavan at slip or leg slip—played a role as important as anyone else on that tour.

THE PATAUDI GENERATION

Like Adhikari, Pataudi manned cover point and was renowned for his agility and quick pick up and throw; and he tried to instil the importance of fielding in the Indian side. He expected the fielders to dive and slide. Unfortunately, most Indian specialist batters and bowlers were reluctant to go the extra mile.

Rusi Surti was an exception. On India's 1967/68 tour of Australia, the local crowds challenged the home batters to 'hit a ball past Surti'. Abid Ali had a gymnast's fitness, won the Best Fielder award while playing for Hyderabad Schools, and could probably make it into most sides on his fielding prowess alone. S. Venkataraghavan and Ajit Wadekar, too, were exceptional fielders.

EKNATH SOLKAR

Though there were many great fielders at the time, there was only one fielding superstar: Eknath Solkar. If one excludes wicketkeepers and puts a 50-catch cut-off, Solkar is the only fielder in the history of Test cricket to have more catches than innings fielded in (53 catches in 50 innings). His catches/Test ratio of 1.96 is another world record. He took 10 catches each in two separate series, against Australia in 1969/70 and against England in 1972/73.

Solkar stood at short leg, often perilously close to the batter. He almost never flinched, even when they attempted full-blooded shots at him in the pre-helmet era. When the ball ricocheted off him, he would yell 'Catch it!' much to the astonishment of his colleagues. He lunged for chances others did not even bother about, sliding his fingertips under balls most would consider too low to be caught.

His most famous catch, of course, was Alan Knott's at the Oval Test of 1971. S. Venkataraghavan got a ball to bounce. It flew off Knott's bat, and Solkar flung himself full-length to take an extraordinary catch. The photograph remains one of the most iconic in the history of Indian cricket. E.A.S. Prasanna hailed it as the Catch of the Century.

RAMNATH PARKAR

Ramnath Parkar played only 2 Test matches, both in 1972/73, but his versatile fielding made him an invaluable asset to any side. While fearless at short leg and silly point, it was his anticipation, speed and accuracy while fielding at positions between point and mid-off that set him apart. Teammate Dilip Vengsarkar rated his speed and throwing ahead of Mohammad Azharuddin's: few compliments can be greater.

GHULAM PARKAR

Bombay used to have a strategy in the 1980s. Captain Ashok Mankad would make Ghulam Parkar field back at mid-on, enticing the unsuspecting batter to go for the extra run. When they fell for it, Parkar would swoop down on the ball and run them out with direct throws that became part of Bombay cricket folklore: years of playing pitthu had helped him perfect his throw.

HOWZZAT!

Dilip Vengsarkar (against Australia, Brisbane 1977/78) and Ashok Mankad (against England, Edgbaston 1974) were both dismissed when their caps fell on the stumps and dislodged the bails.

Cricket in the Crown
Royalty in Indian Cricket

Royal families were the first great patrons of Indian cricket. They considered the sport a way to climb the social ladder and enjoy a status equivalent to that of the British. They had the money to hire the best cricketers and treat them lavishly off the field, maintain world-class personal grounds and fund overseas tours for Indians cricket teams and invite foreign cricket teams to India.

Some members of royal families were fine players themselves: Ranjitsinhji and Duleepsinhji were outstanding cricketers, while contemporaries swear by Tiger Pataudi. There were those though who did not match their peers' talent, but did lead personal teams—what is the point of owning a team if you are not the captain? The Maharaja of Kashmir, however, took this to embarrassing levels. He would arrive at his personal ground at three in the afternoon, smoke the hookah and get ready to bat at about half past four. After being padded and gloved, he would descend on the pitch, an attendant carrying his bat in tow, and he would take the crease irrespective of which side had been batting. For fifteen minutes, every dismissal would go down as a no-ball. Then, when the Maharaja got bored, the umpire would rule him out leg before—though not before the scorers had ensured a minimum of a half century.

Others, however, were not as ridiculous.

NAWANAGAR, BANSWARA AND RAJKOT

As already established, Ranji and Duleep, royals themselves, were also cricketing royalty. We have discussed Ranji, the Jam Sahib of Nawanagar, his nephew Duleep, in the chapter on related Indian international cricketers. Duleep was not the only nephew of Ranji to play first-class cricket though. The others were Samarsinhji, Digvijaysinhji, Himmatsinhji and Lakhajirajsinhji. Digvijaysinhji's son Y.S. Shatrushalyaji's cousin K.S. Chatrapalsinhji's nephew Ajaysinhji 'Ajay' Jadeja led India in 15 ODIs.

Lakhajirajsinhji was also the Thakore Saheb of Rajkot—a designation that qualified for the privy purse—as were his son, Pradyumansinhji, and grandson, Manoharsinhji, both of whom played first-class cricket. While leading Kathiawar in 1948/49, Pradyumansinhji conceded a Ranji Trophy match against Maharashtra to leave B.B. Nimbalkar stranded on 443, 9 runs short of smashing Don Bradman's world record. He did not want a world record against Kathiawar.

Duleep's sister married Chandraveer Singh, the Maharawal of Banswara. Their elder son, Suryaveer, was Rajasthan's wicketkeeper and opening batter throughout their glory days of the 1960s. Hanumant, the younger son, even played for India fourteen times.

K.S. Indrajitsinhji, Ranji's brother Mohansinhji's grandson, played for India in 4 matches. Regardless of their abilities, the royalty invariably preferred to perform the 'honourable' act of batting. That he chose to be a wicketkeeper, often the least thanked member of any XI, made Indrajitsinhji exceptional.

PATIALA

Maharaja Rajinder Singh was a great patron of cricket in India. His son Bhupinder led the first all-India team that toured England in 1911, sponsored several overseas teams on Indian tours, and even donated the Ranji Trophy.

His elder son, Yadavindra Singh, was a reasonably good batter, and scored 24 and 60 in his only Test match, against England in 1933/34. His brother Bhalindra also played first-class cricket.

JAMNAGAR

Yadavindra and Bhalindra Singh's cousin, Ranvirsinhji, was part of the first Test squad of Independent India that toured Australia in 1947/48. His son, Prahlad Singh, was also a first-class cricketer.

VIZIANAGARAM

When Pusapati Alakh Narayanadev Gajapati Raju succeeded his father as the ruler of Vizianagaram in 1922, his younger brother, Vijay 'Vizzy' Ananda, the Maharajkumar, moved to their family estate in Benares. In the 1930s, Vizzy matched Patiala in patronage and outdid him in Machiavellian schemes to get himself appointed as India's captain on the ill-fated 1936 tour of England.

An incompetent cricketer, Vizzy often bribed opposition bowlers to deliberately underperform against him, and created factions within his own team, even treating his supporters to a tour of Paris. He is believed to have rewarded Baqa Jilani with a Test cap for insulting C.K. Nayudu at the breakfast table. He redeemed himself somewhat as an administrator in his later days.

PORBANDAR AND LIMBDI

Royalty played a role so crucial in Indian cricket that selectors had to put *three* men in charge of the 1932 tour of England. Natwarsinhji Bhavsinhji, the Maharaja of Porbandar, was captain. K.S. Ghanshyamsinhji Daulatsinhji, second child of the ruler of Limbdi and brother of Porbandar's wife, Rupaliba Sahiba, was vice-captain. Vizzy had to be kept happy too, so he was made *deputy vice-captain*; he opted out.

Thankfully, both Porbandar and Limbdi were aware of their limited cricketing abilities. They stepped down for India's first ever Test match, which happened on that tour, letting C.K. Nayudu lead. Porbandar actually acquired more Rolls-Royce cars (three) than first-class runs (0, 2, 0, 0—a total of 2) on that tour.

COOCH BEHAR AND BARODA

Nripendra Narayan, the Maharaja of Cooch Behar, was a great patron of cricket in eastern India. His sons, Jitendra Narayan (who succeeded his father), Hitendra Narayan and Nitendra Narayan all played first-class cricket, as did Jitendra's son and successor Jagaddipendra Narayan.

Hitendra played thrice for Somerset in 1910 without any success—though his appearances had more to do with the fact that the cash-strapped club preferred cricketers whom they would not have to pay. They called him both 'Prince' and 'Hitty' over there.

Jitendra Narayan married Indira Devi, the daughter of Sayajirao Gaekwad III of Baroda's famous dynasty. Sayajirao's sons Shivajirao and Dhairyashilrao played first-class cricket, as did Shivajirao's sons, Udaysinhrao and Khanderao, and great-nephews, Fatehsinh, Ranjitsinh and Sangramsinh, while their maternal uncle Jayasinhrao 'Mamasaheb' Ghorpade played 8 Test matches.

In 1963, Fatehsinhrao, known as 'Jackie Baroda' in England, became the BCCI President at only thirty-three. He remains the youngest person to hold that position.

Dattajirao Gaekwad, a distant relation of the royal family of Baroda, led India in 1959. His son, Anshuman, also played for India, while Anshuman's son, Shatrunjay, played domestic cricket.

JATH AND DEWAS

Vijaysinghrao, the Raja of Jath, played 6 matches for Maharashtra. Keeping in tune with royal whims, he decided to learn the googly, and invited Clarrie Grimmett, no less, to coach him. He also brought with him his relative, the Maharaja of Dewas, and an employee called Vijay Hazare.

One of the greatest batters in Indian history, Hazare used to refer to Grimmett as his 'guru'.

PATAUDI

Iftikhar Ali Khan, the eighth Nawab of Pataudi, remains the only cricketer to play for England and India, while he and his son, Mansur, are the only father and son duo to lead India in Test cricket. Saad Bin Jung, Mansur's nephew and Iftikhar's grandson, played first-class cricket as well.

BILKHA

Yajurvindra Singh of the royal family of Bilkha, Gujarat, equalled two world records on Test debut against England at Bangalore in 1976/77: he held 5 catches in the first innings and 7 in the Test match. An outstanding fielder, he held 11 catches in 4 Test matches, and 3 as a substitute against West Indies in 1978/79.

DUNGARPUR

In the early 1960s, Rajasthan reached the Ranji Trophy final six times in seven seasons, only to be beaten by Bombay every time. A stalwart of this Rajasthan side was Raj Singh, the Maharajkumar of Dungarpur, who challenged a royalty-in-cricket stereotype by performing the 'menial' act of seam bowling—and taking 206 first-class wickets.

Raj Singh went on to became one of the most influential figures of Indian cricket in many ways, including stints as BCCI president and national selector, and played a key role in setting up the National Cricket Academy.

HONOURABLE MENTION: THE BRITISH ROYAL FAMILY

Prince Christian Victor, the eldest son of Helena, third daughter of Queen Victoria, was the only member of the British royal family to play first-class cricket (for I Zingari in 1887). His *Wisden* obituary in 1900 said he was 'one of the few men who ever played an innings of over 200 in India, scoring 205 for the King's Royal Rifles v the Devonshire Regiment, at Rawul Pindee, in 1893'.

HOWZZAT!

As per Goa government records, Kapil Dev, Sachin Tendulkar, Sourav Ganguly, Rahul Dravid and even Ricky Ponting, were registered as 'casual labourers' under the Mahatma Gandhi National Rural Employment Guarantee Scheme in 2014. A probe was ordered into the scam.

Curious Selections

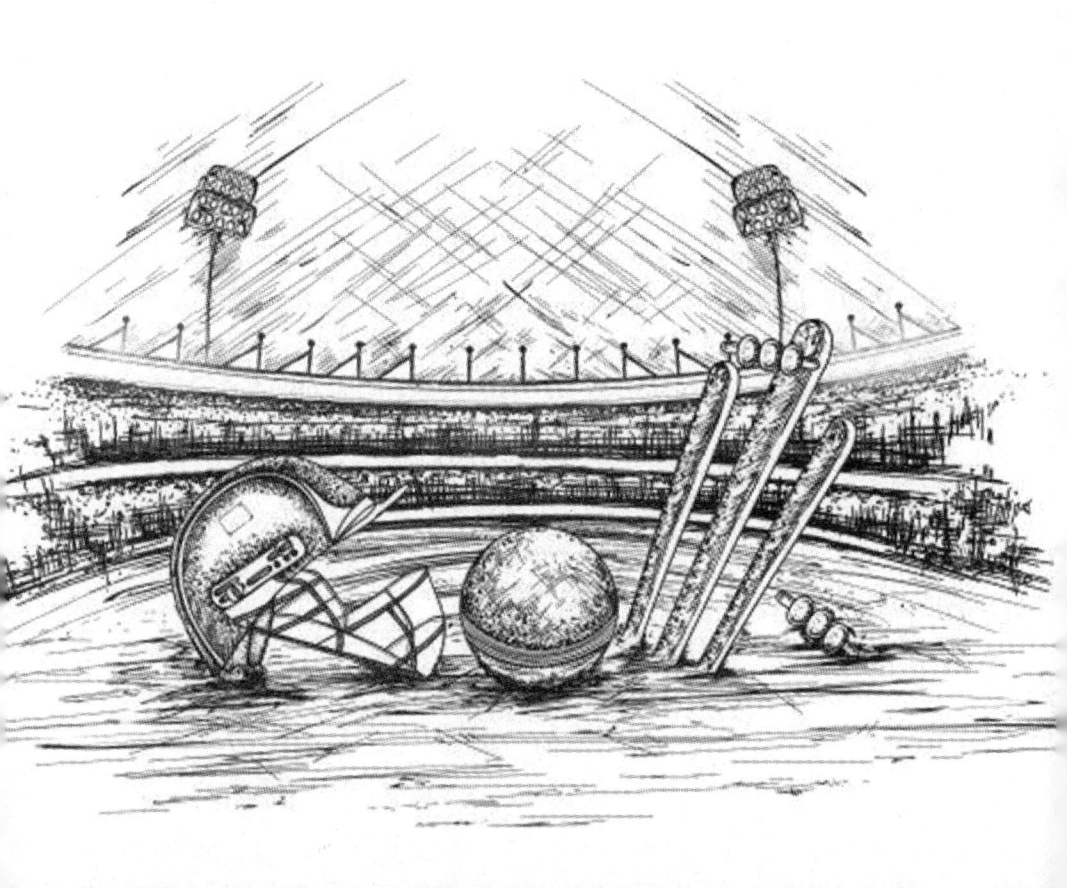

Perhaps no entity in cricket is as unanimously panned by fans as the selection committee, the thanklessness of whose job surpasses perhaps even that of a wicketkeeper or an umpire.

Selection committees of the Indian cricket team used to be entirely different from their counterparts elsewhere. Consider the first All-India team, for example, that toured England in 1911—fifteen years before India became an ICC Full Member. The selection committee consisted of two Parsees (J.M. Framjee Patel and M.E. Pavri), two Hindus (Chunilal Mehta and H.S. Naik) and two Muslims (Ibrahim Rahimtulla and Hadi Tyabji), but was chaired by John Glennie 'Jungly' Greig. The captain was Bhupinder Singh, the Maharaja of Patiala—a Sikh.

Twenty-five years later, the Maharajkumar of Vizianagaram (Vizzy), one of the selectors, appointed himself as captain of India for their 1936 tour of England. Vizzy was an inept cricketer and an autocratic captain, but he had three qualities in surplus—money, power and manipulative skills. A full description of his entire scheme is beyond the scope of this book, or even of Niccolò Machiavelli's *Prince*.

Things became less surreal as the years went on, but only just.

THE MANKAD SNUB, 1952

In 1951/52, India had just won their first ever Test match—against England at Madras. Vinoo Mankad took 8–55 and 4–53, which should have made him an obvious choice for the tour of England in a few months' time.

But there was a problem. Mankad got an offer from Haslingden in the Lancashire League. There was little money in Indian cricket in those days, so Mankad did the obvious thing: he asked Chair of Selectors C.K. Nayudu whether he would be a guaranteed selection on the tour. If Nayudu could assure him, Mankad would turn the Haslingden offer down.

But Nayudu refused, and Mankad and the Indian team went to England in the same summer on different campaigns. India lost the first Test at Headingley by 7 wickets. In the second innings, they lost 4 wickets before scoring their first run.

The Indian team management now had to swallow the bitter pill. An SOS was sent to Haslingden, and Mankad was acquired for the remaining 4 Test matches. In the next Test at Lord's, Mankad scored 72 and 184 and took 5–196 in the first innings.

They still refer to it as Mankad's Test. Even Bollywood plotlines pale in comparison.

THE CURIOUS CASE OF MADHAV APTE, 1953

In 1953, Madhav Apte was being hailed as one of the finest batters in Indian cricket. His numbers—542 runs at 49.27—made for excellent reading. And yet, his entire career lasted only 7 Test matches and less than five months.

When a Commonwealth XI toured India that winter, Apte played the first unofficial 'Test' (these matches were not recognized by the ICC), scored 30, and was dropped for good. He never played for any Indian representative side again.

In his autobiography, Apte speaks candidly about how Lala Amarnath, then chair of selectors, approached Apte's father, Laxmanrao, the owner of Kohinoor Mills, for their cloth distributorship for Delhi. Laxmanrao Apte declined. His son never played Test cricket again.

SIX CAPTAINS IN SEVEN TESTS, 1958/59 AND 1959— AND A TOILET ENCOUNTER

Ahead of the 1958/59 home series against West Indies, Lala Amarnath wanted Ghulam Ahmed as captain. Ghulam was present at the pre-series camp, but he picked up an injury while playing the tourists for the Board President's XI. L.P. Jai and Cotar Ramaswami, the other selectors, wanted him replaced, but Amarnath trumped them with his casting vote. Ghulam himself pulled out of the first Test match at Bombay. Polly Umrigar led instead. India saved the match, but the general discomfort of the batters against the pace of Roy Gilchrist and Wes Hall was evident.

Ghulam was back as captain in the second Test at Kanpur where West Indies won comfortably. India's capitulation triggered crowd violence, and the team had to be escorted by the police back to the hotel. After they were thrashed again in Calcutta during the third Test, Ghulam resigned.

The selectors recalled Vinoo Mankad to the side, and asked Ghulam to withdraw his resignation. He agreed. Then, four days before the next Test match in Madras, he announced *retirement* from Test cricket.

Now the fun began. Amarnath wanted Umrigar to lead. On the eve of the fourth Test, Umrigar even delivered a speech as the Indian captain at a function. He then returned to the hotel and resigned. India arrived at the venue on the day of the match without a captain.

Fifteen minutes before the toss, West Indies captain Gerry Alexander enquired who would lead the Indian side.

'We don't need a captain, it is all communal,' came the response from Subhash Gupte. Meanwhile, the selectors had dragged Vinoo Mankad—who had been recalled to the side a few days before the match, after two years—to the toilet behind the dressing room. Whatever they said must have worked, for Mankad walked out for the toss. India lost the match. And Mankad was sacked.

Who would captain the team for the fifth Test? G.S. Ramchand had led India briefly when Mankad left the field during the fourth Test. But by the time the selectors made up their mind, Ramchand had left to catch his train. They could not reach him, so they decided to *drop* him. But the team still needed a captain, so they sent a message to the army camp in Dharamsala where Hemu Adhikari, who had been dropped two years ago, was posted. Adhikari was not interested, and it took a superior officer's order to convince him to join the Indian team. India drew the Test.

When India toured England a few months later, the selectors dropped Mankad, Adhikari and Ramchand, and appointed Datta Gaekwad as the captain. Gaekwad missed the second Test match at Lord's due to bronchitis, and Pankaj Roy led ('The side showed better form when he led,' wrote *Wisden*), bringing the tally up to six captains in seven Tests.

THE GUPTE MYSTERY, 1961/62

The Indian team was put up at the Imperial Hotel during the Delhi Test of India's 1961/62 home series against England. Subhash Gupte and Kripal Singh were sharing a room.

During their stay, Kripal had asked a receptionist out for a drink. She complained to the team management, and the call was traced to their room. Kripal clarified that the fault was entirely his, but the selectors dropped both men for the next Test in Calcutta.

Ahead of the subsequent tour of West Indies, the BCCI secretary asked Gupte, 'Did you try and stop Kripal making the call?' A bewildered Gupte responded with, 'He is a big man; how can I stop him?'

That was all it took. Gupte, one of the greatest spinners India has produced, never played for the country again. He settled down in Trinidad and spent his last years there.

WHO IS THE INDIAN CAPTAIN? 1974/75

For of the 1974/75 home series against West Indies, the selectors *dropped* captain Ajit Wadekar (for good), replaced him with Mansur Ali Khan Pataudi, and made Sunil Gavaskar his deputy. For some reason, they asked Gavaskar to keep it a secret.

The selectors also left Bishan Singh Bedi out of the first Test match at Bangalore on disciplinary grounds, and called up uncapped Rajinder Goel. A delighted Goel bought new boots in anticipation—but the final squad had Bhagwat Chandrasekhar, S. Venkataraghavan and E.A.S. Prasanna. Goel never played Test cricket.

In the match, Pataudi caught Keith Boyce off Venkataraghavan, dislocated his ring finger and was ruled out for the rest of the match as well as the next Test in Delhi. Gavaskar had to disclose his 'secret' and take charge. He was all set to lead in Delhi when he too broke a finger during a Ranji Trophy match and was ruled out of the Test.

India were now without their captain and vice-captain—and, indeed, anyone to lead them. Ahead of the Test, manager G.S.

Ramchand announced, much to the confusion of the press, 'I know who the Indian captain is but I'm not telling.'

The Delhi & District Cricket Association, for some reason, went ahead and announced Farokh Engineer's name as captain. Eventually, Venkataraghavan led India. Since Bedi was back after his one-match ban, the selectors dropped Chandrasekhar, even though he had troubled a debutant Viv Richards in the previous Test. Richards slammed 192 not out, and India lost by an innings.

Immediately after leading India, Venkataraghavan found himself out of the side. Pataudi returned for the next Test, so did Chandrasekhar.

GAVASKAR SCALES THE WALL, 1984/85

After India lost the home series of 1984/85 to England, there was speculation over Gavaskar staying on as captain for the Benson & Hedges World Series Cup in Australia. The cricketers waited at the team hotel while the selection committee met for over three hours to confirm that Gavaskar had been retained.

Gavaskar was congratulated by his wife, who asked him to meet BCCI Joint Secretary Ranbir Singh. Singh had been waiting in his car to drive Gavaskar to the meeting—but there was a catch. According to Singh's instructions, Gavaskar would have to scale the boundary wall of the hotel to avoid the media waiting outside the entrance.

It was during this bizarre act that Gavaskar made up his mind. Before the tour, he informed Chandu Borde, the chair of selectors, that he would resign from the captaincy after the tour of Australia.

WHO IS NOEL DAVID? 1997

Back in 1967/68, when Bhagwat Chandrasekhar picked up an injury on a tour of Australia, Mansur Ali Khan Pataudi asked for

M.L. Jaisimha as his replacement. A stylish opening batter was hardly like-for-like replacement for a leg-spinner, but it worked. Jaisimha borrowed a bat, practised for a couple of hours, took several flights, landed in Brisbane, took field next day, and scored 74 and 101 to nearly pull off an improbable win.

Things were different in 1997, when Javagal Srinath, India's premier fast bowler, injured his rotator cuff muscle and was ruled out of the West Indies tour. The selectors picked Noel David, an off-spinner, instead.

To be fair, David was handy with both bat and ball, and was one of the best fielders in the country. BCCI secretary Jagmohan Dalmiya also clarified that David was not a *replacement* for Srinath but an addition, that too at the request of the Indian camp.

At this point, the team probably did not want David, and Indian captain Sachin Tendulkar's famous question—'Who is Noel David?'—stumped everyone. David began his international career with 3–21, the best figures for an Indian debutant (the record stood until 2020/21) but he played only 3 more ODIs.

HOWZZAT!

In the 1974 series against England, debutant Madan Lal was dismissed by a ball from debutant Mike Hendrick that knocked over the off and leg stumps, but left the middle stump intact!

Indian International Cricketers Born outside India

Unlike their counterparts Australia, South Africa, New Zealand and the West Indies, the early Indian teams consisted of only cricketers of Indian origin. The trend never changed. There have been, thus, very few examples of cricketers born outside India playing for the country.

LALL SINGH (KUALA LUMPUR, MALAYSIA)

Malaysia-born Lall Singh led the most remarkable life among Indian Test cricketers. While his cricketing talent was evident, options in Malaya were limited. The family reached out to the Maharaja of Patiala, who invited Lall Singh to play in India.

He played in India's first ever Test match at Lord's in 1932. Renowned for his fielding abilities, he famously ran out Frank Woolley inside the first half an hour.

ASHOK GANDOTRA (RIO DE JANEIRO, BRAZIL)

Ashok Gandotra remains the only Test cricketer for any country to be born in Brazil. He came to India at an early age, and played 2 Test matches when India tried out several new faces in the winter of 1969/70. He was named 12th man for the next Test as well, but he opted out: it was clashing with his Rhodes Scholarship interview.

ROBIN SINGH (PRINCES TOWN, TRINIDAD & TOBAGO)

Robin Singh has roots in Ajmer. He was born in Trinidad, and even led the Trinidad & Tobago Under-19s. He moved to India soon after that, made his debut for India in *Port of Spain, Trinidad*, played 1 Test match and 136 ODIs, and—perhaps to retain his roving image—opened an academy in *Dubai*.

AND ONE WHO WAS NOT ... SALIM DURANI (KARACHI, PAKISTAN)

'Prince' Durani was a flamboyant all-rounder who played a key role in India's first series win against England in 1961/62. Contrary to popular belief, especially of quizzers, he was born and brought up in Karachi, not Kabul. In fact, as he revealed in an interview, even as recently as 2020 he had never been to Kabul.

But when Afghanistan played their first ever Test match, against India in Bengaluru in 2018, the BCCI invited Durani as the only Test player linked to both countries. Curiously, he accepted the invitation.

HOWZZAT!

Commandur Rangachari began his Test career with scores of 0 not out, 0, 0, 0 not out and 0 before scoring an unbeaten 8 in his last Test innings.

The Radcliffe Curse
Partition 'Transfers'

The partition of British India into India and Pakistan in 1947 led to widespread violence in the two countries and resulted in the loss of up to two million estimated lives. Millions abandoned their birthplace and ancestral homes to move to the other country.

Cricketers, from either side, were no exception. Some of these cricketers had already moved across the border before Partition, but we shall include them. Do note that the classification is based on birthplaces, not which side of the border the cricketers grew up in.

FROM PAKISTAN TO INDIA

Naoomal Jaoomal (born in Karachi) and Dilawar Hussain (born in Lahore) had played for undivided India in the 1930s. Three other Lahore-borns—Abdul Hafeez Kardar, Gul Mohammad and Amir Elahi—played for both India and Pakistan.

After Partition, Jenni Irani, Gogumal Kishenchand, G.S. Ramchand, Pananmal Punjabi (all Karachi-born) and Man Sood (Lahore) played for India, as did Probir Sen. Comilla, Sen's birthplace, was in East Pakistan at that time. It is now part of Bangladesh.

Salim Durani, born and brought up in Karachi (and not Kabul, as is often perceived), qualifies for this list as well.

FROM INDIA TO PAKISTAN

The reverse list is somewhat longer. Of the 31 Pakistan Test cricketers born in what became India after Partition, most were—not surprisingly—from Punjab, Rajasthan and Gujarat, all of which share borders with Pakistan.

The most famous of them were the Mohammad brothers of Junagadh, Gujarat. Hanif, Wazir, Mushtaq and Sadiq remain the only group of four brothers to play Test cricket. Also from Junagadh was Mohammad Farooq.

From current-day Punjab came Maqsood Ahmed, Waqar Hasan, Fazal-ur-Rehman, Intikhab Alam, Israr Ali, Khalid Wazir, Saeed Ahmed, Younis Ahmed, Majid Khan, while Salahuddin, Shahid Israr, Afaq Hussain, Shahid Mahmood, Javed Burki, Niaz Ahmed all hailed from what is now Uttar Pradesh.

Others on the list include Nasim-ul-Ghani, Javed Akhtar, Ghulam Abbas (all born in Delhi), Ebbu Ghazali, Mohammad Munaf (both Mumbai), Antao D'Souza (Goa), Musafir-ul-Haq (Haryana), Shafqat Rana (Himachal Pradesh), Naushad Ali (Madhya Pradesh), Alimuddin (Rajasthan) and Asif Iqbal (Hyderabad).

HOWZZAT!

In 2013, the Mumbai School Sports Association decided to incinerate the scoresheet of Sachin Tendulkar and Vinod Kambli's world record partnership of 664 in the 1988 Harris Shield. 'You cannot expect us to store files that are twenty-five years old,' explained MSSA secretary H.S. Bhor.

Curious Legacies
Things Named after Cricketers

As we saw elsewhere, Indian Test cricketers have seldom lent their names to cricket grounds in India—though stands, ends and pavilions have been named after them, as have been awards and tournaments. At the same time, they have influenced an assortment of names of objects around the world. The list is long and probably more diverse than one would think ...

ROADS

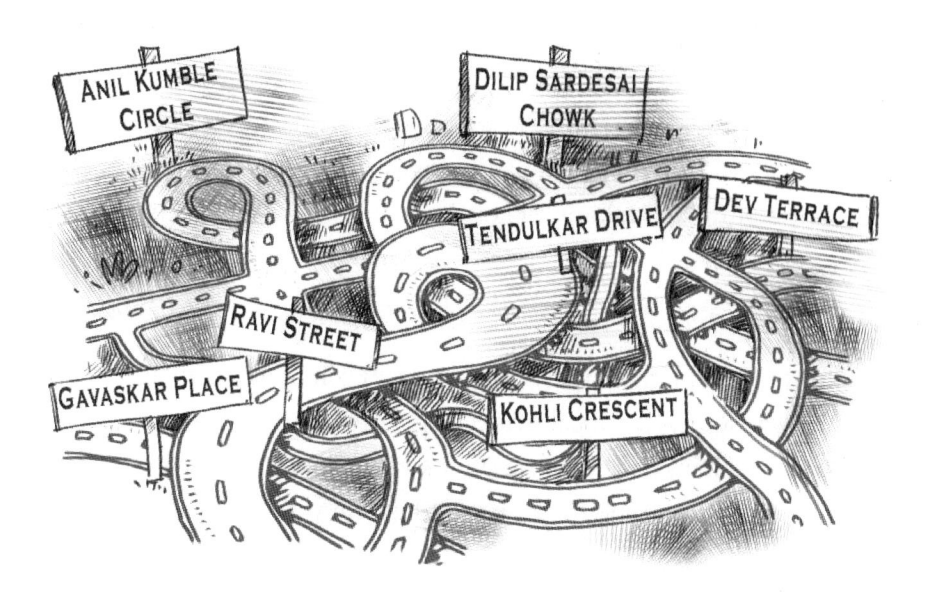

It is not unexpected for Indian roads or landmarks to be named after Indian cricketers. There is an Anil Kumble Circle in Bengaluru as well as an Anil Kumble Road in Kumbla Town (also spelled as Kumble Town), Kerala, where the great man has ancestral roots. There is also a Dilip Sardesai Chowk in Mumbai.

What is interesting is the mark they seem to have made in cities far away from their birthplaces. There is a Gavaskar Place and a Kapil Grove in Khandallah, Wellington, New Zealand—but then, the streets in Khandallah are named after Delhi, Bombay, Calcutta, Gaya, Ganges, Kohima, and so on. There is also a Ravi Street and a Shastri Terrace in Khandallah, though they may not have cricketing connections.

In nearby Australia, in the City of Melton on the 'western rural-urban fringe' of Melbourne, there is a Tendulkar Drive, a Kohli Crescent and a Dev Terrace.

CRICKET GROUNDS

There is a Sunil Gavaskar Cricket Stadium in Zanzibar, Tanzania, and a Sunil Gavaskar Ground in Leicester, England. In fact, two oceans away, in a land where cricket still strives to seek acknowledgement, there is a Sunil Gavaskar Cricket Field in Louisville, Kentucky.

PRISON BLOCK

Delhi's Tihar Jail, the largest prison complex in Asia, had named one of their blocks after local cricketing hero Manoj Prabhakar. The authorities changed the name of the block in 2001 after Prabhakar was named in the match-fixing scandals the year before.

POOL

Not the water body. When the Under-19 World Cup was revived in 1998, the sixteen teams were split into four *pools* for the preliminary round. Hosts South Africa, India, Kenya and Scotland were in the Gavaskar Pool. The other teams were in pools named after Don Bradman, Colin Cowdrey and Garry Sobers.

RACEHORSES

That racehorses have exotic names is well known but not many are named after cricketers. Still, racing historian John Randall has compiled a reasonably long list. Tendulkar came third in the 2001 Dewhurst Stakes in Newmarket, while one Bishan Bedi won several races at Dundalk. Both were trained by Adrian O'Brien.

A DISMISSAL

India were playing an Australian XI in Sydney on their first tour after 1947. At the non-striker's end, Bill Brown took a couple of steps outside the crease before Vinoo Mankad released the ball, and the latter warned him. When Brown repeated the offence, Mankad ran him out. Three days later, Brown pulled off the same stunt in another tour match in Brisbane. Mankad warned him again, but let him go this time.

Then, in a Test match in Sydney, Mankad ran Brown—once again outside the crease at the non-striker's end—out without a warning. Brown found little sympathy; the Australian press generally sided with Mankad, as did Brown's captain, Don Bradman. Years later, this *legal* mode of dismissal by a bowler came to be known, unofficially, as Mankading, something Mankad's family is divided on. By the 1960s, the term had stuck.

A MANGO

Horticulturist Haji Kaleemullah Khan of Malihabad, Uttar Pradesh, develops new varieties of fruits, particularly mangoes which he names after well-known Indians. That has earned him both the Padma Shri and the moniker 'Mango Man'. He famously grew over three hundred varieties of mango on the same tree.

In 2010, he bred a new hybrid mango—a cross between gudshah and chausa—and named it after Sachin Tendulkar.

A SPIDER

While pursuing a PhD in spider taxonomy at the Gujarat Ecological Education & Research Foundation, Dhruv Prajapati discovered two new species of spiders of the 'Indomarengo and Marengo genus of Asian jumping spiders'. He promptly decided to name one of these two species *Marengo sachintendulkar*, after his favourite cricketer.

FOOD AND BEVERAGES

The 'Dravid rasam' at Café Mysore, Mumbai, may not officially be on the menu, but the Feral Brewing Company in Australia does have a Mango Ganguly—'a Mango lassi IPA ... packed with fresh mango, spicy cardamom, lactose and dry hopped with an assortment of American and New Zealand hops'—on offer.

While it is common practice for cricketers-turned-restauranteurs to name the restaurants after themselves, the Dhoni & Kohli Restaurant in Kandivali, Mumbai, is owned by neither.

HONOURABLE MENTION: ALSO A ROAD, BUT…

In 2001, one Tom Gueterbock wanted to sell his GBP 495,000 house in the South London district. There is nothing unusual about that … only the fact that he requested the *Wisden* website to publicize the sale. It would help him attract Indians as clients, he thought.

The house on 10, Dulka Road is perhaps the closest one can get to living in a place that sounds like 'Tendulkar'.

HOWZZAT!

Sourav Ganguly is the only cricketer to have won four Man of the Match awards in a single bilateral series. He achieved it against Pakistan in the 1997 Sahara Friendship Cup in Toronto, Canada.

Did You Know?
Unusual Feats by Indians outside International Cricket

No one has more runs than Mithali Raj or more wickets than Jhulan Goswami in women's ODIs. Rohit Sharma has the highest individual ODI score. Kapil Dev is the only one to achieve the 5,000 run–400 wicket double in Test cricket. Sachin Tendulkar holds too many world records—several of which were once Sunil Gavaskar's—to list.

But what about domestic cricket, or the levels below that? Indian cricketers hold several world records—on their own, shared with others, conventional, quirky. Here are some of them.

SEE YOU AFTER THE ... WORLD WARS

The first Indian centenarian first-class cricketer, Professor D.B. Deodhar debuted in 1911/12 and played until 1947/48. Apart from Bill Ashdown, he is the only cricketer to have played *before* the First World War as well as *after* the Second World War.

THE SARWATE JUDGEMENT

In a tour match in 1932, the visiting Indians declared on 376/6 and bowled out Glamorgan for 149. Vijay Merchant, leading the Indians for the match, enforced the follow-on. There was not much time left in the match, so the last Glamorgan batters, captain John Clay and Peter Judge (who would later play for Bengal), stayed at the crease.

The second innings began without the mandatory break. Clay and Judge opened batting. Chandu Sarwate, who had taken the last wicket, of Judge, opened bowling, and bowled Judge on the second ball. Sarwate, thus, got Judge twice in three balls for two ducks—the quickest pair in first-class history. The whole incident took less time than it took us to write about it.

IBRAHIM'S MARATHON

One of a handful of men to average over 60 with the bat in first-class cricket, K.C. Ibrahim played only 4 Test matches. He also set a first-class record in 1947/48 that still stands.

In the Bombay Festival Tournament, he played *consecutive unbeaten* innings of 218, 36, 234 and 77 in 2 matches—in other words, 565 runs without being dismissed. He then scored 144 in the first innings for Bombay against Sind in the Ranji Trophy before being caught and bowled by Bras D'Cunha.

Ibrahim thus scored 709 runs between dismissals, improving on Vijay Merchant's world record of 634. Since then, Graeme Hick (645) has gone past Merchant, but Ibrahim's record stands.

THE HAT-TRICK MAN

A medium-pacer, Joginder Rao got a hat-trick on his first-class debut for Services against Jammu and Kashmir in 1963/64. He did it two more times in his second match against Eastern Punjab. Only Albert Trott had got a hat-trick twice in the same match until then. Rao remains the only player to have done it thrice in their first two matches. Unfortunately, he played only three more matches before he fractured his ankle during a parachute training, which cut short his cricket career.

Major General Joginder Singh Rao fought for India in the 1965 and 1971 wars.

THE ONE WHO NEVER DUCKED

Abdul Azeem played throughout the 1980s and the first half of the 1990s, mostly for Hyderabad. He had a reasonable career, scoring 4,644 runs at 43.40, including a triple hundred against a strong Tamil Nadu side (who were led by Azeem's elder brother Abdul Jabbar).

What makes Azeem's career truly remarkable is that he never scored a duck. At the time of writing, he holds the world record for the longest first-class career without ever being dismissed for 0.

MAJITHIA MARATHON

In a Ranji Trophy match in 1999/2000, Manish Majithia of Railways returned figures of 20-20-0-1 against Madhya Pradesh, thus setting a world record for most balls bowled in a single innings without conceding a run in first-class cricket.

He had fantastic figures—12.3-9-3-1—in the first innings as well, so his match figures read 32.3-29-3-2. Of the bowlers who have bowled more balls in a match, everyone has conceded at least 10 runs. He also bowled 136 consecutive dot balls across innings, which fell one short of Hugh Tayfield's world record of 137.

SANGHVI SETS WORLD RECORD, NADEEM BETTERS HIM

In 1997/98, left-arm spinner Rahul Sanghvi of Delhi took 8–15 against Himachal Pradesh, setting a new world record for the best List A bowling figures, improving on Michael Holding's 8–21. Twenty-one seasons later, Shahbaz Nadeem of Jharkhand, also a left-arm spinner, bettered Sanghvi's record by taking 8–10 for Jharkhand against Rajasthan. Both Sanghvi and Nadeem later played for India.

AYUB WINS THE RACE

For years, Sonny Ramadhin's 98 overs (the most by a bowler in a first-class innings) in the Edgbaston Test match of 1957 seemed like a record beyond anyone's scope. While Ramadhin still holds the Test record, it was threatened several times by Indians in the Ranji Trophy in the last quarter of the twentieth century, when matches were often played on flat pitches and decided by first-innings leads.

In the final of the 1981/82 Ranji Trophy, Maninder Singh bowled 87.5 overs in an innings for Delhi, but Raghuram Bhat of Karnataka responded with 94 overs in the same match. And in 1987/88, Deepak Sharma of Haryana bowled 97 against Punjab.

But Ramadhin was eventually emulated in 1991/92, when Hyderabad's Arshad Ayub returned figures of 98-24-203-5 against Madhya Pradesh.

THE FORGOTTEN NAYUDU

The Ranji Trophy final of 1944/45—a timeless match between Bombay and Holkar—saw multiple records being set. Two of them, both undesirable feats by C.S. Nayudu, still stand. Nayudu had figures of 64.5-10-153-6 and 88-15-275-5, thus bowling more balls (917) and conceding more runs (428) in a first-class match than anyone else.

THE SEPTUAGENARIAN CRICKETER

In 1950/51, Raja Maharaj Singh, the first governor of Bombay and a prime minister of Jammu and Kashmir, became the oldest to play first-class cricket. He was a few months short of seventy-three.

He was playing for the Bombay Governor's XI (a team named after him) against a touring Commonwealth XI at Brabourne Stadium. Batting at number nine in the first innings, he edged the ball for 3 and got 1 run in before Jim Laker had him caught by George Emmett at slip. He did not take further part in the match.

CRICKET IN YOUR TWEENS

Alimuddin was a mere twelve years and seventy-three days old when he played for Rajputana against Baroda in the 1942/43 Ranji

Trophy. He later played 25 Test matches for Pakistan, between 1954 and 1967. When Samar Bose debuted for Bihar against Assam seventeen seasons later, he missed the world record by three days. Aaqib Javed of Pakistan later equalled Bose, but Alimuddin remains the youngest first-class cricketer.

AGAINST ASSAM, FOR ASSAM

In 2011/12, Ibrahim Khaleel of Hyderabad had 4 catches and 3 stumpings in the first innings against Assam, and held 7 catches in the second. In the process, he broke Wayne James's world record of 13 dismissals in a match. Khaleel's record still stands.

Samarjit Nath played only 1 first-class match for Assam against Tripura in 2001/02. He claimed 7 catches and 1 stumping in the first innings, and added 3 more catches in the second, thereby setting a match haul of 11 dismissals. There are several instances of 11, or even more, dismissals by a wicketkeeper in a match (including Khaleel), but Nath is the only one to do it on first-class debut.

SHANKAR SAINI SNARES SHAKTI SINGH TWICE

A first-class hat-trick is rare; 4 wickets in 4 balls, even more so. But what Shankar Saini of Delhi did in the 1988/89 Ranji Trophy was truly remarkable.

Saini was on a hat-trick, having rounded off the Himachal Pradesh first innings with the wickets of Shakti Singh and Anil Sen with consecutive balls. However, so devastating were Madan Lal and Manoj Prabhakar in the second innings that Himachal Pradesh had already lost 6 wickets by the time Saini got to bowl.

Shakti Singh's wicket got Saini the hat-trick. Saini had dismissed the *same man twice* in *one* hat-trick. William Clarke had got John Fagge twice in his first-class hat-trick back in 1844. Unlike Clarke, though, Saini also got another wicket—Satish Mehra's—in the next ball to make it *four in four*.

THE ROVING HERO

No cricketer in history has played for more first-class teams than Mushtaq Ali, who, in 1936, became the first Indian to score a Test hundred away from home. Mushtaq played for forty-five teams, four more than 'Silver Billy' Beldham, an early eighteenth century English star cricketer.

Mushtaq is not the only Indian cricketer to feature in the top ten on this list. Vinoo Mankad, Lala Amarnath, C.K. Nayudu, C.S. Nayudu and Vijay Hazare all feature there.

THE MILLENNIUM BOY

A.E.J. Collins's 628 not out, scored in 1899, remained the world record individual score in organized cricket until 2015/16, when Pranav Dhanawade not only smashed the record but also became the first batter to hit the four-figure mark.

Dhanawade stopped at 1009 not out, only because Shrimati Kantaben Chandulal Gandhi English School declared. However, it must be mentioned that the opposition, Arya Gurukul Central Board of Secondary Education School, Kalyan, were missing several first-choice players and had to field younger boys. A gap in age is more significant in school cricket than it is at higher age-groups.

FOUR SCHOOLBOYS

Back in 1987/88, Sachin Tendulkar and Vinod Kambli caused a stir with their unbeaten partnership of 664 runs for Sharadashram

Vidyamandir against St Xavier's High School. Both boys became instant sensations.

B. Manoj Kumar (320 not out) and M. Shaibaaz Tumbi (324 not out) broke that world record in 2005/06. They batted through the entirety of the 40-over innings, and St Peter's High School piled up 721/0 against St Philip's High School in the Hyderabad Cricket Association Under-School Under-13 Tournament.

MARATHON MAN

Beginning 22 December 2015, twenty-four-year-old Virag Mare of Pune etched his name in the Guinness Book of World Records for the longest net session. He batted continuously for 50 hours, 5 minutes and 51 seconds in the nets, bettering the previous record by over two hours.

Mare faced 14,682 balls—about five and a half Test matches worth—against a bowling machine and bowlers at the Mahalaxmi Lawns in Karve Nagar.

AND THEN, THERE WERE TWO

As discussed elsewhere, Kerala bowled out Nagaland for a total of 2 runs in the 2017/18 Inter-State Women's Under-19 One Day Competition. Both runs—one of which was a wide—came before Nagaland lost a single wicket. This is the lowest team total in a national-level tournament.

The only other recorded team aggregate of 2 in major cricket came in 2012 (Appleton bowled out Hope Hawks) in the Cheshire Women's Twenty20—a regional competition, one must remember.

EVERYONE GETS A FIFTY

All 9 Bengal batters had scored *at least* a fifty each—Sudip Gharami and Anustup Majumdar both got hundreds—when they declared on 773/7 in the Ranji Trophy quarter-final of 2021/22 in Bengaluru against Jharkhand. Bengal broke the long-standing record of 8 fifties in an innings, set by the touring Australians against Oxford and Cambridge Universities Past and Present at Portsmouth in 1893.

HOWZZAT!

In March 2021, one Salahuddin Abbasi was named Player of the Match in a cricket tournament in Bhopal. Keeping in tune with the steep rise in price, he won a five-litre can of petrol.

The Rovers
Cricketers Who Played for Several Teams

Contemporary fans often complain about cricketers having to switch allegiances almost every year. While that is true, it is hardly a recent phenomenon. Ranji Trophy teams might have been drawn on geopolitics, but that did not prevent cricketers from qualifying and playing for new teams.

Mushtaq Ali's world record of playing for the most first-class teams (forty-five) is unlikely to be broken, but many of them were one-off relief fund matches. He has played for only five teams in the Ranji Trophy—Central India, Gujarat, Holkar/Madhya Bharat, Uttar Pradesh and Madhya Pradesh. That is nothing compared to what some others did.

C.S. NAYUDU

Not for the first time do we have the younger Nayudu brother topping a list in first-class cricket. In a Ranji Trophy career that lasted from 1934/35 to 1960/61, C.S. Nayudu moved from Central Provinces and Berar to Central India to Baroda to Holkar to Bengal to Andhra to Uttar Pradesh to Madhya Pradesh (which included the erstwhile Central India, so he returned to where he had started).

VINOO MANKAD

Mankad's career overlapped with Nayudu's. His first four halts were Western India, Nawanagar/Saurashtra, Maharashtra and Gujarat, following which he went to the opposite side of the country, to Bengal. He switched again, back to the west, to Bombay, before a stint with Rajasthan.

CHANDU SARWATE

Like Nayudu and Mankad, Sarwate too played from before the Second World War until the 1960s. Unlike them, however, he stuck to central and western India. He played for Central Provinces and Berar, Maharashtra, Bombay, Holkar/Madhya Bharat, Madhya Pradesh and Vidarbha, in that order.

JAGDISH LAL

Jagdish Lal's is perhaps the most remarkable story on the list. He played only 16 first-class matches, of which 11 were in the Ranji Trophy. And yet, he managed to played for six teams—Northern India, Hyderabad, United Provinces, Services, Patiala and Railways. His son, the more famous Arun Lal, was not as adventurous: he turned out for only Delhi and Bengal.

GOGUMAL KISHENCHAND

Kishenchand played for six different teams, all of them in the west—Sind, Maharashtra, Western India, Kathiawar, Gujarat and Baroda—but not for Bombay.

VIJAY MANJREKAR

One of India's finest batters in the pre-Gavaskar era, Manjrekar Sr started with Bombay, moved to Bengal, then returned to Bombay before representing Andhra, Uttar Pradesh, Rajasthan and Maharashtra, in that order.

HONOURABLE MENTION: AARON FINCH

Several Indians have played for six franchises, but the honour of the most travelled IPL cricketer lies with Finch, that too after starting in 2010. It perhaps has to do with the fact that, despite an excellent record in T20 Internationals, he has never quite been the IPL sensation. He had a season with the Rajasthan Royals and two with the Delhi Daredevils before playing for the Pune Warriors India, Sunrisers Hyderabad, Mumbai Indians, Gujarat Lions (two seasons), Kings XI Punjab, Royal Challengers Bangalore and the Kolkata Knight Riders.

HOWZZAT!

Sadashiv 'Sadu' Shinde holds the bizarre record of having an average (14.16) higher than his highest score in Test cricket (14).

Did that Really Happen?
Popular Myths in Indian Cricket

It is often difficult to separate rumours from facts, particularly in an age when news spreads at an unprecedented rate on social media. However, some rumours get magnified with every retelling and evolve into myths as the years pass.

MANKAD WAS THE FIRST TO DO 'THAT'

India were touring Australia in 1947/48. During the Sydney Test match, non-striker Bill Brown left the crease before Mankad released the ball. Mankad ran him out. The incident is *unofficially* called 'Mankading', much to the annoyance of Mankad's family.

It is widely believed that Mankad was the first to dismiss a batter in this manner, and that he was criticized when he did. Neither is true.

Between 1835 and 1843, Thomas Barker ran out five non-strikers in the same fashion, the fifth of them at Lord's. This *perfectly legal* mode of dismissal has been used several times. Mankad was not even the first Indian to do it: Narayan Sane ran Ram Singh out in the 1941/42 Ranji Trophy in similar fashion.

Instead of being criticized, Mankad was largely supported by the Australian cricket fraternity. Don Bradman, who led Australia in that match, called Mankad 'scrupulously fair'; eminent journalists like Bill O'Reilly and Ray Robinson lambasted Brown; and readers wrote in to newspapers in support of Mankad.

Perhaps because Mankad did the right thing and Brown did not.

CLIVE RICE'S TEAM WAS THE FIRST SOUTH AFRICAN TEAM TO TOUR INDIA

Led by Clive Rice, South Africa toured India for 3 ODIs in 1991/92 to mark their return to international cricket after being ostracized for over two decades due to their apartheid policies. Since South Africa did not play with non-white nations before being banned, they had never faced India, Pakistan or the West Indies.

However, Rice's men were not the first South Africans to tour India. In November 1921, a group of footballers and cricketers of Indian origin had set sail from Durban. They played 2 cricket (both in Calcutta) and 14 football matches around India. The squad was called 'Christopher's Contingent', after their non-white organizer, Albert Christopher.

Impressed by their performance, Mohun Bagan requested their captain Billy Subban and vice-captain Baboolal Maharaj to play for them in a club match against Ballygunge. Incidentally, this disproves a long-standing claim of Mohun Bagan's, that Chima Okorie was their first overseas player in 1991.

INDIA DID NOT HAVE A WORLD-CLASS PACE ATTACK UNTIL KAPIL DEV

The myth perhaps began in the 1960s and 1970s, when Indian new-ball bowlers often bowled a couple of overs to take the shine off the ball before three of the four spinners—Bishan Bedi, Bhagwat Chandrasekhar, E.A.S. Prasanna, S. Venkataraghavan—came to bowl. M.L. Jaisimha, Sunil Gavaskar and even wicketkeeper Budhi Kunderan opened bowling for India during this period.

India's first Test match, played at Lord's in 1932, featured two world-class pace bowlers, Mohammed Nissar and Amar Singh, backed by the slightly slower Jahangir Khan. In his prime, Ladha Ramji, ten years older than his brother Amar Singh, was the fastest of them all. However, Test cricket came late to him, and he missed the tour—though he did play once, at home in the 1933/34 season. None of the spinners made an impact in India's first 7 Test matches, played during the 1930s.

But India's legacy of pace bowling began decades before that. M.E. Pavri, a fast bowler, starred in the first two major wins by an Indian side against touring British teams: the Parsees against G.F. Vernon's XI in 1889/90 and Lord Hawke's in 1892/93. He also played for Middlesex in the County Championship.

However, as the pitches in domestic matches became flatter and flatter in the 1940s, fast bowlers faded out, while Vinoo Mankad emerged as a world-class spinner. India's pace hopes were dashed further when Fazal Mahmood, after being selected to tour Australia in 1947/48 for India, chose to become Pakistan's first great fast bowler.

FRANCHISE-BASED CRICKET IS NEW IN INDIA

The IPL (and its predecessor, the ICL) changed Indian cricket in more ways than one. For years, cricket in India was played as per the club-state-zone-country hierarchy, with state associations playing key roles. But now, privately owned teams could scout and pick any cricketer, thereby challenging the age-old geopolitical definition of teams.

However, there is nothing new in this. In fact, privately owned teams existed in India as far back as in 1898. Rajinder Singh, the Maharaja of Patiala, led his personal team against the Calcutta Rangers. Apart from the Maharaja himself and six other Indians, the team featured J.T. Hearne, Bill Brockwell, Ranjitsinhji—all of whom were active English Test cricketers—and an 'uncapped' British, H. Priestly.

Bhupinder Singh, his son, continued the tradition of having a personal team. Vizzy joined the fray in 1930. His team comprised Jack Hobbs and Herbert Sutcliffe of England; Ed Kelaart, who would later become the first man to lead a representative Ceylon side; and Indian stars like C.K. Nayudu and D.B. Deodhar.

The cricketers received royal treatment, including generous gifts, and invitations to hunting trips and parties; some were even on the payroll in non-cricketing roles. The Moin-ud-Dowlah Gold Cup, which got underway from 1930/31, featured several privately owned teams.

CONRAD HUNTE RISKED HIS LIFE AT EDEN GARDENS

On 1 January 1967, about 80,000 people entered the Eden Gardens to watch the second day's cricket. The venue accommodated only 59,000 at that time, but numerous counterfeit tickets had been sold on the black market. The spectators and the police clashed; things quickly escalated as the police lathi-charged and fired tear gas. The crowd set fire to parts of the ground, and the violence spilled over to the city.

The West Indian cricketers escaped the ground, and local fans helped them find their way to their hotel. Amidst all this, Conrad Hunte, who had scored 43 on the first day, noticed that the two national flags were about to catch fire. According to some contemporary newspapers, Hunte risked his life to climb the pavilion terrace amidst fire and retrieve the flags.

Hunte had indeed attempted to retrieve the flags. However, he was stopped by a policeman: 'Don't you go, I'll get them.'

Eyewitnesses saw Hunte begin his ascent—and a dark man in white attire retrieve them. From a distance, amidst smoke, they did not realize that these were two different individuals. They assumed it was Hunte, for that made for a better story and over time, it got magnified.

The truth would probably never have been known had Hunte, a Gandhian who would work full-time for the Moral Re-Armament after his cricketing days, not clarified in his autobiography, *Playing to Win*.

WOMEN'S CRICKET WAS NEVER POPULAR IN INDIA

The lack of competitive women's cricket and its scant coverage are part of a vicious cycle. And while some of the blame is attributed to the fans' lack of interest in women's matches, another frequent assumption is that women's cricket was never popular in India to begin with.

Nothing could be further from the truth. The Senior National Women's Cricket Championship of 1974/75, for example, was played across four venues in Calcutta to packed houses, including the vast Eden Gardens. And this was just over a year after the Women's Cricket Association of India was founded.

Later that season, the Australia Under-25s arrived in India for a full tour. They were greeted by a large gathering of fans outside the airport, and a crowd of about 25,000 for the match in Bangalore. The state associations fought with each other for matches—no one wanted to lose out on gate money.

Volunteers were still preparing the outfield when the Australians arrived at the makeshift ground in Jalandhar, where a 20,000-strong crowd awaited them. A lady in the crowd gave birth during a match at the Eden Gardens. All India Radio provided live commentary, print media covered the matches extensively and video cameras filmed them for newsreels.

All this before India Women played even a single Test match.

A BBC STRIKE PREVENTED KAPIL DEV'S 175 NOT OUT FROM BEING TELECAST

There is no video footage of Kapil Dev's iconic 175 not out against Zimbabwe at Tunbridge Wells in the 1983 World Cup. It is generally believed that the match was not televised because the BBC were on strike that day.

There was indeed a dispute—over a GBP 34.84 allowance for hotel accommodation and meals for outstation staff. There was a strike as well, but that was not why the BBC did not cover the match. It was merely a coincidence.

There were 4 World Cup matches on 18 June. The BBC—quite logically—covered the two high-profile matches: one which the hosts were playing (England versus Pakistan at Old Trafford), and the other which featured the world champions (West Indies versus Australia at Lord's).

The commentary teams were at full strength: Richie Benaud, Tony Greig and Frank Tyson went to Lord's, while Jim Laker, Ted Dexter and Tom Graveney were in Old Trafford.

They did not send television crews to cover New Zealand versus Sri Lanka at Derby or India versus Zimbabwe at Tunbridge Wells—because they had never planned to. The schedule had been announced well before the strike.

MAN SINGH OR MAN SINGH?

The story has been recounted many times. David Frith, editor of the *Wisden Cricket Monthly*, was particularly harsh on the Indians, who had beaten only East Africa across two editions of the World Cup until then. Frith even suggested that India should be made to go through the qualifiers, like the Associate Nations, for the next one.

After India won the 1983 World Cup, P.R. Man Singh, the manager of the Indian side, wrote to Frith, asking him to eat his words: 'I will allow him to lace it with chocolate, and wash it down with ale or stout.' Frith sportingly obliged, and *Wisden Cricket Monthly* published P.R. Man Singh's letter as well as a photograph of Frith eating the 'offending paragraph'. P.R. Man Singh has recollected the story himself many times, even during the end credits of *83*.

In 2014, Samir Chopra recollected the incident in a piece in ESPNCricinfo. In response, he received an email from one Panwar Man Singh, who claimed to have written the letter instead. When Chopra asked for evidence, Panwar Man Singh sent him a copy of the original letter, which mentioned that he had been 'living in a country where cricket is almost unknown'. The letter ended with 'Man Singh, New Jersey.'

Like many others before and after him, Chopra had erroneously misattributed the letter to P.R. Man Singh.

SACHIN TENDULKAR WAS THE FIRST OUTSIDE-BORN TO PLAY FOR YORKSHIRE

In 1992, Yorkshire signed up Tendulkar as the replacement for Craig McDermott, thus fuelling the idea that he was their first non-Yorkshire player. However, while the county had always taken pride in fielding only 'home-born' cricketers, there had been several Yorkshire cricketers who were born outside England, let alone the county. Robert Clayton was born in Wales, William Oates and John Usher in Ireland and Geoffrey Keighley in France.

When Yorkshire toured Bermuda in 1964/65, they hired a certain Garry Sobers to play 4 matches for them. Before Tendulkar played for Yorkshire, Lancashire-born Michael Vaughan had played for their 2nd XI and was identified—correctly—as a future star for the county.

And though he was born in Morley Hall, Yorkshire, and played for the county for one summer, Craig White grew up in Australia. He even played for the Australia Under-19s in 1988/89. In 1990, Yorkshire signed him up as an *overseas professional*; he played for Australia Under-19s again, after his stint with the county.

INDIA WERE LATE TO PLAY LONG-FORM CRICKET UNDER LIGHTS

Despite the BCCI's funds (and hence, infrastructure), eight teams had beaten India to playing Test cricket under lights. West Indies hosted a pink-ball first-class match way back in 2010/11. The first ever pink-ball Test match was played between Australia and New Zealand, in 2015, seven months before Mohun Bagan met Bhowanipore in the first competitive pink-ball Test match on Indian soil in the 2016 Cricket Association of Bengal Super League final. Pakistan, West Indies, South Africa, England, Sri Lanka and Zimbabwe soon followed suit. India played their first pink-ball Test match against Bangladesh in Eden Gardens in 2019.

Thus, one cannot blame fans for believing that India were late to take to day-night cricket. But this is far from the truth. India had hosted a first-class match under lights before most other countries: the Ranji Trophy final of 1996/97 between Bombay and Delhi at Gwalior. The match was played with a white ball that was changed every forty overs—though that experiment was subsequently put on hold for almost two decades.

SPRING IN A BAT

Perhaps the most ridiculous of all rumours in Indian cricket took root shortly after the 2003 World Cup final where Ricky Ponting decimated India with an unbeaten 140. 'News' got out that Ponting had installed a spring in his bat, as a result of which he would be disqualified and the final would be replayed again.

Exactly how the rumour spread in the early days of social media in India remains a mystery, but it did. Too many people believed it without questioning what exactly the spring was and how it put Ponting at an advantage.

Similar rumours about Sanath Jayasuriya, one of India's arch nemeses, did the rounds in the 1990s, though in his case it varied between a spring and a steel plate inside the bat.

THE IPL HAPPENED BECAUSE INDIA WON THE T20 WORLD CUP

Barring the shared title in the 2002 Champions Trophy, the 2007 World T20 was India's first major win in a senior global cricket tournament since 1983. The win caused quite a stir, more so because the side, led by a young M.S. Dhoni, were without Sachin Tendulkar, Sourav Ganguly and Rahul Dravid. The first IPL auctions took place soon after, in January 2008. It is easy to see how this sequence of events gave rise to this common misconception.

However, this is far from the truth. In fact India were initially reluctant to even send a team to the World T20 (as it was called back then). BCCI secretary Niranjan Shah made his stance clear: 'T20? Why not ten-ten or five-five or one-one? India will never play T20.' Before that, India had played a solitary T20 International, against South Africa in December 2006. But after the Indian subcontinent's bid for the 2011 World Cup faced rejection, ICC President Ehsan Mani agreed to let them resubmit only if all four Asian teams participated in the 2007 World T20.

As the tournament went on, the initially reluctant India beat Pakistan, England, South Africa and Australia, and Pakistan again in the final. But all these wins came only *after* the BCCI officially announced 'a new Twenty20 competition'—the IPL—in New Delhi on 13 September 2007, the same day when India were playing *their first match of the tournament*, against Scotland.

HOWZZAT!

The first ever Ranji Trophy match got over in one day, 4 November 1934. Madras (130) beat Mysore (48 and 59) by an innings and 23 runs in Chepauk, largely due to A.G. Ram Singh, who took 6–19 and 5–16.

Unholy Smoke
Cricketing Effigies and Posters Burnt in India

While comparing cricketing fans across nations is a difficult, subjective task, there is little doubt that the Indian fanbase is more mercurial than any other in the world. They can hail cricketers as gods, crowd at net sessions and queue outside airports to catch a glimpse—but they can also hurl abuse and objects, and occasionally do worse. Burning effigies of cricketers, an undesirable display of emotions by irate fans, is thankfully not as common as it used to be until a few years ago.

MOHAMMAD AZHARUDDIN

The fans in Calcutta were not content with merely disrupting the semi-final of the 1996 World Cup (the match had to be stopped and rewarded to Sri Lanka). They also burnt posters of captain Mohammad Azharuddin outside the Eden Gardens.

In 2000, after Azharuddin and Ajay Jadeja were named in a match-fixing report by the CBI, angry fans burnt their posters yet again.

MIKE DENNESS

During the Port Elizabeth Test match of 2001/02, match referee Mike Denness fined Deep Dasgupta, S.S. Das, Harbhajan Singh and Virender Sehwag—who was also banned for a Test match—for excessive appealing. He even fined captain Sourav Ganguly for lack of control over his team, and Sachin Tendulkar for ball-tampering. The cricketers leaked the news to the media.

The BCCI demanded the sacking of Denness. They found support from the South African board. When the fans protested outside the South African embassy in New Delhi, the matter was raised at the winter session of the Parliament, and then Sports Minister Uma Bharti asked for a detailed report. Effigies of Denness were burnt in Kolkata. 'I am in the good company of George Bush and Tony Blair,' responded an unperturbed Denness.

When the ICC announced their next Elite Panel of officials four months later, they did not include Denness.

MALCOLM SPEED

Malcolm Speed served as CEO of the ICC from 2001 to 2008, during which time, to quote the *Hindustan Times*, he became 'one of the most disliked men in India'.

Speed often clashed with the BCCI, and was never on good terms with Jagmohan Dalmiya (a man with, in Speed's own words, 'manic determination to make India a world power'). Indian fans burnt his effigies several times. 'It's a traditional way of expressing dissatisfaction with people in positions of power and it was my turn a few times. I look back on with a sense of amusement,' he would recall in his autobiography.

GREG CHAPPELL

In 2005, Sourav Ganguly was sacked as captain and even dropped from the Indian XI. His fans, particularly in Kolkata, hit the streets to protest against coach Greg Chappell, who had written to the BCCI about Ganguly, and chief selector Kiran More. They burnt Chappell's and More's effigies in Esplanade (in central Kolkata), and garlanded their posters with shoes.

Chappell's effigies were burnt again following India's unceremonious exit from the 2006 Champions Trophy, by fans in Patna, Ahmedabad and elsewhere.

THE WHOLE INDIAN TEAM

India scraped through to a win against the Netherlands but were demolished by Australia in their first two matches of the 2003 World Cup. Fans in Kolkata not only burnt effigies of Sourav Ganguly but also performed his mock funeral. Mohammad Kaif's residence in Allahabad was smeared with black paint and tar, while Tendulkar's and Sehwag's posters were torched in Mumbai.

Tendulkar later appealed to the fans to be patient. India eventually reached the final.

THE WHOLE INDIAN TEAM: THE SEQUEL

Following India's shocking defeat against Bangladesh in the 2007 World Cup, angry fans set posters of Sachin Tendulkar and Virender Sehwag ablaze in Jalandhar. The same happened in Amritsar, where fans also burnt posters of captain Rahul Dravid and Harbhajan Singh. The Ahmedabad crowd did the same, though they were all in praise of Sourav Ganguly, who top-scored with 66.

Matters escalated when India were eliminated at the groups stage. A funeral procession (with 11 people dressed as corpses) was held in Kanpur; M.S. Dhoni's house was vandalized and his effigy was burnt in Ranchi; and twenty-eight villages in Haryana banned cricket.

Things turned a full circle for Mohammad Kaif, however, whose residence had been vandalized four years ago; now the fans demanded his recall.

RICKY PONTING, STEVE BUCKNOR, MARK BENSON

Much of the controversies in the 2007/08 Sydney Test was due to sub-par umpiring from Steve Bucknor and Mark Benson, which allowed Ricky Ponting's Australia to win with an over to spare. Ponting himself did not quite make himself popular among Indians when he led appeals for clearly non-existent wickets. Effigies of all three men were burnt in New Delhi after the match.

JOHN BUCHANAN

Ahead of the 2009 IPL, Kolkata Knight Riders coach John Buchanan announced that they would adopt a multiple-captain strategy, which meant that Sourav Ganguly would no longer be the sole leader of the franchise. While the tournament was held in South Africa, the pre-season camp was in the Eden Gardens. Angry local fans burnt Buchanan's effigy outside the ground.

VIRAT KOHLI

Virat Kohli's posters were burnt in Ahmedabad after India's defeat in the 2015 World Cup semi-final against Australia and again after India lost the Champions Trophy final against Pakistan in 2017.

HOWZZAT!

Iqbal Siddiqui opened both bowling and batting in his only Test match—against England in Mohali in 2000/01.

Microphone Men
Iconic, Controversial, Unusual

It started with the humble radio—not the FM stations one can browse through on mobile phones today but enormous box sets. Radio sets were expensive, and it was not uncommon to find the entire population of a locality huddled around one. The commentary was often laced with static, but they would get to hear the scores and familiar names ... in real time. When the large radios were replaced by portable transistor sets, fans began carrying them to venues—and even calling out commentators when they erred. With the advent of satellite television, commentary changed, and the demand for former cricketers increased. Since then, barring glittering exceptions like Harsha Bhogle, Indian cricket commentary has been almost entirely dominated by ex-cricketers.

The ground has been somewhat levelled by ball-by-ball text commentators. If one's internet connection is slow and there is no radio or television set nearby, the browser or a preferred app—where the commentator often slogs away in front of a desk for long hours—becomes handy.

The significance of commentary was identified even in the contest between the Champaner XI and Captain Russell and his men, where Ram Singh (played by Javed Khan) commentated solo during the three-day match, shedding all neutral garb towards the end (*Lagaan*).

THE DOYEN

A.F.S. 'Bobby' Talyarkhan was the first superstar among Indian cricket commentators. Unlike subsequent commentators, he operated *alone* throughout the course of three-, four-, or five-day matches, with perhaps a scorer in the room. Commentating by himself was part of his aura and charm. He had a rich voice, was never short on anecdotes, and could speak incessantly without compromising on quality, breaking only for lunch, tea and stumps.

He debuted in the Muslims versus Parsees match of the 1934/35 Bombay Quadrangular. The tournament owed much of its fame to him. So popular was Talyarkhan that Murphy Radio signed him for a commercial.

He quit All India Radio after India's home series against West Indies in 1948/49, for they wanted a three-member commentary team. He was part of a team only on one occasion: India's historic tour of Pakistan in 1954/55. Barring a brief stint as an end-of-day presenter in 1972/73, he never returned to cricket commentary.

THE EXPERIMENT

When India toured England in 1946, the BBC decided to provide ten-minute coverage of their tour matches against Worcestershire and Oxford University. Abdul Hamid Sheikh provided live commentary *in Hindi* for both matches (from 2053 to 2058 hours Indian time), and John Arlott in English (2140 to 2145 hours). The BBC used Arlott because they found Sheikh's English 'too Indian'—a curious reason, given that their target audience was India.

The British in India were not too excited about having to listen to Indians playing cricket on BBC, but the Indians' response, received through fan mail, was encouraging. Arlott's glorious career behind the microphone was launched—but that is another story.

THE DRONE

Vizzy was as ordinary a commentator as he was a cricketer, but his connections ensured that he commentated not only in India but also on the BBC as a guest during India's 1959 tour of England. His ability to drone on for hours attained cult status of sorts.

The story—perhaps apocryphal—goes that Vizzy once bragged about his tiger-hunting skills to Rohan Kanhai, who responded: 'Really? I thought you left a transistor radio on when you were commentating, and bored them to death.'

THE IRRESPONSIBLE AND THE RESPONSIBLE

Having conceded a lead of 66, India were reeling at 89/7 in the second innings in the Bombay Test match of the 1969/70 series against Australia. Ajit Wadekar and S. Venkataraghavan added 25 before Alan Connolly pitched a ball outside off, Venkat swung his bat, Brian Taber grabbed the ball, and umpire Sambhu Pan ruled Venkat out, caught behind.

Venkat looked aghast, for he—in Taber's words—had 'missed it by a foot'. However, he accepted Pan's decision and walked back. The matter would have ended there, had commentator Devraj Puri not pointed out that Venkat 'did not appear to have got a touch'. Bombay's heat and humidity, combined with India's performance, had already tested the spectators. There were a few transistor radio sets among the crowd. Hearing Puri's comment, the agitated public set stands on fire, smashed chairs and more.

Almost a decade later, during the Calcutta Test match of 1978/79, the West Indies were desperately trying to save the match—with

9 wickets down, Sew Shivnarine wasted time, sometimes even deliberately—until bad light forced the umpires to settle for a draw 11 balls before the scheduled close of play. It is not documented whether commentator Anant Setalvad had the Bombay incident in mind when he requested spectators to keep calm and accept the umpires' verdict. Fortunately, the Eden Gardens crowd curbed their infamous volatile instinct that day.

THE PIONEER

Chandra Nayudu, the first captain of Uttar Pradesh Women, took up commentary as a tribute to her father C.K. Nayudu, the first man to lead India in Test cricket. She debuted as a commentator in a tour match between Bombay and the touring MCC in 1976/77 in her hometown, Indore. She had excellent command over both English—she was a teacher—and Hindi, and was admired for her knowledge of the sport.

Nayudu worked tirelessly towards promoting women's cricket in the country. She was India's first female cricket commentator. Shantha Rangaswamy followed suit in the same decade while being an active cricketer.

THE REBEL

Taking a leaf out of All India Radio's book, Doordarshan hired Shantha Rangaswamy and the Edulji sisters—Behroze and Diana—as commentators in the mid-1990s. It was a move way ahead of its times.

However, Diana Edulji soon found out that their male counterparts earned significantly more for doing exactly the same jobs. This did not sit well with the legend who, after being denied entry to the male-only Lord's Pavilion in 1986, had famously quipped that 'the MCC should change its name to MCP'. She walked out.

THE TRAILBLAZER

In the first half of the 1990s, cricket on the internet was mostly made available by volunteers. Then, in 1996, Cricinfo signed an agreement for live web coverage with PILCOM, organizers of that year's World Cup. The method—PILCOM would send the files, Cricinfo would parse and use them—seemed simple at first. Unfortunately, the PILCOM files needed too much reworking, which slowed down the coverage.

Frustrated with the PILCOM feed, Vishal Misra, a Bhopal-born scientist and co-founder of Cricinfo, decided to use dougie, a code developed by a South African student called Jacques de Villiers in 1992. However, fixes had to be made, for dougie was written for an older operating system. To win the race against time, Louis van Dompselaar from the Netherlands filled in for Misra during his sleeping hours in Massachusetts.

On 1 March, Cricinfo covered the league match between Australia and Zimbabwe. The internet stepped into the hitherto unchartered territory of ball-by-ball cricket commentary. It has not stopped since.

THE PARIAH

Navjot Sidhu's metaphors, vocabulary and controversial choice of words while on air often drew criticism, but the complaints were never serious. In 2003, however, things went a bit out of hand.

While on air, Alan Wilkins casually asked Sidhu to pronounce 'Worcestershire'. Sidhu responded, with thousands tuned in: 'Don't f**king provoke me, Wilko.' While the exact words vary from source to source, they all agree that the F-word was there.

ESPN-Star sacked Sidhu soon after, though both parties denied that the F-word incident had anything to do with it.

THE INSPIRATION

It is not easy for a university-level cricketer to carve a niche for themselves in a galaxy of former international cricketers turned commentators—unless you are Harsha Bhogle, that is. In a career spanning over four decades, Bhogle has emerged as one of the most-loved voices in the world.

In 2004, ESPN-Star Sports launched a talent-hunt programme that would identify and mentor potential commentators. The name was an inspired choice: they called it *Harsha ki Khoj*.

COMMENTATORS TURNED CRICKETERS

It is common for cricketers to take up commentary after retirement or even while playing, but the other way round? Murali Kartik was part of the Neo Sports team for Australia's India tour of 2007/08. After the first ODI was abandoned, Australia were 2–0 in the seven-match series. The selectors included Kartik in the squad to replace out-of-form offspinner Ramesh Powar. In the last match of the series, Kartik took a career-best haul of 6–27, still the best figures by a left-arm finger spinner. Then, he joined Zaheer Khan when India were 143/8 in pursuit of 194, scored 21 not out, and helped India win by 2 wickets to complete one of the greatest all-round performances in ODI history.

While a regular in the IPL, Dinesh Karthik had not played international cricket for over a year when he joined Sky Sports as a commentator in 2020. However, after an outstanding outing in the 2022 IPL, he was recalled to the Indian side for the T20 Internationals against South Africa. He is still going strong.

FAMILY AFFAIR

Sunil Gavaskar had become a commentator shortly after his retirement, and became a regular feature in India's matches, both in India and as a guest commentator overseas. As a result, it took him over a quarter of a century to make his Ranji Trophy debut behind the microphone. When he did, in the 2014/15 Ranji Trophy semi-final between Mumbai and Maharashtra, his teammate in the commentary box was his son Rohan, 'senior' to Sunil in Indian domestic cricket. For a while, they shared space on air.

HOWZZAT!

Two seam bowlers called Rudra Pratap Singh have played for Uttar Pradesh and India—a right-arm medium-pace bowler and right-handed batter in 1986, and the more famous left-arm fast-medium bowler in the 2000s. Both are known more by their initials, R.P.

Standing Out in the Stands

Cricket matches in India often drew large crowds even before India became an ICC member or were granted Test status. Even though television has brought live cricket to the comfort of drawing rooms, packed grounds remain a constant in Indian cricket.

They have cheered and jeered and celebrated and protested and applauded—and even turned violent enough to stop international matches (Eden Gardens alone has at least three notable instances in international cricket). Here are some moments when the crowd grabbed as much attention as the cricketers.

THE GENEROUS LADIES, 1933/34

At the Bombay Gymkhana in 1933/34, Lala Amarnath became the first Indian to score a Test match hundred, sending everyone present into a state of delirium. Even C.K. Nayudu lost his composure and left his crease to congratulate Amarnath.

The crowd went ballistic as people hugged strangers and ran onto the ground to garland Amarnath. As Amarnath returned after the day's play, unbeaten on 102, the women in the enclosures showered their jewellery on him. Kings announced cash prizes for him.

AFTER THE WALKOVER, 1937/38

The Hindus were supposed to face the Europeans in the semi-final of the 1937/38 Bombay Pentangular, at the Brabourne Stadium. Unhappy with the allotment of seats, the Hindus gave a walkover. The Muslims beat the Europeans in the final, much to the delight of their Hindu fans, who had turned up in huge numbers to cheer for them.

In less than a decade's time, communal riots would spread across the nation—but would never touch the Pentangular, despite the teams being defined on religious lines.

THE 'MARTYR', 1961/62

India beat England by 128 runs in the fifth Test of the 1961/62 series at the Corporation Stadium, Madras. The 2–0 win was India's first ever against England.

Chasing 338, England began the last day on 122/5, and were bowled out for 209. During this brief period of cricket, fifty-six-year-old Srivijay Raghavan, from Vellore, had a heart attack in the stands. He did not make it to the hospital.

THE OVERENTHUSIASTIC

There are at least two instances of an Indian male cricketer being kissed on the ground during a Test match. Both incidents took place in Bombay.

The first involved Abbas Ali Baig in the Brabourne Stadium in 1959/60. The incident prompted an on-air sigh from Vijay Merchant, a mention from Rushdie and, decades later, a Cadbury's Dairy Milk commercial. And in 1974/75, Brijesh Patel was kissed in the first ever Test match at Wankhede Stadium.

A season before the Patel incident, Australia Under-25s Women were playing India Women at Eden Gardens. A man from the crowd sprinted onto the field and shook hands with Cathy Garlick when she reached her hundred. It is not known whether the much-acclaimed Dairy Milk advertisement in 2021 was based on this incident.

CHILDBIRTH IN THE STANDS, 1974/75

Thirty-five thousand people had turned up at Eden Gardens in 1974/75 for a match between India Women and Australia Under-25s Women. It turned out to be a thriller—in more ways than one! India, chasing 198, finished on 186/5, and on the third day, a woman in the crowd gave birth in the medical room of the stadium. One of the Australian team doctors was asked to help with the childbirth!

AGAINST THE WAVE, 1996

As Sri Lanka closed in on a famous win in the 1996 World Cup semi-final against India, the angry Eden Gardens crowd erupted in a semi-riot. Objects, particularly bottles, were thrown onto the ground, bringing the match to a halt. Clive Lloyd, the ICC match referee, eventually rewarded the match to Sri Lanka.

Amidst all the madness, someone in the stands decided to go against the tide and put up a *We Are Sorry, Congratulations Sri Lanka* poster. A bold act, undoubtedly, given the temper of the crowd that night.

PROFESSIONAL HELP, 1998/99

The 1998/99 Delhi Test match between India and Pakistan, now immortalized by Anil Kumble's 10-wicket haul, might not have taken place at all had it not been for some unique measures taken by the Delhi and District Cricket Association.

After political extremists dug up the Feroz Shah Kotla pitch, the first Test match had to be rescheduled to Chepauk. But the threats continued when it was announced that Delhi would host the second Test match. There were even rumours that snakes would be released in the stands during matches. To counter this, the DDCA sought the help of, along with police and armed forces, a group of sixteen snake charmers, equipped with pungis (flutes typically used by snake charmers). They placed themselves in front of each section of the crowd.

ONLY IN INDIA? 2004/05

The Kanpur Test match of 2004/05, between India and South Africa, was meandering towards a draw, when a member of the television crew spotted a man with a .38 calibre revolver seated near the boundary, not too far from where Sachin Tendulkar was fielding. The man had an access-all-areas pass. The police identified him as Taslimuddin 'Pasha' Siddiqui, son of Naimuddin Siddiqui, President of Kanpur Cricket Association.

THE TRANSPORTED, 2018

In 2018, the Chennai Super Kings returned to the IPL after serving a two-year ban. The day after they played their first match at Chepauk, the Madras High Court put a stay order on all matches at the venue in the wake of the Kaveri water protests. Chennai's 'home' matches were relocated to Pune.

But what about the dedicated fans, who had missed the home team play for two years? The franchise arranged for a special train to ferry them to Pune. Over a thousand fans boarded the first ever Whistle Podu Express.

THE BETROTHED, 2020/21

India lost the first two ODIs on their 2020/21 tour of Australia, their first international assignment after the COVID-19 lockdown. During the second match, however, one Indian man had his moment of joy.

He proposed to an Australian lady—both had worn the respective jerseys of their teams—and was accepted. As the giant screen displayed his moment of triumph, the crowd at the Sydney Cricket Ground applauded. Glenn Maxwell joined in.

HOWZZAT!

Against Australia at Eden Gardens in 1959/60, M.L. Jaisimha became the first cricketer to bat on all five days of a Test match.

Divine Acts
Religion and Indian Cricket

Perhaps there is some truth in the claim of cricket being a religion in India. Why else would people step out onto the streets to celebrate a team of eleven people beating another similar group late at night, or throng outside airports or hotels to catch glimpses of their favourite stars, or brave the unforgiving heat of May in packed stadia with scant facilities to cheer for teams until their throats go sore?

All that, however, is 'religion' being used in a figurative sense—but religion has been making its way into Indian cricket throughout history In fact, no major cricket-playing nation has been as diverse when it comes to religion.

THE BOMBAY PENTANGULAR

In 1892/93, the Parsees-only Zoroastrian Gymkhana played a two-match series against the Europeans-only Bombay Gymkhana. This became an annual affair called the Bombay Presidency Match. In 1906/07, when the Hindu Gymkhana joined, this became the Bombay Triangular, and the inclusion of the Mohammedan Gymkhana in 1912/13 made it the Bombay Quadrangular.

The qualification rules were extremely stringent. In 1924, the Hindus tried to add P.A. Kanickam to their team, but had to withdraw when they found out he was a Christian. Kanickam qualified for none of the four teams, and thus never played in the tournament. However, the Hindus later became lenient, and included Yadavindra Singh and Lall Singh—both Sikhs—in 1934/35.

To address these qualification issues, a fifth team was added in 1937/38—making this the Bombay Pentangular—which included Sikhs, Buddhists, Jains, Indian Christians (most famously Vijay Hazare), other Indian communities and even the Ceylonese (such as the great Mahadevan Sathasivam).

On 6 December 1940, Mahatma Gandhi said to three representatives of the Hindu Gymkhana: 'I would like the public of Bombay to revise their sporting code and erase from it communal matches. I can understand matches between colleges and institutions but I never understood reasons for having Hindu, Parsi, Muslim and other communal Elevens ... Can we not have some field of life which cannot be touched by the communal spirit?'

Despite the troubled times, and Gandhi's misgivings, there was no serious communal violence in the history of the tournament. The tournament continued for five more years, but was not resumed after 1945/46 as religious riots broke out across undivided India.

No other inter-faith cricket tournament of this magnitude has been played anywhere in the world. Taking a cue, several similar contests sprang up across the nation, but none of them—or any other tournament, for that matter—matched the Bombay Pentangular. Thousands had to be turned away from the stadium in the 1934/35 final. During the 1935/36 final, fans equipped with radio receivers listened to the matches across Bombay. The 1944/45 final attracted 200,000 people—about fifty times the spectators for the Ranji Trophy final the same year.

THE 'QUOTAS'

As is evident from the popularity of the Bombay Pentangular, inter-religion rivalry in cricket was fierce in pre-Independence India. The first All-India team to England in 1911 was selected by a committee of seven members, chaired by redoubtable British cricketer 'Jungly' Greig. The panel also comprised two Parsees (J.M. Framjee Patel and M.E. Pavri), two Hindus (Chunilal V. Mehta and V.J. Naik), and two Muslims (Ibrahim Rahimtulla and Ameeruddin Tyabji). The team was eventually led by a Sikh, Bhupinder Singh, the Maharaja of Patiala, and represented all religions.

Things did not change much over the next two decades. The next Indian team to tour England, in 1932, consisted of seven Hindus, five Muslims, four Parsees and two Sikhs. The Hindus included the captain, the Maharaja of Porbandar, and the vice-captain, K.S. Limbdi, both of whom were essentially non-cricketers.

THE FIRST SUNDAY

For centuries, there had been no cricket on Sundays—for cricket was mostly played by Christian nations. When Test matches were planned, the organizers ensured that the rest day fell on a Sunday. The first five Test-playing nations—England, Australia, South Africa, West Indies and New Zealand—all adopted this practice.

In India, however, there were no qualms about cricket on Sundays. When Vizzy brought Jack Hobbs and Herbert Sutcliffe to play for his personal team, a match was scheduled for 23 November 1930—a Sunday—against Sporting Union in Calcutta. While Sutcliffe played, Hobbs 'did not wish to do anything which might injure Christianity in India' and opted out.

However, when India hosted their first ever Test at the Bombay Gymkhana in 1933/34, the England team did not object to playing on a Sunday which fell on the third day of the match. This was the first time Test cricket was played on the day of the Sabbath. As if to commemorate the occasion, debutant Lala Amarnath became the first Indian to score a Test match hundred on that Sunday.

The other two Test matches of that series—in Calcutta and Madras—also featured cricket on Sundays.

THE PONGAL TEST

Between 1959/60 and 1987/88, Madras hosted 12 Test matches, all during Pongal, which usually falls early in January. The only other Indian city that can boast of anything similar is Calcutta, which hosted 12 New Year's Test matches.

UNITY IN DIVERSITY

The first Indian team featured four Hindus, four Muslims, two Parsees and a Sikh, making it the first time four religions were represented in an XI in the history of Test cricket.

The Indian team against England at Bombay in 1961/62 went a step ahead: there were six Hindus (M.L. Jaisimha, Vijay Manjrekar, Budhi Kunderan, Ramakant Desai, Vasant Ranjane, V.V. Kumar), two Sikhs (the brothers, Kripal and Milkha Singh), a Parsee (Nari Contractor), a Christian (Chandu Borde) and a Muslim (Salim Durani).

There would be several subsequent instances of an Indian XI featuring five religions. The first time the Indian team represented only one religion was in the Edgbaston Test of 1979, almost half a century after their first Test match. This is in stark contrast with most other Test-playing nations, whose early XIs were dominated by one religion.

GANESH CHATURTHI, 1971

The story is so fantastic that it seems incredible that Bollywood has never made a movie on it. Until 1971, India had never won a Test match in England (they had drawn 4—twice because of rain—and lost 15).

In 1971, India were saved by rain in the first two Test matches (though they probably walked away with honours even at Lord's). Then, at The Oval, England secured a 71-run first-innings lead. The fourth day of the Test match coincided with Ganesh Chaturthi, and local Indian fans arranged for Bella, a three-year old elephant from Chessington Zoo, to parade around the ground at lunch.

England collapsed for 101. India scripted history the next day with what is possibly their most famous win.

A BAN ON CRICKET?

In 1998, Swami Nischalananda Saraswati Maharaj, the 145th Jagadguru Shankaracharya of the temple in Puri, Orissa, asked Indians, particularly Hindus, to quit cricket, unless cricket balls were manufactured from alternative materials. Cricket balls, after all, were made of cowhide.

THE TENDULKAR TEMPLE

At the time of writing this book, a Google search on 'god of cricket' returned Sachin Tendulkar. It has been the same for years. There have been other great cricketers, but no other player has been honoured with that title anywhere in the world. Therefore, it was only a matter of time before someone constructed a Tendulkar temple.

The temple, built after Tendulkar announced his retirement in 2013, in Atarwalia village, Kaimur District, Bihar, boasts of an 850 kg life-size marble statue of the cricketer holding the 2011 World Cup.

PITCH POOJA

Visakhapatnam hosted the second ODI of the 2018/19 India–West Indies series. A few days before the match, the pitch curators performed a pooja at the Dr Y.S. Rajasekhara Reddy ACA-VDCA Cricket Stadium. While that is not uncommon, two things stood out. First, it featured M.S.K. Prasad, one of very a handful of Andhra cricketers to play for India, and at that point the chair of selectors. And secondly, the pooja was performed *on the pitch*.

For all that it mattered, the match ended in a tie.

KOHLI SPEAKS UP

In 2021, India lost to Pakistan for the first time in the history of the T20 World Cup. The Indian cricketers were abused on social media, perhaps the digital version of burning effigies on the streets. Unlike his ten teammates, Mohammed Shami—the only Muslim in the XI—was labelled a traitor.

In the press conference ahead of India's next match against New Zealand, captain Virat Kohli slammed the trolls. He labelled them 'spineless', and said that targeting someone over their religion was 'the lowest level of human potential that one can operate at.'

HOWZZAT!

Ghulam Ahmed Hasan Mohammed Parkar is the only Indian Test cricketer with five words in his name.

Not Quite Cricket
Indian Cricketers Who Faced Racism

England, Australia and South Africa, the first three teams to play Test cricket, were represented almost entirely by white men, as were New Zealand. The fourth to play Test cricket, West Indies were racially more diverse, but they were invariably led by white men as well. India, thus, became the first team to field Test XIs consisting entirely of indigenous cricketers. Thus, when they travelled, they faced racism the other colonies seldom did.

That does not, however, absolve the Indians of their own (mis)behaviour. Andrew Symonds had accused Harbhajan Singh of calling him a 'monkey', an allegation that resulted in Harbhajan being banned by the ICC. (The BCCI appealed the ban and Harbhajan was reinstated.) Elsewhere, Darren Sammy recollected how he and Thisara Perera were mocked at by teammates during their playing days at Sunrisers Hyderabad. He found support from Chris Gayle.

In this section we list some Indian cricketers who have been at the receiving end of racism.

RANJITSINHJI

That Ranji would face racism in England in the 1890s was not too unexpected. However, his batting genius helped him win over Stanley Jackson, his captain at Cambridge, who previously had little 'sympathetic interest for Indians'. Ranji made it to first-class cricket, where his Sussex teammates found it difficult to come to terms with an Indian taking field with them. They also addressed him as 'Smith'.

Ranji overcame these hurdles with his delectable stroke play and voracious appetite for runs. His royal status helped, as did unequivocal support from W.G. Grace, the greatest cricketer of the era. He was even considered for England's 1895/96 tour of South Africa, but a coloured man touring that country back then was out of question. A quiet diplomatic word followed, and Ranji opted out.

In 1896, the selectors considered him for the Ashes Test match at Lord's. Unfortunately, presiding over the committee was Lord Harris, who firmly refused to include a 'bird of passage' like Ranji. Ironically, Harris himself was born in Trinidad. Ranji eventually debuted in the next Test match, at Old Trafford, scored 62 and 154 not out and never looked back.

DULEEPSINHJI

At Sussex, Duleep inherited Ranji's nickname of 'Smith'. He played 1 Test match against South Africa in 1929, but that was on English soil. The South Africans played 5 Tests on that tour—but Duleep never played against them again.

By the time England were about to tour South Africa in 1930/31, Duleep had established himself as one of England's finest batters.

The selectors cited illness as the reason for leaving him out. Having scored 2,562 runs at 56.93 the previous season, an 'ill' Duleep, now captain of Sussex, amassed 2,684 runs at 54.77.

VIJAY MERCHANT

Vijay Merchant had played against England in 1933/34, but that was on Indian soil. His incredible batting took the English cricket fraternity by storm when he toured there in 1936. His performance prompted C.B. Fry to famously remark, 'Let us paint him white and take him with us to Australia as an opener.' There was an Ashes tour later that year.

Fry's words, while politically incorrect in 2022, were probably received with a smile in 1936. However, one cannot help but wonder whether mentioning Merchant's complexion was necessary: both Ranjitsinhji and Iftikhar Ali Khan Pataudi had, after all, already toured Australia with English sides by then without being painted.

RUSI SURTI

Rusi Surti, the first Indian to feature in the Sheffield Shield, played 35 matches for Queensland between 1968/69 and 1972/73. Off the field, he also worked at the Queensland Fire Department, where he was called a 'curry cater', an 'Indian bastard', and more. Surti sued his former employers in 1993 and lost. The court dismissed the racist slurs as 'mere banter'.

NEETA TELANG

In 1973, when the first Women's World Cup was played, the Women's Cricket Association of India existed but was not recognized by the International Women's Cricket Council. So, the WCAI sent cricketer-administrator Neeta Telang to watch the World Cup final and to acquire recognition.

Telang succeeded in convincing an organization blissfully unaware of women's cricket in India. Part of her efforts included assuring the administrators that Indians did not play cricket in sarees. Five years later, India *hosted* the second Women's World Cup.

THE INDIAN—AND PAKISTANI—CRICKET TEAMS

Much to the surprise of some, India and Pakistan qualified for the final of the 1984/85 seven-nation Benson & Hedges World Championship of Cricket at the Melbourne Cricket Ground. During the final, the television cameras spotted a banner bearing the text 'Benson & Hedges Final: Bus Drivers versus Tram Conductors'. Three and a half decades later, the Indian players would not be as tolerant of racism in the Sydney Cricket Ground.

AAKASH CHOPRA

Chopra faced racist comments during his days of league cricket in England, particularly during a match when 'two South Africans' in the opposition 'went on an abusive spree'. They used, among other slurs, 'P*ki,' even when Chopra was away from strike.

CHETESHWAR PUJARA

During Pujara's days in Yorkshire, his teammate Jack Brooks found 'Cheteshwar' difficult to pronounce. Pujara did not have a nickname, so Brooks coined the nickname 'Steve', a la Smith for Ranjitsinhji, albeit in an era when racism is a problem more pronounced than it has ever been. Despite Pujara's insistence on being addressed by his first name, the nickname stuck.

Taj Butt, who worked for the Yorkshire Cricket Foundation, claimed this was common practice in the team, and that cricketers of Asian origin were even referred to as 'taxi drivers' and 'takeaway workers'.

Pujara did not play for Yorkshire after 2018, but Shane Warne used 'Steve' multiple times on air to refer to him during India's tour of Australia in 2020/21.

MOHAMMED SIRAJ AND JASPRIT BUMRAH

During the Sydney Test match of India's tour of Australia in 2020/21, a section of the crowd hurled racist abuse at Mohammed Siraj and Jasprit Bumrah on the fourth day. After being called a 'brown monkey', Siraj took it up with captain Ajinkya Rahane, who alerted the umpires, Paul Reiffel and Paul Wilson.

Match was halted for a while. Six spectators were evicted from the ground, and the Indians lodged a formal complaint with match referee David Boon.

IN INDIA: C.K. NAYUDU, ABHINAV MUKUND, L. SIVARAMAKRISHNAN

Indian cricketers did not necessarily have to leave their country to be at the receiving end of racist remarks. When it came to demeaning C.K. Nayudu—his most important competitor for Test captaincy—Vizzy left no stone unturned. One smear campaign ran *'Baahar se kaala, andar se kaala, bada badmash hai yeh Indorewala'* (He is as black outside as he is within, the man from Indore is a rascal').

Shortly after playing his seventh—and, as it turned out to be, last—Test match in 2017, Abhinav Mukund reminisced how he had faced abuse on his skin tone. He stood up on behalf of 'many from our country who experience ridicule based on the colour of one's skin'.

Four years after this, L. Sivaramakrishnan, Mukund's Tamil Nadu and India senior by about three decades, narrated similar experiences from *his* formative days.

HOWZZAT!

Vivek Razdan got 5 wickets in his second Test match, against Pakistan in Sialkot in 1989/90, but never played another Test for India. He also made his Test debut before playing a single Ranji Trophy match.

Comebacks Like None Other
Cricketers Who Overcame Grief to Return to the Field

It seems almost impossible that athletes can absorb blows in their personal lives and still perform at the highest level. Taking time off from cricket would not have lowered the stature of these players, yet they chose to come back as soon as possible, or stayed put and waited for the contest to get over ...

EKNATH SOLKAR

A few days ahead of the Ranji Trophy final of 1968/69, Solkar's father was in an accident and went into a coma. After bowling out Bengal for 387 (Solkar took 3–63), Bombay were 336/5 at stumps on third day. Solkar was unbeaten on 8. His father died that night. Solkar completed the rites, then scored 29 in the morning to help Bombay take the all-important first-innings lead.

PURNIMA RAU

Just ahead of England's 1995/96 tour of India, Rau lost her husband to a battle with viral infection. She still decided to play 'as a way of coping with the grief'. Unfortunately, she lost form completely, and was not the same batter in the series. To relieve her of additional pressure, the selectors appointed Pramila Bhatt as captain for the last Test match and remaining 2 ODIs. Rau found form almost immediately, scoring 46 to help India win a low-scoring match in Madras.

SACHIN TENDULKAR

Tendulkar learnt of his father's death the night before India's match against Zimbabwe in the 1999 World Cup. India suffered a shock defeat, but Tendulkar returned ahead of their next match, against Kenya ('That, it seemed to me, was what my father would have wanted me to do'), and scored an emotional hundred.

By his own admission, Tendulkar was not at his best during the rest of the World Cup. He even donned dark glasses at practice sessions to prevent his emotions from ending up as camera fodder.

VIRAT KOHLI

Delhi were hosting Karnataka at the Feroz Shah Kotla in the 2006/07 Ranji Trophy. After Karnataka got 446, Delhi finished the second day on 103/5, the threat of a follow-on looming. Kohli was unbeaten on 40.

Kohli's father had a brain stroke and passed away that night. Coach Chetan Chauhan and captain Mithun Manhas both advised Kohli to return home, as did the rest of the team, but Kohli stayed back. He walked out to bat with wicketkeeper Punit Bisht.

'*Lamba khelna hai, out nahin hona hai,*' Kohli kept telling Bisht throughout their partnership of 152. Kohli got 90—at that point his highest score—helping Delhi avert the follow-on.

MOHAMMED SIRAJ

When Siraj was playing for the Royal Challengers Bangalore in the 2020 IPL in the UAE, his father had been constantly in and out of the hospital, in Hyderabad, with a lung ailment. Siraj, yet to play a Test match, went directly from the UAE to Australia for a full tour. Soon after he arrived in Australia, he received news of his father's death. Given the quarantine rules in both India and Australia, Siraj could not return for his father's funeral. He debuted in that Test series and finished as the leading wicket-taker for India. He broke down when he took his maiden 5-wicket haul, in Brisbane.

Once back in India, he went straight from the airport to his father's grave.

MANDEEP SINGH

During the 2020 IPL, Mandeep's father—a former athlete—needed to have one of his legs amputated. His condition deteriorated soon, and he passed away. A day later, Mandeep played for Kings XI Punjab against Sunrisers Hyderabad, and scored 17 in a low-scoring match. Punjab dedicated the win to his father.

CHETAN SAKARIYA

Three accidents had left Sakariya's father, the bread winner of the family, bedridden. The onus of looking after the family fell on the brothers, especially the younger son, a year younger—and very close—to Sakariya.

When Chetan Sakariya was playing in the 2020/21 Syed Mushtaq Ali Trophy for Saurashtra, his brother died by suicide. The family took a decision to not inform him for ten days to help him focus on the tournament. When they eventually told him, he broke down. He found it difficult to speak, or even eat, for days. The only solace for him—and the family—was an INR 1.2 crore IPL contract with the Rajasthan Royals. Sakariya impressed on his IPL debut not too long afterwards.

VISHNU SOLANKI

A crucial cog of the Baroda side, Solanki became a father on 11 February 2022, but his daughter died the next day. On 25 February, he scored 104 against Chandigarh. He was overcome when he reached his hundred, and later dedicated the ton to his daughter.

But Solanki's woes were far from over. He received another blow during the same match when his father died of a heart attack. Solanki stayed put. He watched the funeral over a video call, then scored 32 and 28 in his next match, against Hyderabad, four days later.

HARSHAL PATEL

Patel lost his elder sister during the 2022 IPL. He left the bio-secure bubble to be with his family, and missed Royal Challenger Bangalore's match against the Chennai Super Kings. However, he returned after that, and played for the rest of the season, for he had vowed to do everything that would have made his sister proud of him.

HOWZZAT!

After Indian captain Ajit Wadekar and manager Hemu Adhikari negotiated with the BCCI ahead of the 1971 tour of England, the cricketers' daily allowances rose from a meagre GBP 1 to a barely acceptable GBP 3.

Pieces of Wood
Famous Bats of Indian Cricket

For decades, India has been perceived as a batting nation. Though bowlers play a significantly more important role in Test cricket—you cannot win the match unless you take all 20 wickets—a 5-wicket haul seldom receives as much adulation as a hundred. Most cricketers tend to have a special kinship with the bat. In gully cricket, the owner of the bat is inevitably the hardest player to get out—which serves to introduce unsuspecting children to the concepts of power, and perhaps economics, at a very early age.

In a nation that celebrates batting like few others, what bit of cricketing gear can be as important as the bat? Here are some that grabbed the headlines in Indian cricket history.

A HOLE IN ONE

Batting was not Bhagwat Chandrasekhar's forte, as was epitomized by the fact that he had more wickets than runs in both Test and first-class cricket. But the 1977/78 tour of Australia was abysmal even by his standards: he scored 2 twos, 2 unbeaten zeroes and 4 ducks. Gray-Nicholls duly presented him a bat with gigantic hole. Forever the sport, Chandrasekhar posed with it.

THE MOVIE STAR

It is not clear how long Kapil Dev continued to use the bat he slammed his iconic 175 not out in the 1983 World Cup with. However, in Karanjeet Saluja's *Chain Kulii ki Main Kulii*, a bullied orphan called Karan (Zain Khan) finds it, inherits Kapil's genius and performs near-magical feats on the field.

The bat also makes a dramatic entry in Kabir Khan's *83*, when Kapil Dev (Ranveer Singh), halfway through the innings, says '*Talwaar nikaal*' to Yashpal Sharma (Jatin Sarna).

THE LUCKY CHARM

Sandeep Patil gifted Mohinder Amarnath a bat ahead of India's 1982/83 tour of Pakistan. Amarnath had the season of his life, amassing 584 runs in Pakistan, followed by 598 more in the West Indies, and then going on to win the Player of the Match in both the semi-final and the final of the 1983 World Cup.

Unfortunately, his bat was stolen after the World Cup. In the 1983/84 season, Amarnath scored 4, 7 against Pakistan, followed by 0, 0, 1, 0, 0, 0 against West Indies, and was dropped from the side.

FAREWELL AND JAMAICA

Sunil Gavaskar scored 236 not out at Madras in 1983/84, a memorable feat not only because it was the highest Test score by an Indian at that time but also because that was the hundred that took him past Don Bradman's world record of 29 Test tons. During the course of the innings, Jeff Dujon—who had probably seen Gavaskar more closely on the field than any of his teammates—requested the bat.

Gavaskar obliged. The bat now rests under lock and key at the Dujon residence in Jamaica.

MARKETING DONE RIGHT

Sanspareils Greenlands (SG) was founded in Sialkot in 1931, eighteen years before Sunil Gavaskar was born. That the brand and the man share initials is mere coincidence, but the myth of the two being associated grew in India. Sensing a marketing opportunity, SG got Gavaskar to endorse their bats. They even launched a bat—complete with Gavaskar's signature—and called it 'Sunny Tonny'.

MRF ARRIVES

Once matches began to be telecast on television, every time Sachin Tendulkar played his iconic straight drive, the cameras would zoom in on the full face of the bat during action replays, making it the most coveted real estate in Indian cricket. Sure enough, soon after the 1996 World Cup, MRF signed a deal with Tendulkar, who had surprisingly played the tournament without a sticker on his bat.

The next two years were the best of the first decade of Tendulkar's international career. MRF established themselves as a brand that signed up no one barring the greats. They followed up Tendulkar with Steve Waugh, Brian Lara, A.B. de Villiers and Virat Kohli.

THE UNWITTING WORLD RECORD

Sachin Tendulkar had once given his 'favourite bat' to Waqar Younis to take to Sialkot—known for its sports goods industries—to get a replica made.

In 1996/97, Pakistan were playing an ODI against Sri Lanka in Nairobi, when Pakistan promoted a young leg spinner to one-down. Before the youngster walked out, Waqar gave him Tendulkar's bat. This man, Shahid Afridi, slammed a hundred in 37 balls, at that point the fastest in ODI cricket.

MAGNANIMOUS IN DEFEAT

Bangladesh stunned India by 5 wickets at Port of Spain in the 2007 World Cup. Tamim Iqbal set up the chase for Bangladesh with a 53-ball 51, including an outrageous six off Zaheer Khan, India's most senior bowler. After the two teams returned to their hotel, Indian captain Dravid invited Tamim to his room.

After congratulating Tamim, Dravid gifted him two bats, one for him, the other for Mushfiqur Rahim, who had scored a fifty as well.

WILLOW OF KASHMIR

Bijbehara was among several places in Jammu and Kashmir to be hit by the floods in 2014. Parvez Rasool, who had made his ODI debut three months earlier, was trapped on the top floor of his residence for eleven days. Rasool left the house only once during this period—and waded 'neck-deep' to his car.

Anything for a favourite cricket bat.

THE ONE WITHOUT A BAT

Of the many things that added to the regal aura of Mansur Ali Khan Pataudi, one was the fact that he did not carry a bat to Test matches. Indeed, he played some of his best innings by simply picking up the bat closest to the dressing room door and walking out.

WEAPONS

At the Fergusson College Grounds in Pune, Atul Awachat of Golden Cricket Club hit Amit Shinde of Modern Cricket Club on the pads and appealed. Before the umpire could make a decision, the Modern team members and some supporters entered the ground. Soon, cricketers of both sides were attacking each other with bats and stumps. In the scuffle, Shinde hit Awachat on the head with a bat from behind. Awachat was rushed to the nearby Deen Dayal Hospital where he passed away. He was only nineteen, as was Shinde. Awachat's friend Prafulla Deshpande lodged an FIR against Shinde.

In 2017, Chhagan Makwana, forty-five, and his brother-in-law Vipul Bhil had leased a field in Amroli, Gujarat, for farming. One day, they were sitting in the farm when a cricket ball, followed by Aayush, a local youth of twenty, showed up. Aayush wanted the ball back, Makwana refused, and the two got into a scuffle. Bhil left for help and, upon return, found his brother-in-law dead and Aayush standing next to him, holding the bat in his hands.

In the same year, twenty-two-year-old Angad Gupta was hit on the stomach by a ball from a gully cricket match between teenagers in north Delhi. When Gupta asked them to play on a ground, they refused. Gupta slapped one of them, but quickly found himself outnumbered, and could get away only after locals intervened. The matter did not end there, however, for two cricketers from the match—both underage—tracked Gupta down and bludgeoned him to death with a bat.

THE COMMEMORATION

In 1972, the year after India won their first series in both West Indies and England, cricket fans erected the 'Vijay Balla', a 25-foot cricket bat made of concrete bearing the names of the triumphant cricketers, near the Indore Zoo. True to the spirit of Indian cricket fandom, the bat was defaced with tar after India's disastrous tour of England in 1974.

When a corridor had to be constructed in the area in 2009, a 45-foot replica was installed at the city's Nehru Stadium. Ajit Wadekar, who had led India to both series wins, inaugurated the new Vijay Balla.

THE RECORD

On 18 July 2011, three and a half months after M.S. Dhoni hit the six that sealed the World Cup for India, the historic bat was auctioned at the East Meets West charity dinner in London to raise funds for the Sakshi Foundation. It fetched a staggering GBP 60,000—but that is only half the story.

Dhoni himself was on the stage to give away the bat to its new owner. The winner shook Dhoni's hand, took the bat, and announced that he would pay GBP 100,000 instead. At the time of writing this, it remains the most expensive cricket bat as per The Guinness Book of World Records.

HOWZZAT!

Sourav Ganguly made his first-class debut in the 1989/90 Ranji Trophy final against Delhi. He replaced his elder brother, Snehashish.

The Plate Group
Food and Indian cricket

Sunil Gavaskar loves mishti doi. Mohammed Siraj and Yastika Bhatia have quit biryani for fitness. M.S. Dhoni's Twitter bio still says 'perennially hungry for chicken butter masala'. Rohit Sharma's affinity for vada paav is well known. Virat Kohli had to give up junk food. R. Ashwin likes paneer capsicum. Some Indian cricketers have even turned restauranteurs. Food keeps popping up throughout the history of Indian cricket.

So do meals, but that was perhaps inevitable—for cricket is a sport where the longest break of the day is traditionally named after a meal.

BIRYANI CHRONICLES

What better way to start this off than with biryani, consistently rated the most-ordered item on popular food-delivery apps in India? Debabrata Das, general secretary of Town Club, used to tempt a young Mohammed Shami with 'ek wicket, ek plate biryani' during club matches. It always seemed to work. Over the years, Shami has been known to fall back upon red meat as his recovery food.

At three in the morning, after India had won the 2011 World Cup, some members of the triumphant squad began experiencing hunger pangs. Virender Sehwag ordered biryani. For the first—and perhaps the only—time in history was there a biryani party in the company of a World Cup trophy.

In 2014, the Chennai Super Kings were put up at the ITC Kakatiya, Hyderabad, for their 2014 Champions League T20 clash against the Kolkata Knight Riders. Local man Ambati Rayudu arranged for homemade biryani to be sent to the Super Kings cricketers. Chennai captain M.S. Dhoni wanted a biryani party in the hotel boardroom, but the hotel's strict policies barred them from consuming outside food on the premises. The entire Chennai team checked into the Taj Krishna 'in a matter of hours'—though biryani was never cited as the *official* reason.

There are few authorities on Hyderabad cricket greater than P.R. Man Singh, a man unfairly reduced in public memory to simply the manager of the Indian team in the 1983 World Cup. His book on Hyderabad cricket is aptly titled *Cricket Biryani*: 'Much like the famous biryani of Hyderabad this book is rich in history and a blend of different exotic ingredients.'

VEGETARIANS

A young John Arlott followed the Indian team on their tour of England. He invited Vijay Merchant, Vijay Hazare and Vinoo Mankad to his north London residence for dinner. Unfortunately, he did not know that Merchant and Mankad were both vegetarians. The cricketers had to return after a meal of rice, potatoes, and tea.

For a long time, vegetarian Indian cricketers faced similar problems on tours of Australia and England. Vegetarian options, when available, were too expensive. On the 1967 tour of England the Indian cricketers received a daily allowance of GBP 1: the vegetarians were often forced to stick to bread and butter.

Ravindra Jadeja lives in a strictly vegetarian home but loves non-vegetarian food. He satisfies his culinary cravings when he visits his farmhouse where his cook prepares all his favourite non-vegetarian dishes.

THE INFAMOUS BREAKFAST

During India's eventful 1936 tour of England, Vizzy successfully divided the Indian squad into two factions, rewarding his supporters with lavish gifts. These were not restricted to just monetary rewards or a trip to Paris: Vizzy had promised something special to anyone who would insult C.K. Nayudu.

Baqa Jilani, already named 12th man for the Oval Test, verbally abused Nayudu at breakfast a few days ahead of the match. Vizzy rewarded Jilani by including him in the playing XI and leaving out Shute Banerjee. Baqa Jilani scored 4 not out and 12, bowled 15 overs without taking a wicket, and never played another Test match.

TIBB ON A ROLL

In 1967, Amarjit Singh Tibb, a national-level hockey player, tasted a pita wrap in Beirut and decided to adapt it to Bombay's taste buds. Two years later, he and his wife, Surinder, eventually launched a mutton-roll-and-naan outlet in Powai, Mumbai.

Over the years, numerous outlets of Tibb's have opened up across India. They call their version of the roll a 'frankie' after former West Indian captain Frank Worrell, a favourite cricketer of Amarjit's.

ICE CREAM AND CHILLI POWDER

Indian food can pose a challenge to visiting teams, as the touring Australian Under-25s of 1974/75 found out. Even on the occasions when the food was safe for consumption, manager Betty Butcher had to struggle to convince the cooks to prepare their food without chilli powder. It seldom worked—in fact, on one occasion they sprinkled chilli powder even on fruit salad and ice cream.

An exasperated Butcher titled her excellent tour diary *Ice Cream with Chilli Powder*.

DHANSAK

Delve deep into the archives of the Godrej Group, and you will come across cricket. Along with the keenly contested Godrej Golden Jubilee Cricket Cup, you will find mention of the Dhansak Matches that date back to at least the 1950s.

These matches featured both men and women, with the legendary Parsee dish served at the lunch break. This is perhaps the only annual cricket match in India that gets its name from a culinary delicacy.

CHAPATI

At a training camp in Bombay, a young Kapil Dev was served a meal of two dry chapatis and vegetables after a long day's work. Kapil explained to Keki Tarapore, administrator of the camp, that he was a fast bowler and needed more food. When Tarapore laughingly pointed out that India had never produced a fast bowler, Kapil took it to heart—and went on to become the greatest paceman in Indian history.

The humble flatbread found its way into cricket's lexicon as well. The flick off the pads fetched Ravi Shastri enough runs to qualify as his staple stroke, and came to be known as the 'chapati' shot.

ALMONDS

An ovo-vegetarian (an eggetarian, as some would say), Yashpal Sharma knew he had to find alternative sources of protein. While omelettes used to be his standard breakfast order, his affinity for badaam (almonds) was legendary. He claimed the nut was the main source of his power.

This often led to his being teased by his teammates. Once, when a group of girls requested the Indian cricket team to donate blood, Balwinder Sandhu insisted they take Yashpal's blood ('it is full of almonds, and one bottle will be equivalent to four ordinary bottles of blood').

Yashpal's most famous shot was the lofted on-drive that often cleared the boundary. His teammates obviously christened it the 'badaam' stroke.

PORK RIBS

Until the late twentieth century, overseas cricketers often picked up 'Delhi belly', and would even cite unhygienic hotels when they opted out of tours. The ones who did tour were given strict instructions regarding edibles. To be fair, there was some merit in that.

For on the eve of their 1987 World Cup semi-final against England in Mumbai, it was the *Indian* camp that suffered a blow. Dilip Vengsarkar, top-ranked batter in the world and known for his batting exploits *against England*, and his wife, Manali, had ordered a Chinese meal the night before. They had spare pork ribs, which was 'probably infected or stale'.

Manali had to be hospitalized. Vengsarkar fared marginally better and had to be given injections at two in the morning. He missed the match, and India were knocked out.

NOODLES AND ALL THAT

Sachin Tendulkar was having an ordinary run on the 2003/04 tour of Australia. On the eve of the last Test match, in Sydney, he went out with his family to a local Malaysian restaurant, and ordered 'noodles, chicken, and a host of other dishes'.

Tendulkar finished the first day on 73, the second on 220, and got a then career best of 241 not out in India's first innings. Struck by superstition, he went to the restaurant and ordered the same food every night for the initial three days of the match.

VEGEMITE

On the 2003/04 tour of Australia, Harsha Bhogle expressed his surprise at the hype around Vegemite, perhaps the most Australian of all edibles. The ABC audience took it in good humour: throughout the tour, Bhogle would be received with a ceremonious gift of Vegemite.

SAMOSAS

It rained on the morning of India's 2017 World Cup semi-final against Australia in Derby. Mithali Raj and her team, busy with the calculations and possible scenarios, skipped the bacon rolls and chocolate cakes that had been provided for breakfast. The start was delayed, and by the time the ground was ready for practice, the cricketers were starving, having gone without food for so long.

Some Indian cricketers took the field hungry. To the horror of team physiotherapist Tracy Fernandes, others helped themselves to samosas supplied by the supporters. An unconventional fuel for one of India's most famous wins of all time.

RASAM

Founded in 1938, Café Mysore in Matunga, Mumbai, is known for its South Indian cuisine. From Bal Thackeray to Sachin Tendulkar, the café has had its share of famous patrons, but none seem to have left a mark like Rahul Dravid has. His influence has been such that the café boasts a 'hot and fragrant' *Dravid Rasam*.

The name is probably unofficial: it does not feature on the menu.

PLAY FOR MEAT

The annual cricket tournament in Jawhar, Palghar, involves substantial prize money, often leading to rifts, even fights, among teams and players. Umesh Tamore, one of the organizers, came up with an idea in 2017.

This time, the first prize—a goat—remained tied near the ground during the action until Darya Sagar Mitra Mandal, the champions, walked away with it. Royal Teacher 11, on the other hand, struggled to lead their second prize of five roosters away.

As players and spectators lunched together on vegetable pulao, they happily shared the boiled eggs they had won over the course of the tournament for every four and six as well as catches taken in the stands.

THE 'FORBIDDEN' MEAT

Braised beef pasta was on the Lord's lunch menu when India played England in 2018. This caused a furore back home after the BCCI tweeted an image of the menu. Ahead of India's tour to Australia later that year, the BCCI sent an advance party to Australia. One of the items on their to-do list was to ensure there was no beef on the menu for the Indian cricketers.

QUARANTINE CONTROVERSY

On their 2020/21 tour of Australia, Rohit Sharma, Shubman Gill, Rishabh Pant, Prithvi Shaw and Navdeep Saini went out for dinner in Melbourne. Navaldeep Singh, a fan at a nearby table, paid their bill ('It's the least I can do for my superstars'), and tweeted about it.

This backfired, because the cricketers were accused of breaching the strict Australian biosecurity protocols, and were immediately quarantined. However, they were allowed to play in the rest of the series.

HOWZZAT!

Nilesh Kulkarni made his Test debut against Sri Lanka in Colombo in 1996/97. He took a wicket with the first ball he bowled, becoming the first Indian and fifteenth overall to achieve this feat. The batter was Marvan Atapattu.

They Did *That*?
How Indian Fans Have Followed Cricket

Mobile phones, live streaming and high-speed internet have made watching cricket in real time easy even if you are away from the venue or the nearest television screen. However, things were not as easy in the pre-live-streaming era.

Consider this: India are playing, and the fans cannot be at the venue to watch. What will they do? Wait for next morning's newspaper to arrive? Surely not!

RADIO RENDEZVOUS

When India hosted a Test match for the first time, at the Bombay Gymkhana in 1933/34, live English radio commentary was available only in Bombay, that too for certain times of the day. Then A.F.S. Talyarkhan took over, and dominated Indian commentary with his solo stints.

The BBC transmitted parts of India's 1946 tour of England back home, but All India Radio took over from the 1948/49 home series against West Indies and soon the likes of Devraj Puri, Dicky Rutnagur and Anant Setalvad became household names in the country.

What separated India from other cricket-playing nations was languages. All India Radio's Hindi commentary came to enjoy as much space as English over time, while matches in Calcutta and Madras featured additional commentary in Bengali and Tamil respectively.

Once portable transistor sets became available, it was not uncommon for commuters to huddle around the only person in a train compartment with a set or to wait in front of a paan shop and follow live updates, or even ask for scores.

Even after the advent of television, the humble transistor sets scored on two counts: you could carry them with you, and unlike the early days of television in India, you almost never lost signal.

During the 1996 World Cup, some cities came up with a novel idea. They hired youths who, equipped with transistor sets, kept updating basic giant scorecards at important crossings and landmarks.

COMBO OFFERS IN THEATRES

While radio commentary was available throughout the day, it did not satiate cricket fans who wanted to *watch* their heroes. Their best bet used to be a trip to the movie theatres. A newsreel typically preceded the movie, and any major match moments inevitably featured in the newsreel.

Jawani-ki-Hawa, the 1935 Bombay Talkies production, showed parts of that season's Bombay Quadrangular. India's famous win in England in 1971 was showcased for some time—often to thundering applause inside the theatre.

Cricketers availed the benefits as well. When V.V. Kumar took 5–64 on his Test debut against Pakistan at Feroz Shah Kotla in 1960/61, he wanted to watch what he looked like in action. He promptly went to Wellington Cinema for a Dilip Kumar movie to catch a glimpse of himself.

GATHERING OUTSIDE TELEVISION SHOPS

When the West Indies toured India in 1966/67, they played a tour match against a Prime Minister's XI in Delhi. This was the first cricket match telecast in India, while the first international Test match to be televised was the one in Delhi in 1969/70 against Australia. However, the telecast was restricted to only Delhi. In 1972/73, the Kanpur and Bombay Test matches were telecast in the respective cities. For Kanpur, only those within 3–5 miles of the city could watch.

Television sets were still a rarity in India, even in larger cities and metros. This led to resourceful individuals renting halls and charging spectators admission fees to watch cricket. Over time, more television brands appeared in the market, and sales received a boost during the 1987 World Cup in India and Pakistan.

The globalization of the Indian economy in 1991 changed the scenario. Cheaper yet superior television sets flooded the Indian market, which meant that more households—even outside major cities—had access to them, at least communal ones.

The electronics boom of the 1990s, and even the first decade of the new millennium, gave birth to outlets that sold an array of products. Strangers gathering outside the shops to cheer an Indian win or a Tendulkar hundred on the display televisions became a common sight. Over time, sports bars cropped up.

HITTING F5 LIKE A MANIAC

In the 1990s, only a few people had computers in India, and internet was available only in the major cities. One needed to survive a demonic screech for the connection to be established, and no one could make a call to or from the landline while using the internet.

Still, it was better than nothing, particularly for employees stuck in office spaces in an era when smartphones were unheard of. Those desperate for latest scores from live cricket matches had to sit for an eternity in front of a computer—and keep hitting F5 to refresh the page until the ball-by-ball commentary was updated.

SMS CRI

What did one do when there was no access to radio, television, or a computer? Mobile internet had arrived by 2005, but it was often too slow for cricket updates. Apps like WhatsApp and Telegram were still some years away.

The mobile service providers came up with a solution. The users could send a text message, often at two or three times the cost of a normal message, to specific numbers, and get 160-character updates of India's ongoing cricket matches.

Many a board meeting was interrupted thus by the familiar text message beep of a Nokia or a Samsung.

IPL FAN PARK

By the 2010s, cable television and high-speed internet had penetrated the length and breadth of India, and the advent of the IPL revolutionized Indian cricket.

However, one problem remained. The IPL matches were restricted to the home venues of the franchises. Cities like Raipur and Visakhapatnam did get the odd match from time to time, but fans in a majority of Indian cities were unlikely to get that 'stadium' feeling of a live cricket match.

In 2015, BCCI launched the IPL Fan Parks—stadia with giant screens that telecast IPL matches live—in forty-five cities across the country. The count kept increasing until the global lockdown of 2020.

HOWZZAT!

The only Indians to take a wicket with their first balls in ODIs are S. Ramesh and Bhuvneshwar Kumar.

Big Hits
Iconic Sixes in Indian Cricket

A six is special, and it is not merely because of the obvious advantage it brings to the batting side. A six involves lofting the ball—a strict departure from the basic training of protecting one's wickets that batters receive in their formative years—and venturing into the unknown. Six-hitters guarantee box office, and are generally among the most popular cricketers of all time.

NAYUDU'S WORLD RECORD

On their 1926/27 tour of India, Arthur Gilligan's MCC played the Hindus at Bombay Gymkhana and piled up 363. C.K. Nayudu walked out at 67/2—and unleashed carnage. He dispatched Stuart Boyes to the roof of the pavilion once and twice on top of the tents, and Bob Wyatt to the roof of the Gymkhana for consecutive sixes.

In all he hit 11 sixes. As the news spread like wildfire, the crowd swelled, for this was one of their own, demolishing their rulers at their game. Nayudu scored 153 in 100 minutes. His 11 sixes remained a world record in first-class cricket until 1962/63.

But that was not all. Two months later, Gilligan met the Maharaja of Patiala, Grant Govan and Anthony de Mello at the Roshanara Club in Delhi. He requested them to form an Indian cricket board, and promised to talk to the MCC about an Indian tour of England. The BCCI was founded in December 1928 at Roshanara Club. India played their first Test match at Lord's in 1932.

NAYUDU CROSSES A RIVER

Nayudu hit 32 sixes on India's 1932 tour of England. Of visiting cricketers, only Learie Constantine had hit more sixes in a single English summer (37 in 1928) until then. Nayudu's most famous six came on this tour off Hal Jarrett of Warwickshire at Edgbaston.

He hit the ball over square leg and it soared over the rope, over the stands, over the adjacent River Rea, and beyond—into present-day Worcestershire. Had Nayudu played the shot today, he would have hit it from one county to another. Unfortunately, back in 1932, Worcestershire was still about three miles from the river.

EDULJI EARNS A BAT

On India's 1976/77 tour of New Zealand, Diana Edulji spotted Richard Hadlee's Crown bat. Having grown up sharing bats handed down from male relatives, Edulji desperately wanted one of her own. Richard, unimpressed by her slight frame, proposed a wager: he would give Edulji *whatever* she wanted if she hit a six.

During a tour match, she requested captain Shantha Rangaswamy for a promotion up the batting order. Rangaswamy obliged, Edulji duly hit a six, and demanded that Crown bat from Richard Hadlee, who had been in audience that day to watch his wife Karen play.

SIX FOR SURRENDER

India were 136/6 against New Zealand at Brisbane in 1980/81 when Kapil Dev decided to have a go. He hit a pair of enormous straight sixes off Jeremy Coney. Impressed, Coney broke into applause. Then, before running in to bowl the next ball, Coney took out a handkerchief from his pocket and waved it at Kapil. He wanted peace ...

SHASTRI EMULATES SOBERS

At the Wankhede Stadium in 1984/85, Ravi Shastri hit Baroda left-arm spinner Tilak Raj for 6 sixes in an over. The first went straight, the next two over wide mid-on, followed by three more: over mid-wicket, over mid-on and straight. He became only the second cricketer—after Garry Sobers against Malcolm Nash at Swansea in 1968—to hit 6 sixes in an over in first-class cricket.

SHASTRI INFLICTS BIZARRE ORDEAL

Playing for Glamorgan against Middlesex in Abergavenny in 1989, Ravi Shastri put on a superb display of hitting. He scored 127 and 101 not out, smashing 30 fours and 8 sixes across innings. The most famous of these sixes was one that landed in a nearby brook. With no one else available, the Glamorgan secretary had to wade into the brook to fetch the ball.

KAPIL TAKES ON HEMMINGS

Lord's, 1990. India were 9 down, and needed 24 to save the follow-on. At the non-striker's end was Narendra Hirwani, a man with no reputation for, or even the pretence of, being a capable batter. Kapil Dev blocked the first two balls from Eddie Hemmings.

The remaining balls in the over all flew over Hemmings's head: 4 balls, 24 runs, follow-on averted, just like that. 'Well, I suppose it's only logical, if you need twenty-four to save the follow-on why wouldn't you get it in four hits?' Richie Benaud quipped on air.

Kapil became the first to hit 4 consecutive sixes in Test cricket. As if to honour Kapil's keenness to get the job done all by himself, Hirwani got out the first ball he faced.

GANGULY GETS A ROOF

Sourav Ganguly earned quite a reputation for stepping out and hitting monstrous sixes off left-arm spinners. Back in Kolkata, the crowd often referred to the specific shot as *'Bapi, bari jaa'* ('Go home, dude').

In the final of the 1998/99 Coca-Cola Champions Trophy in Sharjah, he lofted Grant Flower of Zimbabwe thrice onto the roof of the stadium. All three balls had to be replaced. An impressed Tony Greig insisted it be renamed 'Ganguly's Roof'.

TENDULKAR GOES AFTER SHOAIB

During the 2003 World Cup, Sachin Tendulkar famously hit Andy Caddick out of the stadium, but the six off Shoaib Akhtar overshadowed that. The ball was short, outside off. Tendulkar 'spotted the ball early' and reached out for a savage slash, and the ball flew over deep third for six. ESPN-Star named it their Sports Moment of the Year for 2003.

SIX TO THREE HUNDRED

At the Multan Test match of 2004, Virender Sehwag zoomed to 295, 5 short of becoming the first Indian to score a triple hundred in Test cricket. The knowledge of history being in the making would have held most back from taking undue risks, but Sehwag's mind seemed made up: 'Whatever will happen, will happen. I don't care, I want to hit a six now.' When Saqlain Mushtaq came to bowl, he did just that, dispatching the ball with a violent slog over mid-wicket.

YUVRAJ DEMOLISHES BROAD

During a 2007 World T20 match in Durban, Yuvraj Singh hit 2 fours off Andrew Flintoff, which led to a verbal battle. Seething, Yuvraj vented his anger on the next bowler: Stuart Broad. With sixes over mid-wicket, square leg, extra cover, backward point, mid-wicket—the largest of them—and wide mid-on, Yuvraj became the first to get the full set in an over in a Twenty20 International.

SEALED WITH A SIX

India needed 4 from 11 balls to win the 2011 World Cup final against Sri Lanka. Nuwan Kulasekara ran in. M.S. Dhoni sent the ball sailing over long on and finished the motion with a twirl of his bat before India erupted in celebrations. The photographs of the six rank among the most famous in the history of a sport, especially the one clicked by Graham Crouch.

TARE BREAKS RAJASTHAN HEARTS

Mumbai Indians needed to chase 190 in 14.3 overs against Rajasthan Royals to qualify for the Playoffs of the 2014 IPL. If they failed, Rajasthan would qualify. They brought the target down to 2 off the last ball, but Ambati Rayudu was run out while attempting a second run.

Then, following an elaborate conference, it was announced that Mumbai would get another shot at qualifying for the Playoffs—*if* they could hit a boundary off the next ball. James Faulkner bowled a full toss, and Aditya Tare dutifully dispatched it over square leg for six.

TEEN TROUBLE

Less than a year after leading India at the 2016 Under-19 World Cup, Ishan Kishan hit 14 sixes—the most by an Indian in first-class cricket—in his 273. Rishabh Pant, Kishan's deputy in that World Cup, responded with 21 sixes *in the match* (8 in the first innings, 13 in the second) to set yet another new record for an Indian.

It was perhaps fitting that the match was played in Thumba, home to the Equatorial Rocket Launching Station.

HONOURABLE MENTION: THE CURSED SIX

Pakistan needed 4 off the last ball to win the Austral-Asia Cup final of 1986. Chetan Sharma bowled a full toss that Javed Miandad sent flying over square leg to seal a historic win.

According to perception, the shot gave Pakistan a psychological edge over India over the next decade. Until the six, India had beaten Pakistan in 8 matches and lost 7. But between that six and Miandad's retirement, Pakistan won 20 times, losing only 5. Of course, correlation is not necessarily causation ...

HOWZZAT!

Virat Kohli's first ball in T20 Internationals was a wide, off which M.S. Dhoni stumped Kevin Pietersen; in other words, Kohli got a wicket with his 0th ball!

End of Innings
Indian Cricketers Who Died Unnatural Deaths

Mantu Banerjee, who played just 1 Test match, used to call the three stumps 'past', 'present' and 'future', while the bails 'formed the timeline connecting the three'. While not a particularly philosophical sport, morbid phrases like 'death overs' and 'death rattle' are often used in cricket, as is 'life', to denote a missed opportunity by a fielding side.

In this section, we shall discuss Indian cricketers—domestic or international—who died of unnatural causes or at unusual places. In some cases, misinformation and rumours have managed to convince the cricket fraternity that the person did not die of natural causes.

BAQA JILANI

The first man to get a hat-trick in the Ranji Trophy, Baqa Jilani's only Test cap—at The Oval in 1936—was almost certainly not based on merit. He suffered from epilepsy, insomnia, somnambulism and high blood pressure, and had a temper—which was often evident on the cricket field.

In 1941, he had an epileptic fit, fell from the balcony of his residence in Jullundur and died on the spot. He was not even thirty. For some reason, rumours of Baqa Jilani hanging himself kept circulating for several decades.

LADHA RAMJI

Eye-witnesses often hailed Ramji as the fastest bowler in pre-Independence India. Unfortunately, he was thirty-two by the time India began playing Test cricket in 1932, and his career was restricted to a solitary appearance. Ramji was forty when he lost his brother, the more accomplished Test cricketer Amar Singh, ten years younger, to typhoid. The blow took a toll on him. He was diagnosed with diabetes soon after that, but refused to cut down on his fifty-odd cups of tea a day. The disease affected his right leg; eventually gangrene set in, and the doctors advised him to get it amputated. Pleas from family members fell on deaf ears, for Ramji would not lead a compromised life.

He ignored the escalating complications, refused treatment, and died at forty-eight.

IFTIKHAR ALI KHAN PATAUDI

Pataudi Sr scored a hundred on Test debut in the Bodyline series of 1932/33, and played 3 matches for England on that tour. In 1946, he led India on their tour of England, and remains the only person to have played for both England and India. He also played hockey for India in 1928—albeit not in the Olympics—and was proficient at polo and billiards.

Pataudi died suddenly while playing polo on 5 January 1952, his son Mansur's eleventh birthday.

RUSI MODI

In 1944/45, twenty-year-old Modi became the first to score a thousand runs in a single edition of the Ranji Trophy, and competed with Vijay Merchant and Vijay Hazare in run-making. He impressed in his 10 Test matches, and was proficient in table tennis, tennis and badminton.

In 1986, Modi, then sixty-two, died at Brabourne Stadium, Bombay. Initial reports mentioned that 'he had fallen to his death from the third floor', which gave birth to multiple theories and speculations. However, it was clarified later that he had died, almost immediately, of a cardiac arrest.

COTAH RAMASWAMY

The only person to play both Davis Cup and Test cricket for India, Ramaswamy was eighty-nine when he disappeared from his residence in Adyar on 16 October 1985. He never returned, nor could he be traced. In the first decade of the millennium, databases and publications started using January 1990 as his date of death.

In a bizarre coincidence Ralph Legall, the only other person to have played both Davis Cup (for the British Caribbean) and Test cricket (for West Indies), too, went missing—and is presumed dead.

MUNI LAL

Muni Lal played 20 first-class matches in the 1930s and 1940s, was an academic of repute and Indian high commissioner to Trinidad & Tobago. His brother Jagdish and son Akash were also first-class cricketers, while Jagdish's son Arun played for India.

In January 1990, a gang of robbers broke into his residence in NOIDA and attacked him, his wife, Shiva, and his grandson, Arsh. Husband and wife both succumbed to the blows, though Arsh survived after being treated at AIIMS.

Muni Lal was the first *known* instance of an Indian first-class cricketer who was murdered.

RAJESH PETER

Peter was good enough to play for Delhi 13 times in the early 1980s, when they were among the top teams in India. He is remembered mostly for his unbeaten 67 in the 1981/82 Ranji Trophy final, where he and Rakesh Shukla added an unbroken 118 to help Delhi beat Karnataka.

On 16 November 1995, Peter was found dead in his flat in New Delhi. Over a quarter of a century later, the cause of his death remains unknown. The local community believed that Peter 'deliberately drank himself to death', probably after his wife had walked out on him.

RAMAN LAMBA

Lamba's meteoric rise—he was named Player of the Series on debut in 1986—culminated in an inexplicable decline. By 1990 he was not in contention for an Indian cap anymore, but continued to play domestic cricket in India and became a superstar in club cricket in Bangladesh.

On 20 February 1998, in a Dhaka club match, Mehrab Hossain pulled Saifullah Khan. The ball hit Lamba, who was standing very close at short leg, on the forehead. Khaled Mashud took the catch on the rebound even as the other players rushed to Lamba, who had collapsed.

Lamba recovered temporarily, but passed away two days later in a Dhaka hospital. He was the first Indian international cricketer to die from an injury during a cricket match.

V.B. CHANDRASEKHAR

Known for his swashbuckling batting, Chandrasekhar—a stalwart for Tamil Nadu—slammed a 56-ball hundred in the 1988/89 Irani Trophy, at that point the fastest century in Indian domestic cricket. He played 7 ODIs, and later became a coach and commentator, and owned the VB Kanchi Veerans in the Tamil Nadu Premier League.

In 2019, he hanged himself at his residence in Mylapore, Chennai. It later came to light that he had been battling a financial crisis.

DIED IN COMBAT

Despite Services featuring in the Ranji Trophy team, no cricketer from the side—or, indeed, any Indian international or domestic cricketer—has died in a war.

However, some cricketers of British origin were killed in the World Wars after playing domestic cricket in India. Most of them played for the Europeans in the Bombay Pentangular, and some featured in the Ranji Trophy too.

Alec Howie was born in Saharanpur, and played once in the 1934/35 Ranji Trophy for the Army—before they became Services—and scored 49. Part of the East Surrey Regiment, Howie died in the Battle of Belgium in 1940.

James Alexander, Stanley Behrend and Alexander Shaw, all played for Bengal, and were killed on Indian soil in the Second World War. And Vivian Chiodetti, who had played for Hyderabad against Aligarh Muslim University Past and Present before the inception of the Ranji Trophy, was killed in Myanmar.

HOWZZAT!

In the 21 Test matches India won under Sourav Ganguly's leadership, Rahul Dravid scored 2,571 runs at 102.84 with 9 hundreds in 32 innings.

Player–Coach Feuds

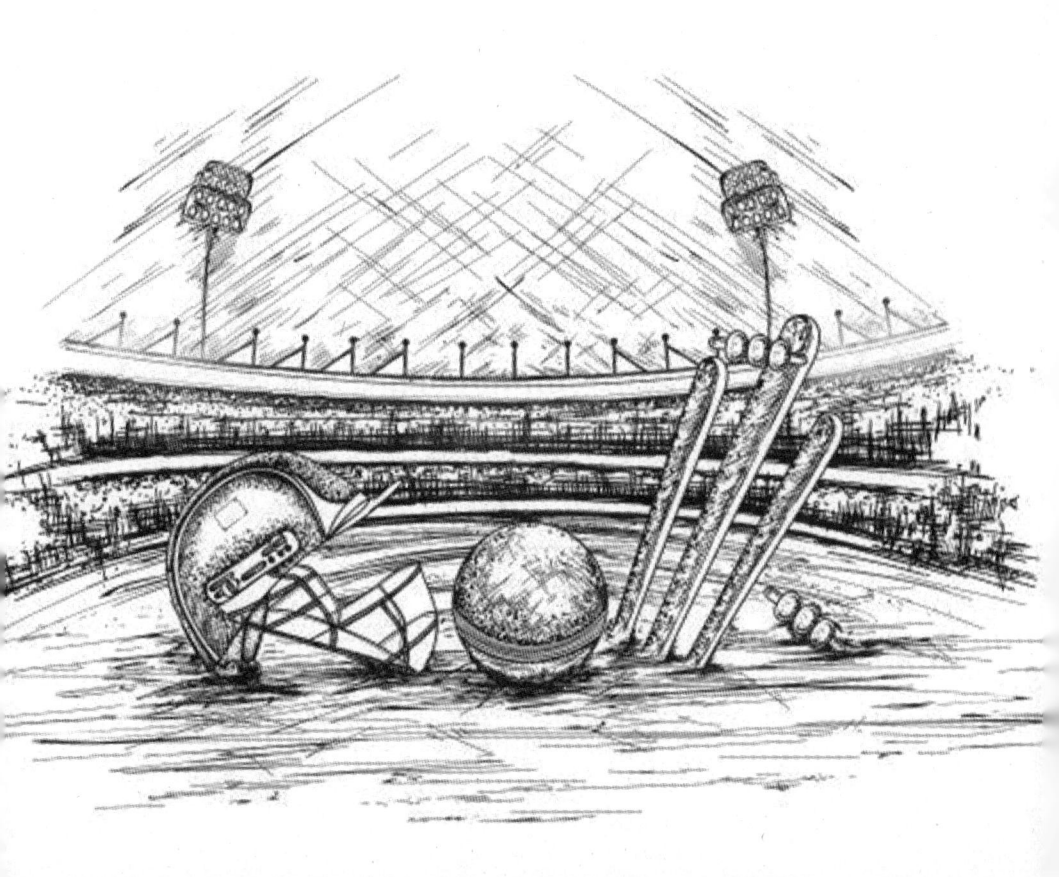

Coaches came much later to Indian cricket—indeed, all cricket. In the past, tours used to have a manager, who doubled, trebled, quadrupled, quintupled ... and more, in multiple roles.

A clash was inevitable, though one possibly did not expect it as early as on India's second ever tour, in England in 1936, when Lala Amarnath was sent back home. The Maharajkumar of Vizianagaram (Vizzy), India's captain on the tour, was the main antagonist in the affair. Major Jack Brittain-Jones, the tour manager, was too aligned with Vizzy to think otherwise.

Over years, there have been numerous instances of fallouts between cricketers—captains or otherwise—and managers, and later, coaches. Here is a list.

MOHAMMAD AZHARUDDIN AND BISHAN SINGH BEDI, 1990

On the 1989/90 tour, India lost the 3-Test series in New Zealand 0-1, and failed to qualify for the final in the Rothmans Cup Triangular Series. After a defeat against Australia, manager Bishan Singh Bedi—never one to mince his words—told the media that 'the entire team should be dumped into the Pacific'.

When New Zealand lost to Australia next day (they were bowled out for 94, in fact), their captain Martin Crowe quipped, 'We are not jumping into any ocean.'

The episode did not go down well with the Indian squad, least of all new captain Mohammad Azharuddin.

Later that year, when the Indian team visited England, Sunil Gavaskar refused to accept an MCC membership. Bedi accused Gavaskar of letting down 'the Indian team, world cricket and more importantly, the Indian people in Britain'. When the media asked Azhar, he calmly responded with, 'The team did not know they were let down by Gavaskar.' Azhar became more vocal about their uneasy relationship once Bedi quit.

PURNIMA RAU AND SREERUPA BOSE, 1994/95 TOUR OF NEW ZEALAND

In 1994/95, India won their first multi-nation tournament—and a great one too, the New Zealand Women's Centenary Tournament. It was a remarkable win, for Australia Women were the third team.

The tour began with a drawn Test match in Nelson. Purnima Rau, the Indian captain on the tour, had not enjoyed the single room allotted to her. Between the Test and the tournament, India had to play an ODI in Christchurch, ahead of which, Rau had requested coach Sreerupa Bose to assign her room to Sandhya Agarwal, the most experienced member of the side. Rau wanted a double room for herself.

When the team arrived in Christchurch, Rau found out that she had been assigned a single room again. When she asked her coach, Bose snapped back: 'How dare you ask me for a room?' and slapped her.

The incident did not hit headlines until the victorious team returned to India. The duo later reconciled.

SOURAV GANGULY AND GREG CHAPPELL, 2005-06

Volumes have been written about the Ganguly–Chappell clash, one of the most tumultuous periods of Indian cricket. Curiously, Ganguly had voiced support when Chappell was appointed coach.

The chain of events began on the Zimbabwe tour of 2005, during which Chappell asked Ganguly—then Indian captain—to leave himself out of the Test XI to accommodate both Yuvraj Singh and Mohammad Kaif. Ganguly refused. Chappell subsequently wrote an email to the BCCI, criticizing the captain. The email was leaked.

Ganguly then missed the first 4 ODIs of a 7-match home series against Sri Lanka due to an injury. He was not recalled even after he recovered, and was left out of the series against South Africa that followed. During the second ODI, at Eden Gardens, Ganguly's home ground, the local fans cheered for South Africa.

Ganguly was subsequently left out for almost the entirety of 2006, including India's historic series win in West Indies after thirty-five years. However, he made a resounding comeback.

Chappell resigned following India's unceremonious exit from the 2007 World Cup.

SOURAV GANGULY AND JOHN BUCHANAN, 2009 IPL

Ahead of the 2009 IPL, Kolkata Knight Riders coach John Buchanan envisaged some radical changes. One of them was using multiple captains throughout the tournament. Buchanan wanted to shuffle between Brendon McCullum, Chris Gayle, Brad Hodge and incumbent captain Sourav Ganguly.

Ultimately, only McCullum led KKR in that year's IPL. The relationship between Ganguly and Buchanan soured. Things took a turn for the worse when Aakash Chopra and Sanjay Bangar were sent back to India from South Africa because 'they did not fit in the "scheme of things"'.

To add to KKR's woes, Anupam Mukherji, a marketing specialist based in Bangalore, published a blog throughout the tournament. The blog targeted the cricketers, with special emphasis on the KKR camp, which led many to believe that he was a member of the squad.

The Knight Riders finished last that season.

VIRAT KOHLI AND ANIL KUMBLE, 2017

It all happened too fast, especially after Anil Kumble's stint as coach seemed to go smoothly for nine months. The first signs of a rift surfaced during the Dharamsala Test match of 2016/17 against Australia. Virat Kohli missed the match with an injury, and India gave Kuldeep Yadav a maiden Test cap—presumably against Kohli's wishes.

Exactly two months later, the BCCI announced their hunt for a new coach. This was unexpected, for Kumble's contract was for a year. Kumble reapplied along with several others. Kohli dismissed any talk of a rift, and the matter was temporarily tabled as India romped their way to the final of the Champions Trophy.

India left England for the West Indies two days after losing the final. Kumble did not board the flight. He resigned that evening.

MITHALI RAJ AND RAMESH POWAR, 2018

India faced a strange predicament during the 2018 World T20 Cup—of finding a role for Mithali Raj. India wanted power hitters at the top for the Powerplay and in the death overs, and she was not one. She was a big scorer, probably the greatest women's cricket has seen, but slogging was not her forte.

Thus, she was not among the seven Indians who got a chance to bat against New Zealand. Promoted to the top, she got serene fifties against Pakistan and Ireland, the weakest teams in the group. She was named Player of the Match in both matches. And then she was left out against Australia—she had injured her knee while fielding—and in the semi-final against England. India lost the last match.

At a glance this feels counterintuitive, but in Raj's case, she did not fit into India's scheme of things. She wrote a letter to the BCCI, accusing Powar of bias. Powar, in turn, accused Raj of 'blackmailing' coaches. Later that month, T20I captain Harmanpreet Kaur and vice-captain Smriti Mandhana voiced their support for Powar.

Powar's five-month stint as coach ended shortly afterwards. He was replaced by W.V. Raman, but got his job back in May 2021. Powar and Raj do not bear grudges.

HOWZZAT!

In 1897, K.S. Ranjitsinhji became the first Indian to be named a Wisden Cricketer of the Year. The first to win that honour while representing India was C.K. Nayudu, in 1933.

Coats, Caps and Bails
Indian Umpires

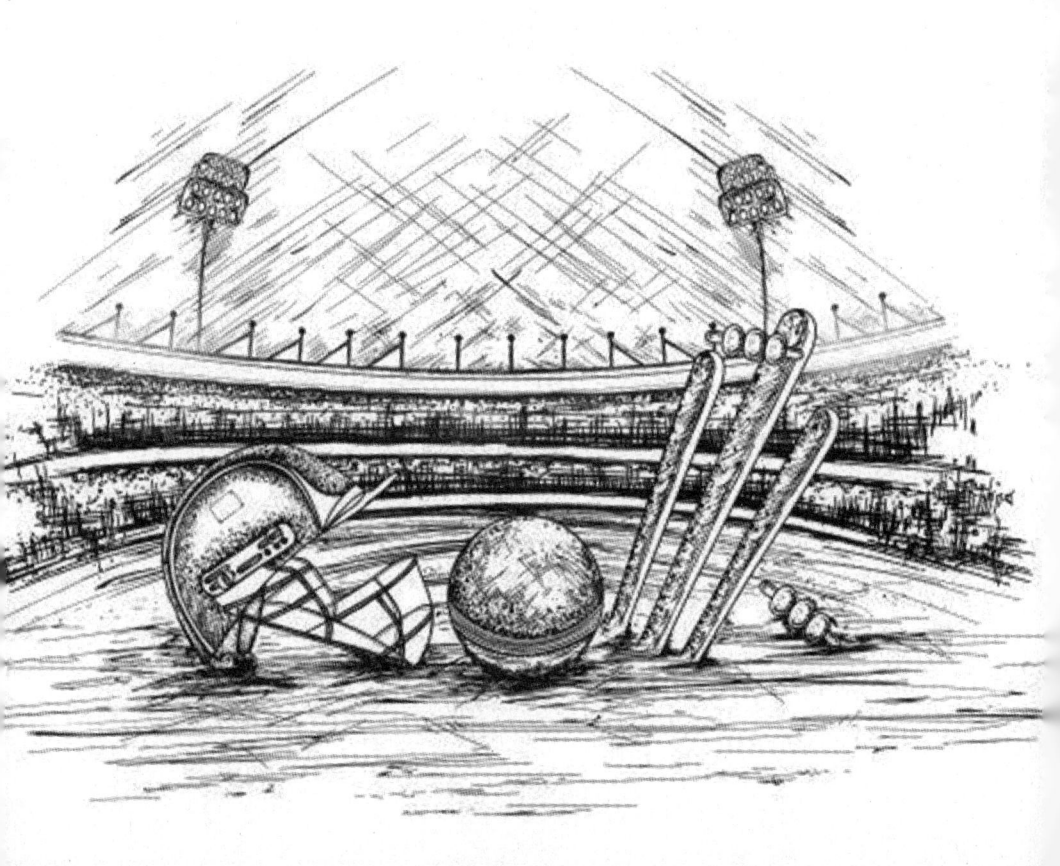

Few jobs in cricket are as lonely or thankless as the umpire's. Unlike a great delivery or shot or catch, an excellent umpiring decision is seldom appreciated. If anything, the advancement of technology has made the on-field umpire even more vulnerable.

India hosted their first Test series back in 1933/34. Of the three umpires, Frank Tarrant was an Australian, while Bill Hitch and John Higgins were British; Indian umpires were not considered. That changed in independent India's first home series, against the West Indies in 1948/49. In that series, Dattatreya Naik and Jamshed Patel became the first Indian Test umpires in Delhi.

Here are some unusual facts about Indian umpires.

ALL IN THE FAMILY, 1933/34 AND 1960/61

Frank Tarrant played first-class cricket for thirty-seven years across three countries. In India, he is known most for his role in Patiala cricket. In 1933/34, he also stood in as umpire in the first two Test matches on Indian soil as well as six other matches. One of these six matches was between Southern Punjab and the touring MCC (England) side. The other umpire in that match was Frank's son Louis.

In 1960/61, M.G. Vijayasarathi (8 Tests between 1951/52 and 1959/60) and his son M.V. Nagendra (11 Tests, 1963/64 to 1976/77), both distinguished umpires in the domestic circuit, officiated together in a Ranji Trophy match between Mysore and Andhra in 1960/61 at Bangalore.

DUAL MISCALCULATION, 1948/49

There is some truth to the claim that Anant Ramchandra 'Bapu' Joshi prevented India from winning their first ever Test match, against West Indies at Bombay in 1948/49.

India were set a target of 361. This was the last Test of the series, and they were 0-1 down, so they decided to go for it. The target came down to 6 runs in 7 balls. A minute and a half remained in the match, so there was enough time to start an over after that final ball.

At this point Joshi miscalculated and called 'over', but that was not all. In the heat of the moment, he also misread the time and took the bails off, declaring a draw. The West Indies celebrated amidst boos from the crowd.

APPEAL AND ENCORE, 1969/70

Sudhir Naik was out caught behind off the first ball of the Calcutta Test match 1974/75 off Andy Roberts. That allowed debutant umpire Har Prasad Sharma to achieve the rare distinction of raising his finger off the first ball of *his* Test career.

But Sharma had also had a forgettable moment five years before that, when the touring Australians were playing North Zone in Jalandhar. He had ruled Vinay Lamba not out when John Gleeson appealed for caught behind. The Australians, led by stand-in captain Ian Chappell, did not give up. They had another go a few seconds later. This time the entire team appealed in unison, irrespective of their fielding positions. Sharma changed his decision.

Decades later, in 2001/02, H.P. Sharma's son Surinder ruled Marcus Trescothick leg-before against Javagal Srinath in an ODI at the Eden Gardens. It was a decision so ridiculous that he was slammed even by the *Indian* media.

SAMBHU, PANNED, 1969/70

During the Bombay Test match of the same tour, umpire Sambhu Pan ruled S. Venkataraghavan caught behind off Alan Connolly. It was an error—even Brian Taber, who caught the ball, admitted so—but Venkat walked back.

It could have been just another forgotten umpiring error had Devraj Puri not voiced his opinion on All India Radio. Many in the crowd had carried transistor sets and after being cramped all day in sub-par facilities in heat and humidity, with an Indian defeat looming, they now erupted. Chairs were smashed, the stand was set on fire. Play continued amidst fire and near-opaque smoke, but not for long.

LUNCH-TABLE APOLOGY, 1976/77

M.V. Nagendra had already entered the record books when he stood alongside his father, M.G. Vijayasarathi, in a first-class match. In the Bangalore Test match of 1976/77, he ruled Mike Brearley out caught by Gundappa Viswanath at slip off Bhagwat Chandrasekhar.

'There was not another pair of eyes on the ground who thought it had carried,' reported *The Times*. A few years later, Viswanath would famously recall Bob Taylor to the wicket—but on this occasion Brearley walked back, and lunch was called.

Then, as Brearley was having a peaceful meal, Nagendra approached him. 'Mr Brearley, I am very sorry. I knew it was not out, but I felt my finger going up and I just couldn't stop it.'

Brearley's response remains undocumented. Perhaps it was unprintable as well.

THE NEUTRALS, 1986/87

Although Pakistan was one of the strongest sides of the 1980s, touring teams did not hold Pakistani umpires in high esteem. The allegations were more about bias than competence. Tired of criticism, Pakistan captain Imran Khan arranged for neutral umpires during their home series of 1986/87 against the West Indies.

Thus, at Lahore, Piloo Reporter and V.K. Ramaswamy became the first neutral umpires in Test cricket since 1912.

THE BULLIED UMPIRE, 1987/88

India needed only 204 in the Nagpur ODI of 1987/88, but Patrick Patterson reduced them to 31/4. Dilip Vengsarkar stood firm until a ball from Winston Benjamin took his edge. Viv Richards caught and appealed, but umpire Rajan Mehra ruled Vengsarkar not out.

Richards turned to V. Vikramraju (of the Madras tied Test match fame) at square leg, who agreed with Mehra. But Richards did not give up. Things turned ugly, and, to quote *Wisden*, 'Richards's tantrum virtually coerced Mr Mehra into reversing his decision.'

NOT A WORD, 1994/95

During a Mumbai–Maharashtra Ranji Trophy match in Solapur in 1994/95, umpire Vinayak Kulkarni warned Mumbai fast bowler Abey Kuruvilla for stepping on the 'danger area'. Mumbai captain Sanjay Manjrekar challenged the decision, even quoting the law, but to no avail. Manjrekar's verbal response was not quite parliamentary. Kulkarni responded with a warning.

'I went up to Kulkarni and needled him again,' Manjrekar later confessed. Kulkarni ended up setting a rare instance by 'banishing' a cricketer—that, too, a captain!—for abusive language.

All this took place in the first session of the day. After lunch, Kulkarni asked acting captain Sameer Dighe about Manjrekar's absence. 'You only sent him off, sir,' Dighe replied. Kulkarni explained that the ban had been for a session, no more.

HOW'S HAT?, 1997/98

Ajay Jadeja edged Chaminda Vaas that day in Margao, during the third ODI of Sri Lanka's tour of India. The deflection was visible to the naked eye, leaving little doubt about the dismissal once Romesh Kaluwitharana caught the ball and appealed. Umpire Raman Sharma raised his finger, Jadeja took his first step back to the pavilion—and then, to the shock of everyone present, Sharma merely adjusted his hat with said finger and lowered his hand. Jadeja stayed put.

The act was so amateurish that all Sri Lankan captain Arjuna Ranatunga—never hesitant to take something up with the umpires—managed was a grin.

Later in the day, Sharma turned down a run out appeal against Kaluwitharana—and changed his mind again, referring to the third umpire. Sunil Gavaskar took a dig at Sharma on air, mocking his 'consistency'.

PIONEERS, 2020

In March 2020, umpires N. Janani of Chennai and Vrinda Rathi of Mumbai became the first Indian women to be inducted into the International Panel of ICC Development Umpires. They joined G.S. Lakshmi, who had already been in the ICC panel as a match referee.

Janani broke another barrier in June 2022, when she stood in a men's professional cricket match between the Salem Spartans and the Nellai Royal Kings in the Tamil Nadu Premier League.

HOWZZAT!

In the Golden Jubilee Test against England in 1979/80, Indian captain Gundappa Vishwanath recalled Bob Taylor after the umpire had declared him out. Taylor and Ian Botham went on to put up a 171-run partnership which won the game for England.

SOS
Famous Call-ups in Indian Cricket

Being called up for a cricket match or series is not too uncommon, but sometimes call-ups happen when you are least prepared. There have been several instances of this at all levels of cricket—though here we shall stick to the national team. The reasons behind these summons varied from genuine helplessness to poor management.

VINOO MANKAD RELEASED BY HASLINGDEN, 1952

In 1952, Vinoo Mankad sought assurance from C.K. Nayudu, then chair of selectors, that he would be picked for the upcoming tour of England. When Nayudu refused, Mankad went ahead and signed a contract with Haslingden in the Lancashire League.

India were blown away in the first Test match at Headingley. In the second innings, they lost 4 wickets before scoring a single run. The team sent an SOS to Haslingden: they wanted Mankad for the Test matches. The club agreed for a sum of GBP 300, a substantial amount given the era. Mankad celebrated his return by scoring 72 and 184 and picking up 5 wickets at Lord's.

HEMU ADHIKARI SUMMONED FROM ARMY CAMP, 1958/59

India had already drawn 1 and lost 3 matches in the 5-match series against West Indies in the winter if 1958/59. Worse, they had had to play under three different captains for these matches. Now, to lead this battered, bruised team, they needed someone else.

Hemu Adhikari had been doing well, but had not played a Test match in over two years. He was posted in Dharamsala on Army duty. The authorities somehow managed to get Adhikari's seniors in the Army to 'order' him to go and take charge of the national side.

That was the first—and only—time Adhikari led India. He scored 63 and 40, picked up 3 wickets, helped his team draw the Test match—and never played for India again.

ABBAS ALI BAIG LEAVES OXFORD TO SAVE INDIA, 1959

India had lost the first three Tests of their England tour of 1959, and were hit further by an injury to their star batter, Vijay Manjrekar. The team management called up a twenty-year-old Hyderabadi student who was studying in Oxford and scoring runs for the university team.

Up against a target of 548, Abbas Ali Baig scored a dazzling 112 despite being hit on the temple by Harold Rhodes. Until 2021, it remained the highest fourth-innings score by a Test debutant.

KRIPAL SINGH SWITCHES SIDES, 1963/64

A string of injuries and ailments had reduced the England camp to a hospital during the Bombay Test of 1963/64. They had exactly ten fit men, and commentator Henry Blofeld was put on standby. On the morning of the match, Micky Stewart, despite not being fit, announced that he would play.

India batted first, and by tea, Stewart had to return to the hospital. He took no further part in the Test series. England needed a fielder. In a magnanimous gesture, Indian captain Mansur Ali Khan Pataudi allowed Kripal Singh to field as a substitute *for* England.

BUDHI KUNDERAN ASSIGNED BIZARRE RESPONSIBILITY, 1967

The tables were turned when India toured England in 1967. For the third Test match in Edgbaston, India were without both their opening bowlers, Subrata Guha and Sadanand Mohol. India were forced to play all of their famed spin quartet. Venkataraman Subramanya, a batting all-rounder and the only other man who could bowl seam, bowled the first over of the Test match. But who would open bowling at the other end?

A desperate Mansur Ali Khan Pataudi turned to Budhi Kunderan, the second wicketkeeper, playing as a batter in this Test match. When Pataudi had asked Kunderan *what* he bowled, the answer was a simple 'I don't know.' Kunderan did take the new ball the next day at the other end. He bowled 4 overs—the only balls he bowled on that entire tour.

M.L. JAISIMHA, NOT QUITE LIKE-FOR-LIKE, 1967/68

India were 0–2 down in the four-match Test series in Australia. When Bhagwat Chandrasekhar was injured, everyone expected the team management to ask for a leg-spinner or a spinner—a bowler at the very least. Instead, to bolster the batting, Mansur Ali Khan Pataudi summoned opening batter M.L. Jaisimha, Pataudi's teammate at Hyderabad.

Jaisimha, who had played some cricket until then, faced Devraj Govindraj in the grounds of the State Bank of India for a couple of hours before hopping onto one plane after another. He then overcame jetlag to score 74 and 101.

MADAN LAL CALLED OVER TO PLAY TEST CRICKET, 1986

Chetan Sharma had destroyed England with 5–64 in the first Test of the 1986 tour at Lord's. When he was ruled out of the next match at Headingley, the obvious move would have been to draft in Manoj Prabhakar. Instead, captain Kapil Dev asked for Madan Lal, who had been playing for Ashton in the Lancashire League.

Batting at nine, Madan scored 20 and 22 in a low-scoring Test match. Opening bowling, he took quick wickets in the first innings to finish with 3–18. With Sharma fit for the third Test match, Madan returned to the Lancashire League.

SUNIL GAVASKAR STEPS IN TO TAKE CHARGE, 1994

India finished second in their group to qualify for the semi-finals of the 1994 Austral-Asia Cup in Sharjah. Unfortunately, team manager-cum-coach Ajit Wadekar suffered from a heart attack ahead of the semi-final against Australia.

Sunil Gavaskar, on commentary duty for the tournament, filled in as manager. India beat Australia easily before losing to Pakistan in the final.

TENDULKAR FLIES HALFWAY ACROSS THE WORLD, 1998

In September 1998, the BCCI demonstrated a classic example of poor planning. When the Sahara Cup—a 5-match India–Pakistan ODI series in Toronto—coincided with the Commonwealth Games in Kuala Lumpur, Pakistan decided to send a full-strength team to Canada and the best of the rest to Malaysia. India, on the other hand, split their best cricketers into what they probably thought were two groups of equal strength.

In Kuala Lumpur, India lost to a nearly full-strength Australia and never made it to the semi-finals. Their campaign ended on 15 September. By then, the Sahara Cup was level 1–1. Utter chaos reigned thereafter, for the planning that should have been in place before the tournaments commenced began after 15 September.

India wanted to reinforce the squad in Canada with Sachin Tendulkar, Ajay Jadeja, Anil Kumble and Robin Singh—all of whom had toured Malaysia. The Pakistan Cricket Board were in no mood to agree: they cited the laws, which clearly mentioned that a team became eligible for replacements only in case of injuries or illnesses.

Eventually they agreed to only Tendulkar and Jadeja, though by then Pakistan had taken a 2–1 lead. It is not clear why Pakistan had issues with only two of the four players. Jadeja made it in time for the fourth match though India lost that one as well. Tendulkar, unaware of all this, was vacationing with his family, and could only play the fifth ODI. It was an exercise in futility, for Pakistan had already taken an unassailable 3–1 lead. They won the series 4–1.

R.P. SINGH CUTS VACATION SHORT, 2011

One would expect Indian cricket to have evolved into a professional outfit by 2011. However, that year, India had been trailing 0–3 in the Test series and were hit by a string of injuries. For the 'dead rubber' fourth Test, they called up R.P. Singh, who had not played Test cricket in over three years and had been vacationing in Miami. Munaf, though in the squad, did not play the match.

The inevitable happened. M.S. Dhoni asked a 'cheerfully overweight' Singh to bowl the first over of the Test match. Singh looked far from match fit from the first ball, which was slow and wide down the leg side. He bowled 34 overs without looking remotely threatening, and never played Test cricket again.

THE COVID-19 ERA REPLACEMENTS

India had to field twenty men over the course of the 2021/22 Test series in Australia for a gamut of reasons. At least two of them—Washington Sundar and T. Natarajan—had come on the tour for the shorter formats that took place ahead of the Test series. They had stayed on as net bowlers, and were drafted into the Test squad when the frontline cricketers were hit by injuries. In the pre-quarantine era, there would have been enough time for India to fly out replacements.

India were hit worse during their 2021 tour of Sri Lanka, where they sent a second-string side to begin with. The ODI series went ahead without a hitch, as did the first T20 International of the three-match series. Then Krunal Pandya tested positive for COVID-19, and he had to be quarantined along with eight of his 'close contacts'.

With nine players unavailable, India had to resort to desperate measures. They had little option but to include all five net bowlers—Ishan Porel, Sandeep Warrier, Arshdeep Singh, R. Sai Kishore and Simarjeet Singh—to the squad. Of them, Warrier played in the third T20I.

HONOURABLE MENTION: LATA MANGESHKAR STEPS UP

After India won the 1983 World Cup, BCCI president N.K.P. Salve announced a bonus of INR 1 lakh for each member of the squad. It sounded excellent on paper, but there was a catch: the board did not have that kind of money. For perspective, Kapil Dev admitted he had never seen a cheque worth that amount until then.

Salve—as we have seen elsewhere in this book—was not someone who backed down on promises. He turned to his friend Raj Singh Dungarpur, who reached out to *his* friend Lata Mangeshkar. An ardent cricket fan herself, she did a two-hour concert at the Jawaharlal Nehru Stadium that was attended by, among others, the triumphant cricketers.

The target was reached. The BCCI could pay the cricketers the amount Salve had promised. The BCCI never forgot Lata Mangeshkar's contribution. Until her death in 2022, she was entitled to two VIP passes for every international match played by India on home soil.

HONOURABLE MENTION: CHARU SHARMA RESPONDS TO CLARION CALL

Auctioneer Hugh Edmeades collapsed during the IPL 2022 auctions held at the ITC Gardenia, Bengaluru. IPL chair Brijesh Patel immediately contacted Charu Sharma, who had some experience of auctions, and more importantly, lived 'fifteen minutes from the hotel'.

Despite the short notice, Sharma conducted the remainder of the auctions without a glitch. Edmeades made an appearance in the end amidst loud applause.

HOWZZAT!

On 17 March 1962, Indian captain Nari Contractor suffered a career-ending head injury from a bouncer bowled by West Indies fast bowler Charlie Griffith. Sir Frank Worrell was the first player to donate blood to the injured Contractor, which saved his life. In remembrance of this act, the Cricket Association of Bengal organizes a blood donation drive on 3 February, the Association's Foundation Day, every year. Since 1981, the day has been celebrated as Frank Worrell Day.

Commercial Gain
Iconic Advertisements in Indian Cricket

Cricketers are celebrated around the world, but India is perhaps the only country where they are as glamorous as movie actors and as recognized as political leaders. Nowhere in the world does everything come to a standstill when the national side plays a cricket match. It is perhaps natural then that cricket and cricketers would feature in commercials.

The list of commercials is long. Here are the most iconic ones.

BOMBAY QUADRANGULAR, *JAWANI KI HAWA*

The Bombay Talkies had acquired the rights (!) for the 1935/36 edition of the Bombay Quadrangular, and showed clips from the match during their first movie, *Jawani-ki-Hawa*, starring the founders, Himanshu Rai and Devika Rani.

The studio promoted the tournament exclusively. During the tenth week of the movie's run, a newspaper advertisement proclaimed: 'In every show, a film of the Cricket matches by Bombay Talkies Ltd, is being shown exclusively at the Cinema along with "Jawani-ki-Hawa".'

SYED MUSHTAQ ALI, BOURNVITA

The Bengali print advertisement of Cadbury's Bournvita appeared—among other places—in the 1938 Eid edition of *Mohammadi*, and is usually accepted as the oldest to feature an Indian Test cricketer. The tagline ran *Poripurno Jibonishoktir Jonyo* ('For a Life Full of Vitality'). Endorsing the brand was the swashbuckling Mushtaq Ali, who had become the first Indian batter to score an overseas Test hundred two years ago.

C.K. NAYUDU FOR BATHGATE & CO. CHEMISTS

C.K. Nayudu, Mushtaq's captain at both Holkar and India, appeared in an advertisement for Bathgate's Liver Tonic. In the advertisement, which mentions a specific date (26 March 1941) and place (Indore), Nayudu claims, among other things, to have 'found that a morning dose of Bathgate's Liver Tonic banishes sluggishness'.

THE BRYLCREEM BOYS

From Denis Compton to Keith Miller to Fazal Mahmood, hair styling brand Brylcreem had a penchant for adopting cricketers as models. Vinoo Mankad—as his son Rahul confirmed—was the first Indian they signed up, followed by G.S. Ramchand and Subhash Gupte.

However, the most popular Indian face of Brylcreem at the time was Farokh Engineer. In the new millennium, the brand signed up M.S. Dhoni as well.

SUNIL GAVASKAR FOR DINESH

In the 1970s and 1980s, cricket fans would turn up outside Sunil Gavaskar's house for *darshan*. He became an easy favourite among brands—in print and, since its advent, television. From Thums Up to Air India to Sentry Soap to Iodex to Cherry Blossom, Gavaskar was ubiquitous. He even featured with son Rohan in a Forhans toothpaste commercial that promoted them as 'the superfighters'.

Indian cricketers had endorsed products before that, but Gavaskar became Indian cricket's first supermodel. To quote Mansur Ali Khan Pataudi, Gavaskar 'opened up entire new vistas of making money'.

Despite this plethora of products, it was Dinesh Suiting that became synonymous with Brand Gavaskar—to the extent that Krishna Kumar, a fan, named his son not Sunil but Dinesh. It was only fitting that Dinesh Karthik caused quite a stir with his singular wardrobe.

SUNIL GAVASKAR AND IMRAN KHAN FOR THUMS UP

Pakistan toured India in 1986/87. Seizing the opportunity, Thums Up paired Gavaskar and Imran Khan, then captain of Pakistan, in an advertisement with the tagline 'Unbeaten partnership'. An advertisement like that would be unthinkable today. Roughly around the same time, Imran also appeared as a model for Cinthol.

KAPIL DEV FOR PALMOLIVE AND BSA SLR

Kapil Dev's rise in the early 1980s gave brands a serious rival to Gavaskar. The difference in how the two legends were perceived, consciously or otherwise, was interesting. While Gavaskar was signed up by suiting brands and airlines, Kapil endorsed a Rapidex English Speaking course.

Before Kapil's *'Palmolive da jawaab nahin'* became one of the most popular television advertisement taglines of the period, the brand had come up with the equally memorable 'As Sunil Gavaskar was perfecting his square drive, Palmolive was perfecting his shaving'.

Later in the decade, BSA SLR bicycles launched a full-fledged one-page comic strip that often appeared in newspapers and Indrajal Comics. Kapil's taxi breaks down en route to the airport. He borrows a bicycle from a young woman to make it in time and catch the flight. At the post-match presentations, he thanks 'a sweet little friend but for whose help I would have missed the match'.

SEVERAL CRICKETERS IN MILE SUR MERA TUMHARA

Doordarshan telecast the iconic *'Mile sur mera tumhara'* for the first time on 15 August 1988. The music video was developed by the Lok Seva Sanchar Parishad to promote unity in diversity across the nation. It featured—among other famous Indians—cricketers E.A.S. Prasanna, S. Venkataraghavan, Narendra Hirwani, Arun Lal, Chuni Goswami (known more for his football) and Diana Edulji.

Edulji had raised her voice against discrimination against female cricketers in commercials in 1984. Of course, her appearance in the video might have been a coincidence.

KAPIL DEV AND SACHIN TENDULKAR FOR BOOST

There have been ensemble casts in advertisements, but seldom has one featured two legends from different generations. Soon after Kapil Dev and Sachin Tendulkar paired up for a double-wicket tournament, Boost, the popular health drink for children, brought them together. After Tendulkar delivers the famous 'Boost is the secret of my energy' tagline, Kapil signs off with 'Our energy.'

Over the years, Tendulkar would emerge as the hottest property in Indian advertisements.

SEVERAL CRICKETERS FOR PEPSI'S AMBUSH MARKETING

Coca-Cola bagged the official sponsorship of the 1996 World Cup held in the subcontinent, but rivals Pepsi outsmarted them with an excellent ambush marketing campaign, running a string of commercials with the tagline 'Nothing official about it'. Along with Mohammad Azharuddin and Sachin Tendulkar, the series featured Courtney Walsh, Ian Bishop, Dominic Cork and Dickie Bird as well as a collage with all six.

RAHUL DRAVID FOR REEBOK

In the second half of the 1990s, several brands came up with ideas to counter Brand Tendulkar. Reebok ran a campaign promoting Mohammad Azharuddin, Anil Kumble and Rahul Dravid. While Azhar's (The Assassin) and Kumble's (The Viper) monikers did not stick, Dravid's stood the test of time. He is referred to as 'The Wall' even today.

SACHIN TENDULKAR, SHANE WARNE AND CARL HOOPER FOR PEPSI

A teenage Tendulkar sprinted in Action Shoes to save a young Kunal Khemu. Two decades later, he strode out in Adidas gear to disprove that cricket was a 'young man's game'. The commercials Tendulkar has featured in deserve a separate book.

Ahead of the 1999 World Cup, Pepsi ran an advertisement where Shane Warne and Carl Hooper try to take advantage of Tendulkar's amnesia and convince him that he is a chef. They try to ship him to Honolulu, but Tendulkar tricks them instead, trapping the duo inside the aircraft and sending them off.

It was in this commercial that Tendulkar famously uttered *'Aila*, plane!' The expression *'Aila'* has been associated with him since, particularly by mimicry artists.

NATIONAL COMMISSION ON POPULATION

The National Commission on Population launched a birth control awareness programme during India's home series against England in 2001/02. Ranging from intelligent to cringeworthy, the taglines included ones like 'Little bouncers—no more please', 'No slips please, population control is not a laughing matter', and 'China stumped—India produced more babies in the last hour!'

SOURAV GANGULY FOR PEPSI

In 2006, Sourav Ganguly was dropped from the national side amidst much furore. In the same year, during the ICC Champions Trophy in India, he appeared in a most unusual advertisement for Pepsi where he introduced himself, mentioned his frustrations, assured the viewers of his being on a comeback trail, and requested his fans to join him in cheering the team.

The commercial added fuel to the murky Chappell–Ganguly controversy. Years later, Ganguly admitted that he had only agreed to it because—as a legal notice from the Pepsi team reminded him—it did not tarnish the image of Brand Ganguly.

JASPRIT BUMRAH FOR JAIPUR POLICE

Jasprit Bumrah had Fakhar Zaman caught behind in the 2017 Champions Trophy final only for the decision to be overturned when the television umpire spotted a no ball. Fakhar stayed put, scored 114, and Pakistan won the match by 180 runs.

Later that week, Jaipur Traffic Police used a photograph of the no ball on traffic rules awareness signboards with the message 'Don't cross the line, you know it can be costly'. Bumrah was not amused; the department clarified that it was not their intention to hurt anyone's sentiments.

THE 'OG' BAND, RAHUL DRAVID, ANIL KUMBLE AND JHULAN GOSWAMI FOR CRED

The advertisements of fintech organization Cred, featuring stars of the yesteryear, are perhaps more popular than their product. After running a series with former Bollywood stars, Cred released their Rahul Dravid commercial during the 2021 IPL where he yells at an old lady, smashes a side mirror with a cricket bat, and claims to be 'Indiranagar ka Gunda'.

Cred launched a second commercial during the same tournament, claiming their

Indiranagar ka Gunda

offers to be 'as rewarding as watching your favourite cricketers in a boy band'. The band in the commercial, featuring Venkatesh Prasad, Javagal Srinath, Maninder Singh and Saba Karim, is shown singing *We were the OGs*.

Cred later used Anil Kumble (who lamented, 'Only Dravid gets to have all the fun,' before signing off) and Jhulan Goswami ('Thank god, you are not doing my biopic').

HONOURABLE MENTION: DAIRY MILK COMMERCIALS

Piyush Pandey, a former Ranji Trophy player, created probably the most popular cricket-based commercial that did not involve any cricketers. It featured a batter on 99 hitting a six to bring up his hundred, and his girlfriend in the stands running out onto the field to celebrate while holding a Cadbury's Dairy Milk bar.

In 2021, Dairy Milk ran a similar commercial with the genders reversed.

HOWZZAT!

Indian captains Sourav Ganguly (in Lumley Castle, Durham, 2002) and M.S. Dhoni (in Langham Hotel, London, 2014) complained that their hotel rooms were haunted. Ganguly slept in Robin Singh's room, while Dhoni asked for a change of room.

And, Sold!
Facts about the IPL Auctions

The pre-season auction has been a salient feature of the Indian Premier League. Cricketers signing contracts or being picked in drafts is one thing; being sold at the auctions is another. Despite the players not being present in person, there have been cries of the entire concept being dehumanizing. However, the cricketers are themselves quite keen to sign up for the auctions, which attract considerable attention from all quarters.

AUCTIONING OF THE BUYERS

It all began on 24 January 2008, with the auctioning of the 8 franchises that featured in the first edition of the IPL. At USD 111.9 million, Mumbai became the costliest franchise: they were acquired by Reliance Industries. Bangalore (bought by Vijay Mallya's United Breweries Group for 111.6 million) and Hyderabad (Deccan Chronicle, 107 million) also crossed the 100-million-dollar mark.

ICONOLOGY

At this point, the IPL franchises were without strong local identities. To establish loyalty among local fans, they identified marquee cricketers who would receive 15 per cent more than the most expensive cricketer for their respective franchises. These 'icon cricketers' were Sachin Tendulkar (Mumbai), Sourav Ganguly (Kolkata), Rahul Dravid (Bangalore), V.V.S. Laxman (Hyderabad), Virender Sehwag (Delhi) and Yuvraj Singh (Chandigarh, Punjab). All of them became the first captains of their teams.

Laxman opted out of his 'icon' status, allowing the Deccan Chargers, the Hyderabad franchise, to spend more in the auctions. The Chargers duly spent USD 1.35 million on Andrew Symonds, the most expensive overseas cricketer of the year.

HOW IT ALL STARTED

The inaugural edition of the IPL featured two days of auctions, conducted by Richard Madley. The first, on 20 February at the Trident Hotel in Nariman Point, Mumbai, began with Shane Warne and M.S. Dhoni. They were acquired and appointed as captains by the Rajasthan Royals and the Chennai Super Kings, respectively, the two teams that made it to that year's final.

On 11 March 2008, there was a second round of auctions, followed by a draft of Indian Under-19 players. The latter consisted of the triumphant Indian team at that year's Under-19 World Cup in Malaysia and a sixteenth player: Viraj Kadbe.

Curiously, Pradeep Sangwan was picked by the Delhi Daredevils ahead of Virat Kohli, captain of the World Cup-winning side; Kohli went to the Royal Challengers Bangalore. Of the current IPL cricketers, Kohli remains the only one to have never featured in an auction.

Dimitri Mascarenhas, at that point without a central contract from the England and Wales Cricket Board, became the first English cricketer to get an IPL contract—from the Rajasthan Royals. Mohammad Yousuf, part of the rebel Indian Cricket League, went unsold after both rounds—but got his retainership amount as per the rules of the 2008 editions.

A BIZARRE CONFUSION

After the auctions, the franchises reached out to various Indian cricketers, with base prices set at USD 50,000 for Ranji Trophy players and USD 20,000 for others. As frantic scouting and acquisitions began, Delhi and Bangalore both claimed to have got Praveen Kumar, a star in the Commonwealth Bank Series in Australia in early 2008. It turned out that Bangalore had already signed him up for USD 300,000, but Delhi tried to better the offer. Bangalore raised a complaint and eventually acquired him.

Praveen bowled the first ball in IPL history to Sourav Ganguly.

ROYAL FINE

In the first edition of the IPL, the Rajasthan Royals invested in inexpensive, relatively unheralded cricketers like Yusuf Pathan, Ravindra Jadeja, Kamran Akmal, Swapnil Asnodkar, Munaf Patel,

Sohail Tanvir and Siddharth Trivedi. Despite that, they emerged as champions, losing only 3 of their 16 matches, and earned the moniker of the Moneyball Team.

Ironically, they had to cough up quite a bit of money before the tournament began. They had spent only USD 2.925 million, falling short of the cut-off of USD 3.3 million. They had to pay the difference (USD 375,000) to the IPL committee.

CRAZY BIDDING

The centrally contracted English cricketers became part of the IPL from 2009. At USD 1.55 million each, two Englishmen—Andrew Flintoff and Kevin Pietersen—were the most expensive players that season. However, theirs was not the surprise buy at that season's auctions.

There was frantic bidding between the Kings XI Punjab and the Kolkata Knight Riders over Bangladeshi seamer Mashrafe Mortaza. Kolkata eventually got him for USD 600,000, twelve times his base price of USD 50,000. On his IPL debut, Mortaza had to defend 21 off the last over against the Deccan Chargers. He conceded 26 to finish with 4-0-58-0. He never played another IPL match.

THE SILENT TIEBREAKER BID

For the 2010 auctions, the IPL committee put a cap of USD 750,000 on cricketers. This led to the obvious problem of a tie between multiple franchises that were interested in a particular cricketer. To resolve this, the IPL announced a secret bidding between franchises for cricketers who had reached cap price. The surplus amount would go to the IPL and not the cricketer.

The Mumbai Indians, thus, acquired Kieron Pollard for USD 2.75 million, while the Kolkata Knight Riders got Shane Bond for USD 1.3 million.

NO TAKERS FOR PAKISTANIS ... AND JADEJA

In the aftermath of the terrorist attacks in Mumbai on 26 November 2008, the franchise either terminated or suspended contracts of every Pakistani cricketer for the 2009 auctions. The Pakistanis returned in 2010, but this time no franchise was interested in them.

Ravindra Jadeja fared even worse, for he was not allowed to be part of the auction. Despite having signed a contract with the Rajasthan Royals until the 2010 season, he had been on the lookout for other opportunities after 2009 and had even exchanged contract documents with the Mumbai Indians. When this came to light, he was suspended for a year.

THE PRODIGAL SONS

In 2007, Subhash Chandra's rebel Indian Cricket League had lured many from Indian domestic cricket who were promptly banned by the BCCI. However, when the ICL dissolved, the cricketers accepted amnesty and found their way back into mainstream cricket. They were part of the 2010 IPL auctions, along with non-Indian ICL cricketers like Damien Martyn and Shane Bond.

THE MISSES

The 2011 auctions witnessed significant overhaul in squads for the first time, as franchises revamped their teams entirely, while two new teams—the Pune Warriors India and the Kochi Tuskers Kerala—entered the fray. While retaining or buying back some players, the squads became unrecognizable from their 2010 versions.

The Kolkata Knight Riders released Sourav Ganguly, and got Gautam Gambhir to lead them. Not retained by the Royal Challengers Bangalore, Rahul Dravid went on to lead the Rajasthan

Royals. Yuvraj Singh went from the Kings XI Punjab to the Pune Warriors India.

Ganguly was one of the marquee cricketers who went unsold in 2011. He was eventually acquired by (and led) Pune, but that was only after Ashish Nehra was ruled out with an injury. Another unsold cricketer, Chris Gayle, went to the Royal Challengers Bangalore after Dirk Nannes opted out. Gayle won the Orange Cap that season, and again in 2012.

Brian Lara was not as fortunate. Probably the greatest cricketer of his generation, Lara never played in the IPL. What if he had batted alongside Tendulkar for the Mumbai Indians?

A BOYCOTT

Two new franchises—Kochi Tuskers Kerala and Pune Warriors India—were introduced in the IPL in 2011. The Kochi franchise was disbanded after their first season, and the players were back in the auctions the next edition.

Yuvraj Singh was undergoing cancer treatment at that point and had opted out of the 2012 tournament. Pune wanted his value—USD 1.8 million—to be available to them at the auctions. When the BCCI refused, Pune not only boycotted the auctions but also threatened to pull out of the IPL.

They eventually played, but not after 2013.

A CHANGE IN CURRENCY

Until 2013, the IPL auction prices were listed in US dollars, with the amount in Indian rupees mentioned for reference. That changed in 2014: the Indian rupee became the default currency at the auctions.

MORE DRAFTS

The Chennai Super Kings and the Rajasthan Royals were suspended for the 2016 and 2017 editions of the IPL. They were replaced by the Rising Pune Supergiants and the Gujarat Lions. Ahead of the 2016 auctions, the two teams participated in a draft, where each team could pick at most five players from the pool of former Chennai and Rajasthan cricketers.

While Pune opted for M.S. Dhoni (who would lead them that season), Ajinkya Rahane, R. Ashwin, Steven Smith and Faf du Plessis, Gujarat backed Suresh Raina (they would name him captain), Ravindra Jadeja, Brendon McCullum, James Faulkner and Dwayne Bravo.

Two new teams—the Gujarat Titans and the Lucknow Super Giants—entered the fray in 2022. Ahead of that season's mega-auctions, they attended a draft. While Gujarat got Hardik Pandya, Shubman Gill and Rashid Khan, Lucknow opted for K.L. Rahul, Ravi Bishnoi and Marcus Stoinis.

IDENTITY CRISIS

Harmeet Singh had played for India Under-19 and in the IPL. In 2017, he drove a car on a train station platform in Andheri, and was promptly arrested. ANI News tweeted the story, but with an error: they used 'Harpreet' as the name of the cricketer.

Now, Harpreet Singh had also played for India Under-19 as well as in the IPL, and had registered for the 2017 auction, which took place shortly after ANI's error. By then, Harpreet's name had been all over the internet.

When *The Indian Express* probed, 'a franchise official' admitted to not picking Harpreet to prevent the franchise getting 'a bad image'.

ANI issued a clarification, but it was too late. Harpreet did return to the IPL in 2023, a full eleven seasons after his last IPL appearance. The broadcasters refer to him as Harpreet Bhatia these days, which may not be a coincidence.

THE RESCUE ACT

After a long stint, Richard Madley made way for Hugh Edmeades as IPL auctioneer in 2019. Edmeades had three successful years. Then, on the first day of the 2022 edition, he collapsed during the auctions. Former commentator Charu Sharma responded to the crisis on SOS basis and took over as auctioneer. Edmeades made an appearance in the end amidst loud applause.

HOWZZAT!

Pakistan included their seven-foot-one fast bowler Mohammad Irfan—the tallest international cricketer—for an ODI in 2012/13. As a result, the Eden Gardens authorities had to raise the sight screens, and cordon off several rows of seats for the first time at the historic venue.

What Do They Know of IPL Who Only IPL Know?

There is little doubt that the Indian Premier League, Lalit Modi's 'recession-proof product', changed the structure of cricket. Cricketers have been known to turn their backs on international contests now and then, but never on official leagues which are run by every cricket board in the world.

ONSITE PROJECT

Royal Challengers Bangalore were the first IPL franchise to sign up cheerleaders. They got on board the troupe of the Washington Redskins (now the Washington Commanders), an NFL team.

The cheerleaders became part of cricket history at the M. Chinnaswamy Stadium when they performed at the inauguration ceremony of the first ever IPL, in 2008, along with Shankar Mahadevan—an unusual example of Americans working 'onsite' in India.

WHAT'S IN A NAME?

Ahead of the first season of the IPL, at least three teams changed their name. Co-owner Shah Rukh Khan initially wanted to name his Kolkata-based franchise the 'Ball Breakers'. Thankfully, he was talked out of it. The team was eventually named after the 1980s American television series, *Knight Rider*.

Mumbai wanted to be 'Razors' before becoming Indians at the request of their icon player, Sachin Tendulkar. However, their logo still features a wheel-blade. And Delhi eventually chose Daredevils over 'Sultans'.

In 2010, the new Kochi-based franchise owners decided to call their team the 'Indi Commandos'. This resulted in severe criticism on social media, for every IPL team in history has included a city, a state or—like the Deccan Chargers—a zone in their name. The owners then ran a poll on their website, where the voters had to choose one word between Kochi and Kerala, and a second from Titans, Commandos, Tigers, Tuskers, Heroes and United. While

Tuskers won by a clear margin, the owners retained both Kerala and Kochi.

The Pune franchise that played in 2016 and 2017 went by the name Supergiants. After they finished seventh in the first season, the Rising Pune Supergiants dropped the 's' at the end of their name. It somehow favoured their cause: they reached the final, where they lost to Mumbai by 1 run.

In December 2018, the Delhi Daredevils switched to being the Capitals, triggering an instant change in fortune. Having finished in the bottom three in five consecutive seasons, Delhi made it to the top three 2019, 2020 and 2021.

No such fate befell the Kings XI Punjab, who became the Punjab Kings in 2021. They finished sixth in the next two editions.

CATCH 'EM!

Ahead of the 2008 edition, all 8 IPL franchises were assigned catchment areas, from which they had to select a minimum of 4 cricketers. These were mostly based on proximity to the home venues of the teams.

The Mumbai Indians, for example, were assigned all of Maharashtra—in other words, the Ranji Trophy teams of Mumbai, Maharashtra and Vidarbha. However, there were exceptions, because the teams were not uniformly distributed across India. Madhya Pradesh, for example, was assigned to the Delhi Capitals, Railways to the Chennai Super Kings, and Services to the Royal Challengers Bangalore.

The Kings XI Punjab's catchment area included Kashmir, Jammu, Himachal Pradesh, Punjab and Haryana, as indicated by their original logo which bore the acronym KJHPH.

SOME HEROES WEAR CAPS

A week into the first edition of the IPL, Brendon McCullum of the Kolkata Knight Riders was awarded the Orange Cap, a rolling in-tournament award for the leading run-scorer of each edition. The cap would change 'heads' if someone else usurped the top spot. Soon afterwards, a Purple Cap was announced for the leading wicket-taker. The colours were chosen with care, for they did not appear on the jerseys of any of the 8 franchises.

However, from 2010, the Kolkata Knight Riders went from black to purple at the behest of co-owner Juhi Chawla, who thought black was inauspicious (the franchise had finished last in 2009). And Sunrisers Hyderabad have been donning orange since their inaugural season, in 2013.

ENDGAME STRATEGIES

The first three editions of the IPL featured two semi-finals and a final. In addition to that, IPL 2010 also had a third-place decider match. However, this did not reward teams for finishing at the top in the league stage. To combat this, the organizers revamped the final stage by incorporating the Page Playoff System—a feature of the Australian Rugby League Championship from 1954 to 1972—from 2011.

In the IPL Playoffs, the top two teams now played in Qualifier 1, the winner of which went directly to the final. The losing side got a second chance, in Qualifier 2, where they played the winner of the Eliminator, a match between the third- and fourth-placed sides.

IT'S A FAKE!

The Kolkata Knight Riders had a dismal campaign in 2009, replete with controversies and a bottom-of-the-table finish. The Fake IPL

Player—an anonymous (at that point) blogger—merely added fuel to the fire. The blog became one of the most-followed websites during the IPL, registering up to 1,50,000 simultaneous visitors.

Throughout the season, the blog published unflattering content about cricketers, mostly those from the Knight Riders camp, triggering numerous speculations about the identity of the blogger. The Kolkata franchise slammed it as 'poison pen of the dirtiest variety, but far too many factual errors'.

In 2010 Anupam Mukherji, a Bangalore-based marketing specialist, owned up to being the person behind the blog. He also admitted that he had made up the stories.

DAWN OF A NEW ERA

The first decade of the new millennium saw the expansion of broadband internet connection in India, but *legal* live streaming of cricket matches was virtually unheard of. That changed in 2010, when the IPL became the first cricket tournament in history to be streamed live on YouTube. While there was a five-minute lag compared to the television coverage, the user could watch live cricket free of cost.

The idea caught on. As smartphones flooded the Indian market and internet became cheaper, faster and mobile, live streaming—albeit paid—provided serious competition to television channels.

CRICKET MARCHES ON

On 16 April 2010, the US State Department issued the following travel alert: 'The U.S. Government continues to receive information that terrorist groups may be planning attacks in India.'

Oblivious to this, a packed house turned up to watch the Royal Challengers Bangalore host the Mumbai Indians at M.

Chinnaswamy Stadium the next afternoon. Two bombs exploded inside the ground before the match, injuring at least fifteen people and blowing away parts of a wall. A third bomb was diffused.

Yet, the match was played in its entirety, albeit after an hour's delay. However, organizers subsequently moved both semi-finals from Bengaluru to Navi Mumbai.

By the end of the year, the Bengaluru police made at least two major arrests.

THE LANKAN BAN

A conflict between the Sinhalese and Sri Lankan Tamils seemed imminent just before IPL 2013. Tamil Nadu Chief Minister J. Jayalalithaa expressed her concern about Sri Lankan cricketers playing in the home matches of the Chennai Super Kings at Chepauk to Prime Minister Manmohan Singh.

Soon after, the IPL committee barred Sri Lankan cricketers from playing at Chepauk that season. The other franchises protested, because some of them were more dependent on their Sri Lankan players than Chennai, despite the latter missing Nuwan Kulasekara and Akila Dananjaya. Delhi, for example, had Mahela Jayawardene and Jeevan Mendis; Kolkata had Sachithra Senanayake; Mumbai had Lasith Malinga; Pune had Ajantha Mendis and Angelo Mathews; Rajasthan had Kusal Perera; Bangalore had Muttiah Muralitharan and Tillakaratne Dilshan; and Hyderabad had Kumar Sangakkara and Thisara Perera.

But the decision stayed.

Things improved over the next decade. In 2023, Sri Lankan cricketers Maheesh Theekshana and Matheesha Pathirana played key roles in Chennai Super Kings' fifth IPL triumph.

IPL REACHES OUT

By 2015, the IPL had become a roaring success. Yet, fans across the vast nation had to remain content with watching the action on television—for the matches were restricted to a handful of venues.

That changed with the eighth edition, with the launch of the IPL Fanpark in other cities. The weekend matches, often double headers, and Playoffs were telecast live on giant screen inside stadia. The entry was free, and on first-come-first-serve basis.

The first edition featured 15 venues, and was a hit. Despite the break caused by COVID-19, as of 2023, the count is up to forty-five.

CRICKET CRISIS

In 2016, the Maharashtra government declared a drought in the state. Following this, the Lok Satta Movement filed a petition, requesting to shift all matches of IPL 2016 outside Mumbai, Pune and Nagpur.

On 13 April—four days after the Mumbai Indians hosted the Rising Pune Supergiants at Wankhede Stadium—the Bombay High Court ordered all IPL matches to be moved from the three venues to 'some other state where water is in abundance'.

The BCCI first assured that they would be using tankers for water, then petitioned the Supreme Court, even as Mumbai and Pune continued to host matches. On 27 April, the Supreme Court stayed the High Court's order and ordered 13 matches to be moved outside Maharashtra.

Mumbai's initial choice, Jaipur, was far from ideal, as Rajasthan had also been hit by drought that year. The Rajasthan High Court stepped in then … the Maharashtra matches were finally played in Visakhapatnam, Mohali, Bengaluru and Delhi.

UNITY IN DIVERSITY

Unlike previous editions, each of which began with a single, grand opening ceremony, the 2017 IPL had one ahead of the first match at each ground. Thus, Hyderabad, Pune, Rajkot, Indore, Bengaluru, Mumbai, Kolkata and Delhi had separate ceremonies with separate performances.

EXPRESS MEASURES

After being banned from IPL 2016 and 2017, the Chennai Super Kings returned in 2018 to win their third title. However, just after the season got underway, the Kaveri Water Protests triggered a controversy in the city. There were calls to move the matches way from the city. Nagapattinam legislator M. Thamimun Ansari even threatened to arrest the cricketers.

Chennai beat the Kolkata Knight Riders at Chepauk amidst all this, but the next day, the Madras High Court put a stay order on all matches in Chepauk. Chennai had to play the rest of their home matches in Pune.

The Chennai team management, eager to have their loyal fans at the stadium, arranged for special trains to ferry them from Chennai to Pune. Over a thousand fans boarded the first of these—affectionately called the Whistle Podu Express.

INDIAN EXPANSION LEAGUE

A two-month annual tournament led to a barren window of ten months. With the intention of making the months count, the IPL franchise owners began to acquire teams in other franchises. In the Caribbean Premier League, the Trinbago Knight Riders (the Trinidad & Tobago team), the Barbados Royals and the Saint

Lucia Kings now share owners with the Kolkata Knight Riders, the Rajasthan Royals and the Punjab Kings respectively.

When the International League T20 was launched in the UAE, the Knight Riders acquired the Abu Dhabi team, Delhi the Dubai Capitals and Mumbai the MI Emirates.

However, when Cricket South Africa announced the CSA T20 League, *all six teams* were bought by IPL franchises. The names—the Johannesburg Super Kings, MI Cape Town, the Pretoria Capitals, the Paarl Royals, Sunrisers Eastern Cape and RPSG Durban—are self-explanatory. Continuing with the trend, the Major League Cricket—in the USA—will feature Los Angeles Knight Riders, MI New York, and Texas Super Kings among its six teams. The GMR group, who own the Delhi Capitals, co-own the Seattle Orcas with Satya Nadella.

HOWZZAT!

Chandu Borde has played Test cricket with two generations of Mankads—with Vinoo in the 1958/59 Madras Test against the West Indies, and with Vinoo's son Ashok in Bombay against Australia in 1969/70.

Why This Book?

Indian cricket.

As much about triumphs and trophies as it is about the fans who fast for their favourite stars, queue in the rain or scorching heat outside ticket counters, and wait for hours outside team hotels just for one fleeting glimpse.

As much about mighty teams and masterful performances as it is it is about blunders and mess-ups that leave us fuming and laughing at the same time.

As much about the children playing in a park as it is about the quadragenarian passer-by swallowing their ego and asking to face just one ball.

As much about the superstars we see on billboards as it is about the teenager hoping that the sport will be their ticket out of poverty.

This book is a humble tribute to the curiously diverse, gloriously unpredictable, absurdly hilarious madhouse of Indian cricket.

A Note from the Authors

Separating facts from myths for the chapters dealing with numerical records and scorecards was challenging, but it was nothing compared to researching anecdotes which turned out to be an uphill task.

We have verified every fact in the book from as many sources as possible. When the sources contradicted each other, we made a mention of that as well.

The book is updated until 2022. However, in some (but not all) cases—our editors deserve all the credit for bearing with us—we added events from 2023.

Acknowledgements

R. Ashwin, for the support, the inspiration, and for finding time from a packed schedule to pen the preface.

Surojit Bhattacharjee, whose delightful illustrations brought this book to life; and Mohit Suneja and Saurav Das, for a cover that captures the soul of the book.

Diya Kar, who turned this dream book into reality. And Poulomi Chatterjee, who made sure it reached the finish line. Thanks for your faith, Poulomi, we didn't drop the ball this time!

Separating facts from myths has been a challenge throughout a book like this. It would not have been possible without the meticulous Shatarupa Ghoshal, who would keep asking questions until she was satisfied.

Abhishek and Joy

Joy Bhattacharjya, whose ping and subsequent call began this journey, over the course of which no question was too random, no factoid too mundane, and no topic not worth exploring. The collaboration has been a delight.

Acknowledgements

There is a saying in cricket circles that if B. Sreeram checks a fact, it remains checked. To add to that, he has always been a ping away, and is never annoyed irrespective of the hour. We shall quiz each other again on cricket with returns skewed in your favour (sigh), Sreeram, as they have been over two decades.

Arunabha Sengupta, university senior, friend, philosopher, guide, cricket rant listener, myth buster, and co-author of my first book.

Mayukh Ghosh, Sumit Gangopadhyay, Ankit Verma, Michael Jones—extraordinary researchers capable of excavating facts from sources I did not know existed.

Vijay Lokapally, whom I read growing up, and over the years, a go-to person for cricket questions: always patient, often with an indulging smile.

Sharda Ugra, an institution, and forever an inspiration.

My colleagues at Wisden, both India and the UK, for making work a delight. With you, I learn every day.

Shakuntala Khan Bhaduri and Prodipto Pal, for seeing me through the lowest ebbs of my life.

Suvasree Basu, Anushtup Sett, and members of the Sobuj Songho WhatsApp group (do not ask)—friends I have made over the years.

My parents, brother, and sister-in-law—for every moment of support over the years.

My daughter, who always believed I should write a book.

Koi, whose canine exuberance continues to border on the ridiculous.

And Rituparna Chatterjee, for making life, the universe, and everything better than they once used to be.

Abhishek

Acknowledgements

Abhishek Mukherjee. This is honestly his masterpiece. His prose is excellent, his facts are amazing, his research is bulletproof, and he has spared us his terrible puns. Now that's true dedication and self-control!

Indrani Lahiri and Sravani Banerjee, my doting sisters, whose senior member cards at British Council Library meant new cricket books every week.

Rohit Brijnath, Andy O'Brien, and the good folks at Sportsworld, for both the magazine and the annual Sportsworld Sports Quiz, the most anticipated event of our student lives. And all my amazing teammates, Debkumar, Jaideep, Angshuman, Jayaditya, Soumyadip, and Rathin.

Bhaskar Bhattacharya at BITV, who actually allowed me to create and present a cricket quiz in a news channel.

Lawrence Duffy and Peter Hutton, who let me continue that cricket quiz journey at IMG/TWI.

Dave Tully, who got me doing yet another cricket quiz for Star Sports, and Ray Hume, who changed my life at ESPN Star Sports. Ray, we have one more good project in us, I promise.

Jeet Banerjee, for getting me on an unforgettable seven-year journey with the KKR, and Dav Whatmore and Trevor Bayliss for ensuring I had something to show for all those years.

Harsha Bhogle, friend, guru, guardian angel. Yes, it's possible to be all three.

And Veena Venugopal, minder of 'its' and 'it's', and the reason I smile most of the time.

Joy

Bibliography

Books

Allen, David Rayvern, *Arlott: The Authorised Biography* (HarperCollins, 1996)
Apte, Madhav, *As Luck Would Have It – An Autobiography* (Global Cricket School, 2015)
Archer, Jeffrey, *A Quiver Full of Arrows* (Pan Macmillan, 1980)
Bamzai, Sandeep, *Guts and Glory: A Bombay Cricket Story* (Rupa, 2002)
Bandyopadhyay, Kausik, *Mahatma on the Pitch: Gandhi & Cricket in India* (Rupa, 2017)
Bose, Mihir, *A History of Indian Cricket* (André Deutsch, 2002)
Bose, Mihir, *A Maidan View* (Penguin Random House, 2006)
Bose, Mihir, *The Nine Waves* (Aleph, 2019)
Botham, Ian, *Beefy's Cricket Tales* (Simon & Schuster, 2014)
Brodribb, Gerald, *Hit for Six* (Heinemann, 1960)
Buruma, Ian, *Playing the Game* (Farrar, Straus and Giroux, 1991)
Butcher, Betty, *Ice-Cream With Chilli Powder* (B. Butcher, 1996)
Bhagat, Chetan, *The 3 Mistakes of My Life* (Rupa, 2008)
Bhatkal, Satyajit, *The Spirit of Lagaan* (Popular Prakashan, 2002)
Bhattacharjya, Joy and Bhattacharjya, Vivek, *Junior Premier League: The First XI* (Penguin Random House, 2014)

Bhogle, Harsha, *Azhar: The Authorised Biography of Mohammad Azharuddin* (Penguin Random House, 1995)

Bond, Ruskin, *Cricket for the Crocodile* (Puffin, 1986)

Bradman, Donald, *Farewell to Cricket* (Hodder & Stroughton, 1950)

Cashman, Richard, *Patrons, Players and the Crowd* (Orient Blackswan, 1980)

Chambers, Diana R., *The Star of India* (Penguin Random House, 2020)

Chand, Dhyan, *Goal!* (Sport & Pastime, 1952)

Chauhan, Anuja, *The Zoya Factor* (HarperCollins, 2008)

Das, Suprita, *Free Hit: The Story of Women's Cricket in India* (Harper Sport, 2018)

Doshi, Dilip, *Spin Punch* (Rupa, 1991)

Dev, Kapil, *Straight from the Heart: An Autobiography* (Laxmi Publications, 2003)

Foot, David, *Sunshine, Sixes and Cider: History of Somerset Cricket* (David & Charles, 1986)

Frith, David, *Bodyline Autopsy* (Aurum Press Ltd, 2003)

Frith, David, *Silence of the Heart: Cricket Suicides* (Mainstream Publishing, 2001)

Ganguly, Sourav and Bhattacharya, Gautam, *A Century is Not Enough* (Juggernaut, 2019)

Gavaskar, Sunil, *One-Day Wonders* (Rupa, 1986)

Gavaskar, Sunil, *Idols* (Rupa, 1983)

Gavaskar, Sunil, *Runs 'n' Ruins* (Rupa, 1984)

Gavaskar, Sunil, *Sunny Days* (Rupa, 1976)

Guha, Ramachandra, *A Corner of a Foreign Field: The Indian History of a British Sport* (Picador, 2003)

Guha, Ramachandra, *The States of Indian Cricket: Anecdotal Histories* (Permanent Black, 2005)

Hunte, Conrad, *Playing to Win* (Hodder & Stroughton, 1971)

Kidambi, Prashant, *Cricket Country: An Indian Odyssey in the Age of Empire* (Oxford University Press, 2019)

Laxman, V.V.S. and Kaushik, R, *281 and Beyond* (Amazon Publishing, 2018)

Lokapally, Vijay, *Driven: The Virat Kohli Story* (Bloomsbury, 2016)

Majumdar, Boria, *Eleven Gods and a Billion Indians* (Simon & Schuster, 2018)

Manjrekar, Sanjay, *Imperfect* (Harper Sport, 2017)

Man Singh, P.R., *Cricket Biryani* (Marine Sports, 2008)

Marqusee, Mike, *Slow Turn* (Cardinal Friends, 1986)

Menon, Suresh, *Pataudi – Nawab of Cricket* (Harper Sport, 2013)

Mukherjee, Abhishek and Sengupta, Arunabha, *Sachin and Azhar at Cape Town* (Pitch Publishing, 2021)

Mistry, Rohinton, *Tales from Firozsha Baag* (Faber & Faber, 1987)

Narayan, R.K., *Swami and Friends* (Hamish Hamilton, 1935)

Oborne, Peter, *Wounded Tiger* (Simon & Schuster, 2015)

Odendaal, André; Reddy, Krish; Merrett, Christopher and Winch, Jonty, *Cricket and Conquest: The History of South African Cricket Retold 1795–1914* (BestRed, 2016)

Pataudi, Mansur Ali Khan, *Tiger's Tale* (Stanley Paul, 1969)

Patel, J.M. Framjee, *Stray Thoughts on Indian Cricket* (Times Press, 1905)

Keshav, Karunya and Patnaik, Sidhanta, *The Fire Burns Blue* (Westland Sport, 2018)

Levison, Brian, *Amazing & Extraordinary Facts: Cricket* (David & Charles, 2012)

Ratnakar, Pramesh, *Centurion* (HarperCollins, 2012)

Raiji, Vasant, *India's Hambledon Men* (Tyeby Press, 1986)

Rushdie, Salman, *The Moor's Last Sigh* (Random House, 1995)

Sandhu, Balwinder Singh, *The Devil's Pack* (Rupa, 2011)

Scott, Les, *Bats, Balls, and Bails* (Bantam Press, 2009)

Speed, Malcolm, *Sticky Wicket* (Harper Sport, 2011)

Sen, Ronojoy, *Nation at Play: A History of Sport in India* (Columbia University Press, 2015)

Sengupta, Arunabha, *Bowled Over* (Writers Workshop, 2004)

Sengupta, Arunabha, *Apartheid: A Point to Cover* (CricketMASH, 2020)

Sengupta, Arunabha, *Elephant in the Stadium* (Pitch Publishing, 2022)

Tendulkar, Sachin and Majumdar, Boria, *Playing It My Way* (Hodder & Stoughton, 2015)

Rice, Jonathan, *Wisden on India* (Wisden, 2011)

Wadhwaney, K.R., *Indian Cricket and Corruption* (Siddharth Publications, 2005)

Wadhwaney, K.R., *Indian Cricket Controversies* (Diamond Pocket Book, 2017)

Waingankar, Makarand, *A Million Broken Windows: The Magic and Mystique of Bombay Cricket* (Harper Sport, 2015)

Wynne-Thomas, Peter, *England on Tour* (Hamlyn, 1982)

Newspapers, journals, periodicals, almanacks

The *Indian Police Journal*, Volume 5 (1959)
Sport
The *Guinness Book of World Records*
Wisden Almanack
Wisden India Almanack
Sportstar
Wisden Asia
Cricinfo Magazines
The *Cricketer* archives
Sports & Pastime archives
Indian Express archives
Yugantar archives
Wicket Women archives
The *Internet Movie Database (IMDb)*
Godrej archives
Official match scorecards (*Wisden, ESPNcricinfo, CricketArchive*)
The Association of Cricket Historians and Statisticians archives
Z-score's Cricket Stats Blog

Web links

Acharya, Shayan, 'Distraction Spoiled My Career: Noel David' (https://timesofindia.indiatimes.com/sports/new-zealand-in-india-2016/interviews/distraction-spoiled-my-career-noel-david/articleshow/17842585.cms)

Alter, Jamie, 'Franchises for Board's New Twenty20 League' (https://www.espncricinfo.com/story/franchises-for-board-s-new-twenty20-league-310819)

Banerjee, Sandipan, 'Mohammed Shami: An Incredible Journey from Sahaspur to the Indian Dressing Room' (https://www.cricketcountry.com/articles/mohammed-shami-an-incredible-journey-from-sahaspur-to-the-indian-dressing-room-198248)

Bhogle, Harsha, 'Comedy of Errors – Cricket at the 1998 Commonwealth Games' (https://www.indiatoday.in/sports/commonwealth-games-2010/story/comedy-of-errors-cricket-at-the-1998-commonwealth-games-77825-2010-06-30)

Chokhani, Priyanka A., 'Now, A Tendulkar Drive and a Dev Terrace in Melbourne' (https://timesofindia.indiatimes.com/sports/off-the-field/now-a-tendulkar-drive-and-a-dev-terrace-in-melbourne/articleshow/76378550.cms)

Chopra, Samir, 'When an Editor Ate His Words' (https://www.espncricinfo.com/story/samir-chopra-when-an-editor-ate-his-words-703921)

Chopra, Samir, 'The Mystery of the Letter Writer Solved' (https://eye-on-cricket.blogspot.com/2014/01/the-mystery-of-letter-writer-solved.html)

Coutinho, Ashley, 'Frankielicious!' (https://economictimes.indiatimes.com/frankielicious/articleshow/1874207.cms?from=mdr)

Deeley, Peter, 'Tendulkar Injury the Concern for India' (https://www.espn.in/cricket/story/_/id/23255904/tendulkar-injury-concern-india-4-february-1999)

Deogharia, Jaideep, 'It's Picture Perfect for This Dhoni Fan' (https://timesofindia.indiatimes.com/sports/off-the-field/its-picture-perfect-for-this-dhoni-fan/articleshow/4943007.cms)

Ezekiel, Gulu, 'Afghan Cricket: The Indian Connection' (https://www.rediff.com/cricket/report/afghan-cricket-the-indian-connection/20170627.htm)

Farooq, Omer, 'Dhoni Fights for Biryani, Takes Team Out of Hotel' (https://www.dailypioneer.com/2014/page1/dhoni-fights-for-biryani--takes-team-out-of-hotel.html)

Ghosh, Sayan, 'Anshuman Rath – Former Hong Kong Skipper Pursuing India Dream' (https://www.hindustantimes.com/cricket/anshuman-rath-former-hong-kong-skipper-pursuing-india-dream/story-ZnVRXJstdlgTK4FWVQJ2rO.html)

Gonsalves, Michael, 'Irate Batsman Knocks Bowler Dead In 'Friendly' Cricket Tie' (https://m.rediff.com/news/1999/may/03ball.htm)

Gupta, Gaurav, 'Believe It or Not, Kanga League Opener Put Off Due to No Rain' (https://timesofindia.indiatimes.com/sports/cricket/news/believe-it-or-not-kanga-league-opener-put-off-due-to-no-rain/articleshow/59510566.cms)

Jones, Michael, 'C.K. Nayudu's Cross-County Hit' (http://cricmash.com/myths/ck-nayudus-cross-county-hit)

Johal, Vikramdeep, 'Stumped on Screen' (https://www.tribuneindia.com/2005/20050828/spectrum/main4.htm)

Karmakar, Rahul, 'WC Cricket Fever: Court Orders Cable TV For Guwahati Jail Inmates' (https://www.hindustantimes.com/worldcup2015/wc-cricket-fever-court-orders-cable-tv-for-guwahati-jail-inmates/story-Al8IyWgSatM3dW2AGA7aWI.html)

Krishnan, G., 'Aditya Tare Becomes 1st Batsman to Score Double Ton in Kanga League'
(https://www.cricketcountry.com/news/aditya-tare-becomes-1st-batsman-to-score-double-ton-in-kanga-league-32442)

Krishnan, Sankhya, 'The Colonel Receives His Just Desserts'
(https://www.espn.in/cricket/story/_/id/23221601/the-colonel-receives-just-desserts)

Kumar, Solomon S., 'Pitch "Puja": MSK's Mantra for Team India's Success'
(https://timesofindia.indiatimes.com/sports/cricket/west-indies-in-india/pitch-puja-msks-mantra-for-team-indias-success/articleshow/66350100.cms)

Lokapally, Vijay, 'Slow, Left-Arm Orthodox!'
(https://www.thehindu.com/sport/cricket/slow-leftarm-orthodox/article5116590.ece)

Menon, Suresh, 'The Man Who Put India on the Cricketing Map'
(https://www.espncricinfo.com/story/nkp-salve-1921-2012-the-man-who-put-asia-on-the-cricketing-map-559492)

Mohan, Sai, 'Dujon Cherishes Gavaskar Souvenir'
(https://www.mid-day.com/sports/cricket/article/dujon-cherishes-gavaskar-souvenir-143406)

Mishra, Prasun K., 'A Temple for God of Cricket Sachin in Bihar'
(https://www.hindustantimes.com/india/a-temple-for-god-of-cricket-sachin-tendulkar-in-bihar/story-ETQfMpSOLsrPb1eSZdv8ZM.html)

Misra, Vishal, 'One Night in 1996'
(https://www.espncricinfo.com/story/vishal-misra-the-birth-of-proper-ball-by-ball-commentary-on-cricinfo-637331)

Monga, Sidharth, 'Gavaskar Place, Kapil Grove'
(https://www.espncricinfo.com/story/gavaskar-place-kapil-grove-614840)

Mukherjee, Abhishek, 'Fake IPL Player, 2009: The First Great IPL Scam'

(https://wisden.com/stories/controversies/fake-ipl-player-2009-first-great-ipl-scam-kkr-blog)

Murzello, Clayton, 'Mumbai's Cricket Cradle' (https://www.espncricinfo.com/story/mumbai-s-cricket-cradle-565891)

Murzello, Clayton, 'Ashok "Kaka" Mankad Was Rajesh Khanna's Big Fan' (https://www.mid-day.com/sports/cricket/article/Ashok--Kaka--Mankad-was-Rajesh-Khanna-s-big-fan-173144)

Muzumdar, Amol, 'Looking Back: Day-Night Ranji Final' (https://sportstar.thehindu.com/cricket/indian/looking-back-daynight-ranji-final/article8788579.ece)

Nair, Sandhya, 'In Cashless Cricket Tourney, Goat, Roosters & Eggs are a Prize Catch' (https://www.hindustantimes.com/india/small-joints-big-clients/story-kvkoRzWA20XlO5Gowe5FaM.html)

Nair, Roshni, '"Frankie" Speaking: Meet the Magicians Behind On-the-Go Delicacy' (https://www.dnaindia.com/lifestyle/report-frankie-speaking-meet-the-magicians-behind-on-the-go-delicacy-2078661)

Nayar, K.R., 'Yuzvendra Chahal: Chess' Loss Was Cricket's Gain' (https://gulfnews.com/sport/cricket/ipl/yuzvendra-chahal-chess-loss-was-ipls-gain-1.1326048)

Ninan, Susan, 'Paint My Love' (https://www.espncricinfo.com/story/susan-ninan-meets-sudhir-gautam-the-sachin-tendulkar-fan-now-supporting-his-badminton-team-1086121)

Pal, Suvam, 'Indian Cricket's First Broadcast Rights: How Devika Rani And Himansu Rai Won It In 1935, Long Before IPL Era' (https://www.outlookindia.com/sports/indian-cricket-s-first-broadcast-rights-how-devika-rani-and-himansu-rai-won-it-in-1935-long-before-ipl-era-news-202173)

Pal, Suvam, 'The Incredible Life of Lall Singh'

(https://www.mid-day.com/sunday-mid-day/article/the-incredible-life-of-lall-singh-23233089)

Patil, Sandeep, 'I Knew Sachin Tendulkar Was Special When He Was 10'
(https://www.thequint.com/sports/cricket/sandeep-patil-on-the-growth-of-sachin-tendulkar)

Patra, Sajal Kumar, 'Man Drives Car Onto Pitch During Ranji Trophy Match, Gautam Gambhir, Ishant Sharma Left Amazed'
(https://sports.ndtv.com/cricket/man-drives-car-onto-pitch-during-ranji-trophy-match-gautam-gambhir-ishant-sharma-left-amazed-1770864)

Pandey, Aditya, '"Called Me A Gaddar": MS Dhoni's Biggest Pakistani Fan On Supporting Mahi In A Rival Nation'
(https://www.mensxp.com/sports/cricket/95318-ms-dhoni-pakistani-fan-chacha-chicago.html)

Pandey, Devendra, 'IPL 2017 Player Auction: Wrong Name, Wrong Picture, Wrong Story Costs Harpreet Singh Berth'
(https://indianexpress.com/article/sports/cricket/ipl-auction-unsold-2017-harmeet-singh-harpreet-singh-wrong-name-wrong-picture-wrong-story-cost-him-ipl-berth-4538865/)

Pandey, Devendra, 'J&K High Court Order Stalls Jammu & Kashmir's U-23 Game Over Selection Row'
(https://indianexpress.com/article/sports/cricket/high-court-order-stalls-jammu-and-kashmirs-u-23-game-over-4881149/)

Phatarpekar, Kushal, 'Tendulkar-Kambli Record 664-Run Partnership Score-Sheet Lost Forever'
(https://www.hindustantimes.com/cricket/tendulkar-kambli-record-664-run-partnership-score-sheet-lost-forever/story-QjNnmPYYV9p2r1N8f1IwvM.html)

Purohit, Abhishek, 'Life's Biggest Achievement – Chatterjee'
(https://www.espncricinfo.com/story/life-s-biggest-achievement-soumik-chatterjee-600183)

Prasad, R.S., 'Meet Ram Babu, Skipper Dhoni's Die-Hard Fan'

(https://timesofindia.indiatimes.com/sports/new-zealand-in-india-2016/top-stories/meet-ram-babu-skipper-dhonis-die-hard-fan/articleshow/49554269.cms)

Rajan, M.C., 'VB Chandrasekhar Was Under Great Mental Stress, Says Police'
(https://www.hindustantimes.com/cricket/vb-chandrasekhar-was-under-great-mental-stress-says-police/story-QDhBBCPeagqdQzcLzYkCZN.html)

Sen, Sumant, 'IPL 2018: CSK Fans Whistle Away to Pune, Literally'
(https://www.thequint.com/sports/cricket/whistle-podu-express-ferries-csk-fans-pune)

Sundaresan, Bharat and Veera, Sriram, 'Untold Story of Pranav Dhanawade's 1000 Runs Record: 25 Chances, 10-Year-Old "Pacers", 30-Yard Boundaries'
(https://indianexpress.com/article/sports/cricket/pictures-tell-a-1000-runs-25-chances-10-year-old-pacers-30-yard-boundaries/)

Tatia, Jatin, 'Day/Night Ashes Test Breaks Viewership Record'
(https://sportsmintmedia.com/day-night-ashes-test-breaks-viewership-record/)

Thompson, Jenny, 'Boxing Not So Clever'
(https://www.espn.in/cricket/story/_/id/22963930/boxing-not-clever)

Thompson, Jenny, 'A Mystic, A Musical and a Mistaken Identity'
(https://www.espncricinfo.com/story/a-mystic-a-musical-and-a-mistaken-identity-250062)

Ugra, Sharda, 'Girls Aloud'
(https://www.thecricketmonthly.com/story/1013165/sharda-ugra-on-how-the-ipl-is-redefining-television-commentary)

Williamson, Martin, 'Compton, Ranji and The Missing Rupees'
(https://www.espncricinfo.com/story/compton-ranji-and-the-missing-rupees-252651)

Williamson, Martin, 'The Denness Affair'

(https://www.espncricinfo.com/story/the-denness-affair-when-tendulkar-was-accused-of-ball-tampering-496743)

Williamson, Martin, 'The Umpire's Word is Final ... But Wrong' (https://www.espncricinfo.com/story/the-umpire-s-word-is-final-but-wrong-321553)

Waingankar, Makarand, 'Eknath Solkar: All Heart and Lots of Soul' (https://timesofindia.indiatimes.com/sports/new-zealand-in-india-2016/top-stories/eknath-solkar-all-heart-and-lots-of-soul/articleshow/12617976.cms)

'A New Mango Variety Named After Sachin Tendulkar' (https://www.dnaindia.com/india/report-a-new-mango-variety-named-after-sachin-tendulkar-1378429)

'Army Organises Siachen Cricket League' (https://www.greaterkashmir.com/sports/army-organises-siachen-cricket-league)

'Beef on Team India's Menu at Lord's, Fans React on Social Media' (https://www.indiatoday.in/sports/cricket/story/india-vs-england-second-test-lord-s-beef-anti-nationals-1312269-2018-08-12)

'Cheteshwar Pujara Receives Apology from Yorkshire Teammate for "Steve" Nickname'
(https://indianexpress.com/article/sports/cricket/jack-brooks-apologises-to-pujara-for-steve-nickname-during-yorkshire-stint-7629760/)

'Couldn't Make Sachin Play Bridge' (https://www.telegraphindia.com/sports/couldn-t-make-sachin-play-bridge-mehta/cid/503754)

'Cricket Crisis: Thunder Down Under' (https://www.news18.com/photogallery/sports/cricket-crisis-thunder-down-under-755053.html)

'DDCA Begins Hot Weather Tournament' (https://sports.ndtv.com/cricket/ddca-begins-hot-weather-tournament-1613262)

'Fans Burn Effigies of Cricket Players'

(https://timesofindia.indiatimes.com/fans-burnt-effigies-of-cricket-players/articleshow/1775872.cms)

'Farmer Killed with Bat for Not Returning Ball' (https://timesofindia.indiatimes.com/city/surat/farmer-killed-with-bat-for-not-returning-ball/articleshow/58690751.cms)

'"Go Back Buchanan": Shout Protesting Kolkatans' (https://www.dnaindia.com/sports/report-go-back-buchanan-shout-protesting-kolkatans-1242902)

'Helicopter Lands Play in Indian Cricket Match' (https://www.reuters.com/article/idINIndia-38144620090222)

'ICC T20 World Cup Delivers Record Viewership Globally' (https://indianexpress.com/article/sports/cricket/icc-t20-world-cup-delivers-record-viewership-globally-7641435)

'Inclusion of Sports Disciplines in the List of Games for Recruitment of Meritorious Sports Persons to Any Post in Group "C" – Tennis Ball Cricket: DoPT OM Dated 29.01.2021' (https://www.staffnews.in/2021/02/inclusion-of-sports-disciplines-in-the-list-of-games-for-recruitment-dopt-om-dated-29-01-2021.html)

'IPL 2021: MI-CSK Match In New Delhi Most Watched Mid-season Game Ever' (https://www.news18.com/cricketnext/news/ipl-2021-mi-csk-match-in-new-delhi-most-watched-mid-season-game-ever-3741038.html)

'Just Learnt What Kalu Meant: Darren Sammy Furious At Racial Barb Directed During IPL' (https://www.indiatoday.in/sports/cricket/story/darren-sammy-says-he-thisara-perera-were-called-kalu-playing-in-ipl-1686277-2020-06-06)

'Indian Villages Ban 'Meaningless' Game' (https://mg.co.za/article/2007-04-04-indian-villages-ban-meaningless-game/)

'Man of the Match in Bhopal's Cricket Tournament Wins Five Litres of Petrol as Prize'
(https://www.news18.com/news/buzz/man-of-the-match-from-bhopals-cricket-tournament-given-five-litres-of-petrol-as-prize-3489932.html)

'Man Thrashed with Bat by Two Juveniles, Dies'
(https://www.dailypioneer.com/2017/delhi/man-thrashed-with-bat-by-two-juveniles-dies.html)

'Mango Ganguly – Feral Brewing Co.'
(https://www.feralbrewing.com.au/beer/mango-ganguly/)

'Marengo Sachintendulkar: Rare Species of Asian Jumping Spider Gets Sachin Tendulkar's Name'
(https://www.outlookindia.com/website/story/sports-news-marengo-sachintendulkar-rare-species-of-asian-jumping-spider-gets-sachin-tendulkars-name/342157)

'Patel of a Day of Cricket'
(http://news.bbc.co.uk/sport2/hi/funny_old_game/1447033.stm)

'Ravindra Jadeja: The Relentless "Rockstar"'
(https://www.dnaindia.com/analysis/column-ravindra-jadeja-the-restless-rockstar-1813369)

'Sachin Tendulkar: How the Media Loved Him'
(https://wisden.com/stories/wisden-almanack/sachin-tendulkar-how-the-media-loved-him)

'Sachin Tendulkar Listed As a 'Casual Labourer' in Goa government's Records'
(https://www.mid-day.com/sports/cricket/article/Sachin-Tendulkar-listed-as-a--casual-labourer--in-Goa-government-s-records-15256060)

'Sixer Kills Horse, FIR Lodged'
(https://timesofindia.indiatimes.com/city/chandigarh/sixer-kills-horse-fir-lodged/articleshow/1839789.cms)

'Students of Calcutta's South Point School Pay Lavish Tribute to Kapil Dev'

(https://www.indiatoday.in/magazine/eyecatchers/story/19940315-students-of-calcuttas-south-point-school-pay-lavish-tribute-to-kapil-dev-808871-1994-03-14)

'Tendulkar Appeals for Calm'
(http://news.bbc.co.uk/sport3/cwc2003/hi/newsid_2770000/newsid_2775900/2775931.stm)

'Thanks for Losing, Mr Dhoni'
(https://timesofindia.indiatimes.com/city/lucknow/thanks-for-losing-mr-dhoni/articleshow/46720918.cms)

'Virat Kohli and "That Boy" at the Other End: Punit Bisht Recalls Emotional Stand with Old Buddy'
(https://timesofindia.indiatimes.com/sports/cricket/sri-lanka-in-india/virat-kohli-and-that-boy-at-the-other-end-punit-bisht-recalls-emotional-stand-with-old-buddy/articleshow/89920514.cms)

Social media

BCCI
(https://twitter.com/BCCI/status/750277796899934208)
Bumrah, Jasprit
(https://twitter.com/Jaspritbumrah93/status/878221654479876096)
Karthik, Dinesh
(https://twitter.com/DineshKarthik/status/1368111183295770631)
Mukund, Abhinav
(https://twitter.com/mukundabhinav/status/895324499154841600)
Nair, Sajan
(https://twitter.com/SajSpeak/status/684393386132963328)
Sathaye, Vikram
(https://twitter.com/vikramsathaye/status/890154794089709569)
Yadav, Yogendra
(https://twitter.com/_yogendrayadav/status/807843435184959488)
Delhi Food Walks
(https://www.facebook.com/watch/?v=3204232059814766)

Podcasts, videos

I Was Called a P*ki, Aakash Chopra
Managing Cricket, featuring Amrit Mathur ('22 Yarns with Gaurav Kapur')
Managing '83, featuring P.R. Man Singh ('22 Yarns with Gaurav Kapur')
K.L. Rahul on What the Duck (with Vikram Sathaye)
Yuzvendra Chahal on Breakfast with Champions (with Gaurav Kapur)

About the Authors

Abhishek Mukherjee is the content head at Wisden India. He co-authored *Sachin and Azhar at Cape Town*; won the Anandji Dossa Award for the Cricket Statistician of the Year in 2019/20; used to be the assistant editor at the Wisden India Almanack and the chief editor at CricketCountry; and has written for several media houses, including The Cricketer, Moneycontrol, The Quint, and Yahoo! Cricket.

Joy Bhattacharjya is a cricket analyst with Cricbuzz, the world's largest online cricket platform, and also runs a professional volleyball league. He was the project director for the FIFA U-17 World Cup, which in October 2017 became the most attended junior tournament in the history of FIFA. His previous engagements include being team director for the Kolkata Knight Riders which included two championship seasons, head of programming for both History Channel and National Geographic channel for South Asia, and ESPN Star Sports' first Indian head of production. He also designed India's first ever fantasy sports game, Super Selector, for ESPN Star Sports. Joy writes regularly on sport for *The Economic Times* and has also written on cricket for *The Times of India*, *India Today*, BBC, *The Telegraph* and the *Hindustan Times*.

30 Years *of* HarperCollins *Publishers* India

At HarperCollins, we believe in telling the best stories and finding the widest possible readership for our books in every format possible. We started publishing 30 years ago; a great deal has changed since then, but what has remained constant is the passion with which our authors write their books, the love with which readers receive them, and the sheer joy and excitement that we as publishers feel in being a part of the publishing process.

Over the years, we've had the pleasure of publishing some of the finest writing from the subcontinent and around the world, and some of the biggest bestsellers in India's publishing history. Our books and authors have won a phenomenal range of awards, and we ourselves have been named Publisher of the Year the greatest number of times. But nothing has meant more to us than the fact that millions of people have read the books we published, and somewhere, a book of ours might have made a difference.

As we step into our fourth decade, we go back to that one word – a word which has been a driving force for us all these years.

Read.

Harper Collins 4th HARPER PERENNIAL HARPER BUSINESS HARPER BLACK हार्पर हिन्दी

HarperCollins *Children's Books* HARPER DESIGN HARPER VANTAGE Harper Sport